T0114096

Praise for
A WHALE HUNT

"A rip-roaring sea story and a painfully funny portrait of a modern
Native American tribe searching for its soul."
—Beth Rattray, *Vogue*

"A rich story, at turns ironic and bemusing, sad and funny."
—Bob Minzesheimer, *USA Today*

"A compelling, insightful account of the Makah tribe's return
to whaling on the Olympic Peninsula, with particular
emphasis on the clash of cultures that ensued."
—*Seattle Post-Intelligencer*

"Sullivan's style as a journalist in this and his previous book,
The Meadowlands, is to look very hard for what 'just is.' He parks
in a place, as only a freelance journalist can do. He is called to
a question, a dilemma, a situation, a story, and he stalks it,
reporting with great clarity and humor."
—Susan Salter Reynolds, *Newsday*

"Sullivan goes beyond the fray to craft a hilarious, bone-true portrait
of Makah life. . . . Here Sullivan captures, with curiosity and empathy,
the sighing and breathing of a culture fighting to stay alive."
—Bruce Barcott, *Outside*

"A story that is stirring, infuriating, and often laugh-out-loud
hilarious. . . . Even those who reflexively turn away from the subject
should read this book and think about its lessons. Everyone else will
simply savor its delights: a good story, a diversity of characters,
even a running commentary on Melville."
—Stephen Bodio, Minneapolis *Star Tribune*

"A fascinating look at a clash of cultures and philosophies."
—Lewis Beale, *Daily News*

"Full of adventure—and irony."
—Lee Milazzo, *The Dallas Morning News*

ALSO BY ROBERT SULLIVAN

The Meadowlands:
Wilderness Adventures at the Edge of a City

A WHALE HUNT

Robert Sullivan

How a Native American Village Did What No One Thought It Could

A TOUCHSTONE BOOK
PUBLISHED BY SIMON & SCHUSTER
New York London Toronto Sydney Singapore

TOUCHSTONE
Rockefeller Center
1230 Avenue of the Americas
New York, NY 10020

First Touchstone Edition 2002

Portions of this book originally appeared in different form in *The New York Times Magazine.*

For information regarding special discounts for bulk purchases,
please contact Simon & Schuster Special Sales at 1-800-456-6798
or business@simonandschuster.com

DESIGNED BY ERICH HOBBING

Manufactured in the United States of America

1   3   5   7   9   10   8   6   4   2

The Library of Congress has cataloged the Scribner edition as follows:
Sullivan, Robert, 1963–
A whale hunt: two years on the Olympic Peninsula with the
Makah and their canoe/Robert Sullivan.
p.   cm.
1. Makah Indians—Hunting. 2. Makah Indians—Social life and customs.
3. Makah Indians—Public opinion. 4. Whaling—Washington (State)—Neah Bay.
5. Public opinion—United States. 6. Neah Bay (Wash.)—Social conditions. I. Title.
E99.M19 S85   2000
639.2'8'089979079799—dc21   00–030108

ISBN 13: 978-0-684-86434-1   ISBN 10: 0-684-86434-7

For Suzanne

CONTENTS

CONTENTS / 11

1 / Editorials

Before there was a whale hunt; before seven members of the Makah—a small tribe of Native Americans situated at the very northwestern tip of the United States—climbed into a canoe and paddled out into the ocean that first was calm and then swelled like a man drunk with power, oblivious to the paddlers who were singing and praying and carrying a harpoon and a rifle capable of killing an elephant, much less a whale; before the whale came; before that canoe and the men in the canoe paddled after it and a harpoon was launched and the whale dragged the canoe and a bullet was fired and the whale was killed and then nearly lost but then recovered; before the whale was towed into Neah Bay, the tiny and tired little fishing village that is for all intents and purposes the capital of the Makah reservation; before the people of the town rejoiced because it had been so many years—an entire generation, in fact—since a whale had been hunted and killed and because the hunting of the whale is what has for thousands of years made the Makah the Makah, what identified them among the tribes that live along the northwest coast of Canada and the rest of America as the tribe that hunts the whale; before the party that ensued, before hundreds of aboriginal people came from Canada and all over the Western United States to Neah Bay to sing songs and give thanks and eat whale; before all that, there were editorials:

Whaling has been part of our tradition for over 2,000 years. Although we had to stop in the 1920s because of the scarcity of gray whales, their abundance now makes it possible to resume our ancient practice of whale hunting. Many of our tribe members feel that our health problems result from the loss of our traditional sea food and sea mammal diet. We would like to restore the meat of the whale to that diet. We also believe that the problems which are troubling our young people stem from lack of discipline and pride and we hope that the restoration of whaling will help to restore that discipline and pride. But we also want to fulfill the legacy of our forefathers and restore a part of our culture which was taken from us. . . . In fact, one of our whalers has said that when he is in the canoe whaling, he will be reaching back in time and holding hands with his great-grandfathers, who wanted us to be able to whale.

—Keith Johnson,
president of the Makah Whaling Commission,
in an Open Letter to the Public

The Makah Indian tribe's pending whale hunt creates an awkward Catch-22 for Northwesterners: oppose the hunt and deny an undeniable treaty right, or support the Makahs and sanction the slaughter of [a gray whale]. . . . Uncertainty about techniques, motivations and repercussions has made *The Times'* editorial board reluctant to support a gray whale hunt off the Washington coast. Both the Makah tribe and the U.S. government, however, have made a compelling case that the hunt embodies restrained stewardship after a species' triumphant comeback.

—Editorial, *The Seattle Times*

Officials have given the green light for the hunt. Now the only way to stop the tragic killing of whales is a moment of compassion by the Makah tribe. Their days of hunting precious whales ought to stay in the past. The Makah tribe is troubled in many ways. Over 70 percent unemployment [and] drug and alcohol addiction plague many tribal members living on the North Olympic Peninsula. But there ought to be a better way to heal the Makah's social problems than bringing back the vicious killing of gray whales. . . . There are other ways to revive their tribe without hurting innocent whales in the process.

—Editorial, *The Everett Herald*, Everett, Washington

A society can never evolve by adopting archaic or inhumane rituals. Progress affects everyone living in this new era of the Global Village. No legitimate argument can be made that the Makah, or any other ethnic group, can move their culture forward through ritual killing.

—Michael Kundu, Pacific Northwest coordinator,
Sea Shepherd Society, an ocean conservation group

The Makah tribe received various threats of violence in recent weeks as it prepared to resume its traditional whale hunt. One of the ugliest came when the director of the Makah Whaling Commission found 25 messages left on her answering machine. Each recording consisted of a gun being loaded and fired. This is not a new phenomenon. Washing-ton state has long harbored a streak of anti-Indian bigotry, much of which focuses obsessively on tribal hunting and fishing rights. Histori-cally challenged Washingtonians see these rights as "special privileges." In fact, they are ancestral practices the Indian nations insisted on retain-ing when they ceded most of the state's territory to the U.S. government in the 1850s. Some Indian-bashers are using the Makah whaling dis-pute as a politically correct cover for venting genuinely vicious feelings.

—*The Tacoma News Tribune*

The real reason for this initiative by the Makah is because they know very well that whale meat goes for $80 per kilo in Japan, and that one of those whales is worth close to one million dollars. So—what they have their mind set on here is a commercial whaling operation. And that doesn't just mean the five whales that they say they want to kill—which will probably escalate quite rapidly after they get it off the ground—it will have implications for literally thousands of whales because Norway and Japan and those other nations that want to go whaling, like Russia and Iceland, are looking at this very closely because they know that if the Makah are given permission to take whales that it will undermine any integrity the United States has in the international marine conser-vation movement.

—Captain Paul Watson, president and founder
of the Sea Shepherd Conservation Society, *MSNBC News Forum: The News with Brian Williams,* January 1997

It's not for—we're not going to hunt the gray whales for commercial purposes, you know, even though we've heard the rumors that we are going to sell them to the Japanese, or you know, different countries like that. Our purpose for the whaling is for ceremonial and subsistence. We've requested five gray whales but that's not to say that we'll take them all. You know, after our first hunt we may find that we'll only need one a year. To resume whaling it would be, you know, like another piece of the puzzle that's been kind of out of place, and by doing this it will help push that piece back into the puzzle to make a complete picture.

—Marcy Parker, a member of the Makah Tribal Council,
MSNBC News Forum: The News with Brian Williams, January 1997

If the Makah whale hunt is allowed to proceed, the whale sight-seeing business is finished—whales won't come within a mile of any boat, and the owners might just as well put up their boats for sale now.

—Letter to the editor, *The New York Times*

The Makahs should continue on their path of renewing tradition in the face of fanatical, irrational opposition. Protecting the last vestiges of Native American culture from extinction is as important as protecting whale species from extinction.

—William Sommers Quistorf,
member, Oneida Indian Nation of Wisconsin,
living in Everett, Washington, in a letter to the editor,
Seattle Post-Intelligencer

The Neah Bay whale hunt controversy could be resolved if the Makahs would take a page from the fly fisherman's book and adopt a "catch-and-release" policy.

—Letter to the editor, *Seattle Post-Intelligencer*

What is endangered here is an irreplaceable culture, not an appealing sea mammal.

—Letter to the editor, *The New York Times*

Gray whales are going to be slaughtered in U.S. waters in October. This is wrong!

—In the Path of Giants,
a sea-kayak-based documentary group,
filming the migration of the gray whale

Whale, I have given you what you wish to get—my good harpoon. Please hold it with your strong hands. . . . Whale, tow me to the beach of my village, for when you come ashore there, young men will cover your great body with bluebill duck feathers, and the down of the great eagle.

—Makah tribal song

Gray whales have lost their fear of humans and their boats in North American waters. In fact, they are well known for approaching people in a curious and friendly manner. When the Makahs move in for the kill, the whales will be unafraid.

—Pamphlet entitled *Gray Whales in Danger*,
published by the Progressive Animal Welfare Society,
a group commonly referred to by its acronym, PAWS

I have come to see how your house is. Is it prepared for large crowds?

—"Song of the Whale,"
as sung by Wilson Parker, 1855–1926,
as quoted in *National Geographic*, October 1991

This is possibly the most important whale hunt in the past 25 years.

—Capt. Paul Watson of *Sea Shepherd*,
as quoted in *The New York Times Magazine*

We ought to just go out there and get a whale.

—Wayne Johnson,
captain of the Makah whaling crew, to me

I'm not too good with the spiritual stuff.

—Wayne Johnson,
also to me and on numerous occasions

2 / *The Car Ride*

I remember exactly where I was when I read that the Makah were going whaling, when I felt suddenly compelled to go to my map and point to Cape Flattery, when I felt the place calling me. I was at home in the kitchen and it was one and a half years before the Makah actually threw a harpoon at a whale. I'd just heard on the radio that they wanted to try, and I was amazed, of course, that anybody would want to even attempt to hunt a whale, what with a whale's size and its connotations, and I was amazed that whale hunting was part of the tradition of this place I'd never even heard of before, even if that tradition had died or was disused. But in the beginning, it was the cape itself that most amazed me, just the idea of the place. I'd been living in the great Pacific Northwest for several years, and Cape Flattery was always one of those spots that cried out to me from my atlas as I studied it in the evenings, prowling America's far corner and all its farthest-away places for the nourishment of my about-to-go-to-bed soul: it is a place where the road north and west ends emphatically, a peninsula that reaches out to the sea, to the vast aquamarine-colored area that is—in the color codes of my map, anyway—not described, as if infinite and immeasurable. It's where the tip of America meets the North Pacific, where the water seems charged and about-to-be roiled, like the water off the bow of a ship.

My work being what it is, I generally go to places as a reporter, as a filer of facts for hire, so after Cape Flattery called me, I made a few calls myself, and, in time, found a magazine editor who hired me to type up a quick and simple report on the tribe's plans, a few paragraphs that would pay for my way there. I set aside a few days to check things out. Then, just before dawn on a drizzly fall morning, I stuffed the trunk of my car with raincoats and boots, filled a thermos with coffee, grabbed my brand-new copy of *Moby-Dick,* which I had never read and which seemed like a good book to take along, and I set off to see how the Makah would go about hunting a whale.[5] If I had known then that as a result of that day's drive I would be compelled to repeat that six- and sometimes seven-hour drive so many times over the course of the next two years that I can now describe every chain-saw sculpture along the road in my sleep; if I had known that I would be living for weeks on the edge of the woods in a cold, damp shack or often in an old tent that was so leaky that I finally had to break down and buy a new one, which was better but still leaked sometimes; if I had known that I would eventually be compelled to temporarily abandon my family and drive for days along the length of the West Coast of North

---

[5] I spent a long time in the bookstore trying to decide which edition of *Moby-Dick* to buy. I found the selection daunting, like the book. I finally decided on the Penguin Classics version because I liked the cover, which showed a detail of a painting from the New Bedford Whaling Museum in which a sperm whale was in the midst of furiously staving a whaling boat, the men thrown about like flotsam. I also liked that the Penguin Classics edition included a lot of commentary, which I felt I needed in order to understand what Melville was going for in terms of references and allusions and so forth. Later, after I had read the book more than once, and had already decided that it was one of the most significant book-reading experiences I'd ever had, I was hanging out in another bookstore and paging through various other *Moby-Dick* editions, and I found one with an introduction that said: "To read *Moby-Dick* is to change."

America in hopes of touching a whale in a tropical lagoon in Mexico; if I had known that I would sit in a hot, dark sweat lodge and think about my soul or the soul of anybody else, for that matter; if I had known that I would end up diving nearly naked into the ice-cold winter water around Cape Flattery or end up going out on little boats that were chased by animal rights activists whom I didn't have anything against really—if I had known any of that before I took off that drizzly fall morning, I might have stayed in bed.

On that autumn morning, shortly after I pulled out of my driveway in Portland, I felt the secret expectancy of the beginning of a long trip, an excited shiver. I got on the interstate and crossed the wide Columbia River, which runs through the Northwest like a spinal cord, and I saw Mount Hood, the glacier-topped volcano that stands up in the Cascade Range, cutting a black silhouette against the red rising-sun sky. I drove past suburban developments and car dealerships, past Mount Saint Helens and the huge drumlins of ash left over from Mount Saint Helens' last explosion, past tree farms and paper mills and aluminum plants and rivers such as the Lewis and the Kalama, the Cowlitz and the Skookumchuck. Sometimes, I passed trucks carrying cut trees and sometimes the same trucks passed me in a plume of forest rain, violent sixty-five-mile-an-hour weather systems. Above me, gray clouds herded over the road faster than I could believe.

For the first couple of hours on my trip, I was headed in the direction of Seattle, which is a sophisticated city, a city with happening restaurants and specialty coffees and whole-grain muffins, a city filled with people who walk around in technologically advanced outdoor fabrics, who work for software companies and Internet sites and live on a series of beautiful lakes and bays—a place where, in general, you will not see a lot of whale hunting going on, much less hunting of any kind. But halfway to Seattle I turned left, which is to say west, and I worked my way onto the Olympic Peninsula. The Olympic Peninsula is *not* Seattle; it is Seattle's sometimes-still-wild backyard, the place where residents go to commune with nature or to ponder their place in the universe or to do what most people in Seattle do when they head for the woods, what is a kind of postindustrial ritual: utilize state-of-the-art outdoor gear.

The Olympic Peninsula is a Connecticut-sized land of mountains and rivers, of state parks and timber mills, of vistas that sometimes look scenic and sometimes look chewed up, fields left for logged. At the heart of the

count office-supply stores (piles of logs that are small compared with what they have been traditionally). I passed through Hoquiam, another old logging town; through a logging town called Humptulips, and then through the logged and unlogged woods and over the rivers raging down from the peaks of the Olympics. I passed a clear-cut that had recently been set on fire—a forest management practice that halfheartedly mimics an actual forest fire burn: a faux inferno. I drove through an alley of huge cedar and Douglas fir trees that darkened the road despite the clearing sky. And then, all of a sudden, the woods opened up like a curtain to feature the Pacific Ocean. From the edge of the Olympics' forest, the Pacific looks so big and vast that it commands you to park at the tree line and walk into the dark gray sand and feel the foamy coldness on your feet and wade in a ways. When I was back on the road, the glacier-covered mountains at the heart of the Olympics peeked over not-so-faraway ridges. Just past the town of Forks, a road sign advertised the ancient land of the Makah at last. It said: MOST N.W. POINT.

The road to Neah Bay is serpentine, a thin twist of wet double-yellow-lined gray. It flirts for twenty miles with the edge of cliffs that seem to stand at the mercy of the Strait of Juan de Fuca and its wide swath of soon- to-be Pacific Ocean. Mapmakers mark it as scenic when it would be better marked IMAX: waterfalls and cliffs and mud slides on the left; white-capped blue water dotted with tall, just-off-the-shore rock formations on the right. I could see Vancouver Island, in Canada, across the vast strait and through the clearing sky. Its mountains were topped with snow and clouds.

And out in the water, I looked for whales—I looked as long as I dared, that is, until I remembered the road and the hairpin turns and then jerked the steering wheel back toward land. And while I was looking and jerking and swearing and doing my best to stay alive, I got whale on the brain: the idea of one floated in my head like a portent.

The sight of this creature in my mind's eye contributed to the concerns I had vis-à-vis my life on this dizzyingly beautiful cliff-side road, so that by the time I pulled into Neah Bay, and saw the boats tied up peacefully in the marina, and the little houses tucked gently beneath the Olympic Peninsula's most western peaks (the very last hills before the sea), I was hunched over the wheel and exhausted.

3 / Cape Flattery

It was late in the afternoon when I hit town that fall day. I drove through the ragged little village that is downtown Neah Bay and wondered if the young guys I saw in pickup trucks or if the kids hanging out on the main drag were whalers-to-be. I passed out of town and along the Waatch River as it made its final run through a swampy prairie of reeds and dry grass to the Pacific. An eagle circled overhead. At the end of the road, a few hundred yards from the crashing waves, I parked in back of the Makah tribal government center, an evacuated U.S. Air Force base. I sat down in a little office in a neat but run-down office complex and I met two men—George Bowechop and Gary Ray.

A former tribal chairman, George Bowechop is a distinguished-looking man in his late sixties. He is compact and bespectacled, and he was wearing khakis and a polo shirt. He was extremely polite. He asked me about my drive, which he said he had made many times. Gary Ray, on the other hand, didn't say much. He is thin but muscular and he seemed to me taller than he is. He was wearing jeans and a flannel shirt, and as I spoke with George, he took page after page of copious notes, and in so doing made me nervous.

I asked questions about the Makah Nation, and George and eventually Gary told me many things. They told me that, until they signed a treaty with the U.S. government, in 1855, their land had stretched miles and miles back farther east into the peninsula, nearly to Port Angeles, a two-hour drive away. They told me that with this treaty their ancestors signed away their land but not their rights to fish in the rivers and the sea and to whale, which was very important to them. They told me that tribal attorneys and tribal leaders had been working to prove their treaty valid almost since it was signed, and that the right to whale was, in a way, the final test of the treaty, proof that it was still a valid document. They told me that they had a museum that they also called their cultural center because they wanted the things of the past to be alive and not dead. They said that even though the American government tried to eradicate the Makah language, some people still speak it and it is being taught again. They told me that Makah is not their real name, but the name given to them by the American government, which took the name Makah from a non-Makah translator who referred to them as Makah, which in the translator's native language meant "people who are generous with food." They told me that the real name of the Makah is $q^{w}idi\check{c}\check{c}\cdot a\,tx$, which means, "people who live by the rocks and seagulls," or "people who live on a point of land projecting into the sea," or "people of the cape."

I wrote everything down, and proceeded to ask questions about the upcoming whale hunt, which seemed relatively imminent. At that point, the International Whaling Commission had just approved the Makah's request to restart their traditional hunt. I asked about dates, names, facts regarding preparations.

George said the tribe was beginning to make preparations for the hunt; that the hunt might take place as soon as the following fall; that the town was in the midst of forming a whaling commission; that the whaling commission would soon choose a crew. George described these as the final steps in a long process that had begun years before in 1994, when the gray whale was taken off the Endangered Species List. At that time, the Makah notified the federal government that it intended to whale, and the government, in turn, assisted the Makah as they presented their plans to the IWC. (The tribe's request was initially turned down by the IWC in 1996.) George also described all of this as a difficult process, given that the last whale hunt happened seventy years before. He also said that the tribe was well aware of public opposition to their plan. "It's a war out there, and we know it," he said, then added, "they want us in the museum. They'd rather we just said, 'Oh, the Makah were great whalers,' and leave it at that. They want us to have a dead culture. But it's been our way of life. We look at the ocean and we feel we not only have a legal right but a moral right to whale."

As I took more of my own notes, Gary stopped taking his notes and began talking. He told me that as a result of the plan to resume the hunt, Makah young people who lived off the reservation had begun to move back for the chance to whale. At this point, I was wondering about phone numbers and names of people who might be involved in the hunt but neither George nor Gary offered any. At the time, I thought they were being vague, but in retrospect they weren't. They didn't have any names and some of the whalers who eventually ended up being chosen for the crew didn't have phones. Also, I had the distinct feeling that both men thought it wasn't any of my business.

Gary did mention one further thing about the whale hunt, though. He leaned over and looked at me intently and he said, "Just remember, the whale knows it's being hunted."

I had more questions, but, as it was getting dark over the river outside the office window, Gary interjected, saying, "Have you been to the cape?" He was talking about Cape Flattery.

I said I hadn't.

"There's some time before dark," he said. He told me to drive, and in a minute, he had folded his long legs into the front of my car. We drove out toward the ocean and then up a dirt road into a forested hill curving around Archawat Peak. We came to a lookout where you could see all the way south down the coast, down the length of the Makah Nation and the West Coast: a chain of crescent-shaped bays that linked south into infinity, a shore of hills that descended into cliffs and then beaches and then seabird-circled foam. Just off the shore were tall stacks of sandstone, primordial statuary that seemed headed away from the peninsula, back to the sea.

Gary told me to stop the car and look out. "To keep this spot, we had to be great defensive warriors," he said.

We drove on.

We parked at the trailhead at the tip of the cape and hiked for a few minutes down a path of gnarled cedar and hemlock, over little streams decorated with ferns. We padded over moss and mushrooms, passing turned-over trees, their roots the hair of Medusa. On the way, Gary talked about the whale hunt. "It's gonna be like a blood transfusion for this community," he said.

And then we came out into a clearing and a little wooden platform that the tribe had built on the edge of a tall cliff. We stepped up and looked out at the ocean and Tatoosh, the little island just in front of us, and we didn't say anything. The ocean smashed against the base of the cliffs, churning around the rock roots of this last little bit of land until Asia. The sun had almost disappeared down into the sea.

Gary was just looking out at the horizon, beaming.

The place felt the way it looked on the map in my kitchen: like the very edge of the world.

Finally, Gary said something. "This is our place," he said. "This is where we have always been."

4 / The Cape Motel

Checking into a room at the Cape Motel in downtown Neah Bay, you notice that no lights can be seen on the shadowy hump across the strait and out the window that is Vancouver Island. You notice that the super-tankers and aircraft carriers and giant, new-car-carrying barges move across the almost-dark horizon slowly, silently, like ghosts. You get a room for one that has enough beds for two and is a favorite with visiting fishermen, and you turn on the TV and lie down and stretch your legs out and put your hands behind your head and notice that the Seattle TV stations barely come in on the little TV—a snowy, static-filled picture that can drive you crazy in its lost horizontal hold. You discover that you are better off tuning in a Canadian radio station—specifically a station from Victoria—and you listen to the Canadian coastal weather forecast and the traffic reports for urban British Columbia and feel as if Neah Bay is a place between the United States and Canada, newscast-free.

I chose the Cape Motel because it was the first motel on the left as I drove into Neah Bay and it looked good to me. After the Cape Motel, there are two other motels, a gas station, a general store, a post office, a marina, a boat launch, two restaurants, a fish storage house, a building used to store the surplus cheese and butter that the U.S. government gives to the tribe, a dock where felled trees are loaded onto barges, a community hall, a high school, a health clinic, three churches, a jail, four pay phones, five soda machines, and an espresso stand, open seasonally.[b] The soda machines are

[b] The espresso stand does not sell Starbucks coffee. I mention this for several reasons. First of all, the brand of coffee called Starbucks is ubiquitous in the Pacific Northwest, where the coffee company is based, so the fact that there is no Starbucks coffee store in Neah Bay is a further measure of the remoteness of the village. Second, Starbucks takes its name from the character Starbuck in *Moby-Dick*. When the company was first founded, in 1971, their publicity material referred to "the coffee-loving first mate named Starbuck." The company stopped referring to Melville's character, however, after the Herman Melville Society contacted the company to say that Starbuck doesn't drink coffee anywhere in Melville's novel. Naturally, I watched to see if Starbuck drank any coffee as I was reading my way through the novel on my trips to Neah Bay (he didn't). This attention to fictional coffee-drinking had the side effect of causing me to pay close attention to the history of the creation and publication of *Moby-Dick* and to the personal history of Melville. Reading *Moby-Dick* became an adventure in itself. Accordingly, I soon learned that the actual whale Melville is thought to have based the story of *Moby-Dick* on was named after an island in the Pacific Ocean off the coast of Chile. The island is called Mocha, and the whale that allegedly terrorized whaling ships in that area was known as Mocha Dick.

Neah Bay's late-night hot spots; cars stop by them up until midnight and a little later on the weekend, and the sound of the soda machines is one of the sounds of the typical Neah Bay night. The other sounds are an occasional car, kids driving around town or standing around one of the soda machines or walking down the dark bay-front street aimlessly while kicking the flattened beer or soda cans, a foghorn on the island in the bay, seals barking by the fish docks, the barking of one of the several small packs of stray dogs, and in the spring, frogs croaking in the swampy ditch alongside the market. Those are the sounds after about nine, when everything shuts down. There are no bars; Neah Bay is a dry town. The closest bar is in Clallam Bay, which is twenty miles back down the winding road. Once, I was talking to the Presbyterian minister in town, and he told me that the only other place he had ever lived that felt anything like Neah Bay was on the coast of Alaska.

Approximately 1,500 people live in Neah Bay, 1,200 of whom are members of the Makah tribe, and if you spend any time there at all you soon discover that nearly everyone in Neah Bay knows everyone else. When someone new arrives in town, most of the town knows immediately—an atmospheric disturbance. With very few exceptions, drivers wave at one another from their cars. When you are downtown—which is the term residents use to refer to the area along the main street that runs along the bay front—it is considered a sign of affection to swerve your car toward someone else's as it comes toward you in the road. This is possible mostly because there are usually only three or four cars on the main road at any given time. The exceptions are at noon, when people come downtown to check their mail and eat lunch, and at around seven-thirty in the morning, when the dozen or so people in town who work at the state penitentiary in Clallam Bay set out down the road to work, causing a tiny little rush hour.

Before the Makah signed the treaty of 1855 without really having any choice and gave over their land and agreed to be administered by the U.S. government, they lived among five villages: Waatch, Sooes, Baada, Ozette, and Diah. Neah Bay is built at the site of Diah. The people in the villages were united by shared customs and by a language unrelated to the languages spoken on the rest of the Olympic Peninsula and understandable only to the tribes on the coast of Vancouver Island, the tribes that were once called the Nootka tribes by visiting Europeans, but are now commonly known as the Nuuchahnulth, which means "long hills." The names of the five original villages are on the flag of the Makah Nation. In the early 1900s, when the federal government wanted all the villagers to move to Neah Bay to school their children in English, the Makah resisted at first but then eventually moved, often settling in town in neighborhoods as per their family's ancestral village. (The villages still exist, even if they can seem invisible to an outsider. "Oh, you Sooes folk!" one woman once said to another in front of me.) Today, most of the Makah living on the forty-seven-square-mile reservation live in Neah Bay, though there are still a sprinkling of people in the hills and along the road that runs south along the Pacific. Anyone living out of town is said to be living "in the country," an expression that can seem redundant to visitors.

The road into Neah Bay was built in 1931. Before that, all traffic in and out was by boat or by trail, both of which could be grueling. "When I was on the back of an Indian pony, climbing the mountain and holding on for dear life, I regretted I had not taken the route by sea. On the ocean, in a frail canoe, every motion felt, sometimes on the crest of a mighty wave, and then diving down in the trough of the sea until the land was lost to our view, I was then quite positive that the mountain trail was the smoothest," wrote John P. McGlinn, a federal Indian agent in the late 1800s. Recently, on a rainy winter day, there was a landslide and the road was blocked. For a couple days no one left town. During this time, a young man was wounded in a gunshot accident and needed to get to the hospital in Forks. It was still raining—it rains all winter in Neah Bay—and the road had yet to be repaired. An ambulance crew drove to the landslide and carried the stretcher across a path dug out by the Makah forestry crew and into an ambulance on the other side.

Two peaks tower over the town—Bahokus and Archawat. Each is half logged and, as a result, give the town a shopworn majesty. They cradle the village, and every afternoon as the sun sets behind them, it scatters its dying light like a cymbal crash. In the morning the wood stoves in the little ramshackle houses and trailers puff out thin trails of smoke that drift up into the hills and decorate the green slopes like garlands. When bad weather is on the way, the ocean clouds seep over the peaks to break the news. Once the peaks were lookout posts for whalers; from a thousand feet up and in the panoramic view of the Northwest Coast, they could spot the gray whale migration as it came south from Alaska or north up from Mexico. Now the peaks have several different uses. An Air Force radio tower on Bahokus monitors air traffic out over the Pacific. (During the Cold War, the Soviets were monitored from Neah Bay.) The National Oceanic and Atmospheric

Administration also houses air quality monitoring equipment on another peak. (The air is often said to be some of the cleanest in the world.) People not affiliated with government agencies drive up to the top of the peaks just to look around. They leave empty beer cans and empty wine cooler bottles and sometimes the remnants of little fires.

The first time I ever went up to the peaks, on a beautiful autumn morning, I had a guide—a woman named Harriette Cheeka. In addition to being a Makah, Harriette is a single mother, an Army veteran, the personnel director of the tribe, a volunteer ambulance driver, one of the people who helped paint the totem poles at the marina, a member of the Neah Bay dart team, a police dispatcher, and a poet. She wears her dark, silver-streaked hair short and she has bright eyes and a warm smile. She was not involved in the whale hunt in any official capacity; she was just someone I ran into in Neah Bay, and, like everyone in Neah Bay, someone I would run into again and again. On the day she took me on my first trip up to the peaks, she was with her mother, who was wearing a windbreaker and reading a magazine in the front seat of Harriette's large, comfortable 1998 Oldsmobile sedan. Harriette prefers a sedan to a four-wheel-drive sport utility vehicle, which most non–Neah Bay residents drive when visiting Neah Bay, because she believes in driving in comfort. Her comfort comes at the expense of the comfort of the car, however. Like many residents of Neah Bay, she drives her car where most non-Makah drivers would not dare drive. "The last car I traded in was beat to shit because I boondocked it," she told me. "It was a ninety-five Buick. I was way off on a logging road, and a logging truck driver saw me and said, 'What are *you* doing here?'"

On our way to the peaks, she drove me over to the tribe's designated sacred lands, low rolling hills beside the ocean and near the mouth of the Sooes River, just out of town. I sat in the backseat and her mother was in front. Harriette talked of being in the Army and about a dream she had that involved a horse, which, to her, had something to do with Christianity being forced on Indian people, and which became a poem. We drove slowly along the rutted, muddy dirt road that led onto the sacred lands and then we got out of the car, while her mother sat in the front seat and continued reading. We stood in the short and bristly green grass that grew on the low sandy hill, in view of peaks and cliffs and the roaring ocean. I asked Harriette what she saw there, as a poet, the way you'd ask an innkeeper to describe his rooms. "Today, I see the potential in the fog banks and clouds that are just kind of misting gently. I see the clouds and fog banks that, to me, are in transition. And I feel the wind off the ocean." She had a lot to say about the wind. "That's my Stolichnaya, the breeze that blows off the ocean. It can be anything. It can be a soft caress or a frigid winter slap." About the cold rain, she said: "The cold—I don't like the cold. But the rain to me is like the sky scrubbing. It's purifying the air." About the sound of the ocean, which was crashing its waves a few dozen yards away, she said: "Oh, I love that sound. It's like listening to the earth itself. How do you say it? It's like listening to its vital sounds, as though the earth is sighing and breathing. I spend as much time as I can out here breathing it up, so that I can take it with me."

As we got back in the car and started up into the peaks, we began talking about the general public's perception of Makah. She mentioned that she had been interested in visiting Germany, where she had heard the public was interested in Native American issues, but a group of German filmmakers who work in Neah Bay suggested that the kind of Indian culture that Germans were most interested in was the culture of the Plains Indians, as opposed to the very different culture of the Northwest coast tribes. At this point, Harriette's mother looked up from the magazine she was reading. "They want to see long black hair," she said.

"Even today, people don't know," Harriette said. "They say we live in teepees."

"Even the people in cities around here," Harriette's mother said, "cities that are close by."

We didn't talk about whaling—though Harriette did mention that she was worried about the controversy whaling might cause and she wondered if maybe the tribe couldn't come up with a kind of mock hunt or if maybe the government could pay the tribe not to hunt whales, the way farmers are paid not to grow corn. She said she felt the threat of violence looming.

We were making our way up a rutted road, up to the top of Bahokus Peak. "Once, while I was in here, I had an eagle bless my car," she said. "A golden eagle. Its right wing and long tail feathers brushed up my hood and then against my windshield." She pointed to her windshield, to where the eagle would have been, and she looked back at me. "Now, *that's* something you tell your grandkids," she said. We drove around huge ditches, through pond-like puddles, across ruts that seemed impossible to cross and then turned onto logging road after logging road, until finally we came to a clearing at the top of Bahokus Peak. We were directly behind the abandoned Air Force base that the tribal government occupied, though you couldn't see the old base and you couldn't see the sewage treatment plant. You could just see forever down the Northwest coast, down into a house-less view of fir trees and low cottony clouds and gray sky through which the sun struggled mightily. It was amazing—the best view in the house. Harriette got out of the car, put her hands on her hips, waved her arm, and said, "Now, how does *that* make you feel?"

5 / The Museum

On my first visit to Neah Bay, I walked around a lot and tried to figure out how whale hunting fit into this place, and eventually I landed in the Makah museum. The Makah museum is not just a museum but a kind of shrine to the Makah's ancient way of life: it is a repository for all the arti-facts dug up in the late seventies at the site of an ancient whaling village that operated for centuries on the southern tip of the reservation, the place where the symbolic tools and daily-life equipment of an entire culture are displayed in a dim, church-like light. Over the course of my time in Neah Bay, I spent a lot of hours in the museum, buying postcards and pricing the locally carved cedar paddles and the phantasmagoric cedar masks, and, of course, pondering all the displays and exhibits, often in the com-pany of tourists, for few are the Olympic Peninsula–touring visitors to Cape Flattery who fail to visit the spot.

Read the brochure, I would say to myself, as I began my self-guided tour. Read the brochure, which says, "Our exhibits will give you a chance to look back in time and see how our people lived," and then goes on to add, "Perhaps you will be able to experience a portion of our appreciation of the One Above who taught our ancestors how to live in this place. The items you will see and the ingenuity behind them were inspired through prayer."

See the cedar boxes made from cedar planks that are ingeniously carved with creases and then folded and nearly welded, like a state-of-the-art alloy. See how the boxes are smoothed not with sandpaper but with the dried skin of a dogfish, which is a kind of shark. See how they are decorated with the characteristically oval-shaped rectangles, the incredibly stylized drawings that are based on creatures that actually live in the nearby woods and forests—drawings that would make the perfect trademarked logo for the Northwest's nature if the Northwest's nature were a brand-name corporation.

See the cedar baskets woven tightly enough to hold water.

See the wooden halibut hooks that were taken away from the Makah, who were not farmers but who had farm tools forced upon them anyway, who took the steel in the farm tools and bent it and made the same uppercase U-shaped halibut hooks with steel that are now what even the non-Indian fishermen use. See the sealing harpoons, which are long and thin and two-pronged.

See the whale fin carved from cedar and decorated with seven hundred otter teeth, a constellation's worth.

See the doughnut-shaped rock that the sealer tossed from the boat when a shark followed—so that the shark was tricked, so that the shark followed the rock down, down, down, and away from the canoe.

See the huge dugout cedar canoes, which were for sealing and whaling and traveling far along the strait and the coast, out onto the high seas, out in the evening, not to return for several days, until the halibut were hooked, until the seals were caught, until the whale gave itself up to the whalers.

See the mussel-shell-pointed, cedar-roped, yew-shafted whaling harpoon.

See the tools, the art, the remnants of a village where life was simultaneously productive and artful, where life faced toward the sea and the greatest creatures were the whales and the highest-ranked and most esteemed villagers were the men who caught the whales—especially the whaling captain.

See in the museum, in the place that celebrates the Makah-ness of the cape—see over and over, a picture of a bird that appears in the motels and on the business cards of the elected tribal representatives, and on the flag and the Web site of the Makah Nation, a bird that is not just any bird but is Thunderbird, the great bird-like god who lives in the far-off icy peaks of the Olympics, the being, who, when he is hungry, flies out into the ocean and with his huge claws and weapon-like lightning fish that he uses like great electrical harpoons, captures a whale.

See this, the symbol of the Makah, for it was Thunderbird, according to the stories, according to what people still to this day say, who—in a time of great famine, when the community needed food if not hope—first brought the whale here.

After a while, staring at the museum's displays, touching the whaling canoe and pondering the whale floats and harpoons like Stations of the Cross I didn't understand, I saw that these were the very symbols of the Makah whaling quest. Now, all the tribe had to do was flesh out the details.

A man who remembered the dig from which the musuem sprang was Edward Clapanhoo; he was the chairman of the tribal council at the time of the Ozette dig. A stocky and nearly bald man, he lives over on the western edge of town in a little house that is two blocks from the bay, and one afternoon, after spending more time in the museum, I knocked on his door and he invited me into his home. On the wall were photos of relatives and some Northwest Coast art. He had a large shelf of books, many of them about the Makah, some of which mentioned him. He offered me a seat on a big comfortable couch, then he went to the kitchen and came back after a while with some smoked salmon to offer me. He sat down and folded his hands over his chest. He said, "Oh yes, I remember the dig.

"You know, back in the sixties, you've gotta remember that the feds came to us and they said they were going to declare Ozette deserted and they were going to take the land away from us. And we told them that Ozette belongs to us. It's our land. And then they said, 'Can you prove that place belongs to you?' And we said that on our treaty Ozette was Makah. And they said we need more proof. So that's where Doc Daugherty came in. We called him Doc. I knew him from my days at Washington State University. Before that, you know, archaeologists were raping the land. They would just come in and take everything. But he was different. He came to the tribal council and he said that he had walked pretty much the entire coast from Vancouver Island all the way to California and he said no other site had excited him so much. So we said, 'Welcome to the Makah Nation.' He came in 1965 and 1966 and he dug a trench and he determined that there was life there for twenty-five hundred to three thousand years and that the Makah and the Ozette were basically one."

In the summer of 1966, when they dug the trench at Ozette, Daugherty and his assistants found modern things—rusted nails, coins, parts of a muzzle-loading rifle—and older things—fishhooks and hair combs made from bone.[5] They found seal bones, sea lion bones, the bones of dozens of species of fish, and so many whalebones that they had to be sawed through to allow digging to continue. The workers used whalebones as stools, and the shoulder blades of whales jutting from the walls of the trench served as tables for note takers. When winter came they closed up the dig, convinced they were close to something big. "There is a persistent tradition among the present Indians of a landslide which carried 40 people to their deaths in a large house," Daugherty told the *Port Angeles Evening News*. "We think we have a pretty good idea of where that house is but we haven't had time to prove it."

Four years passed. It was the winter of 1970. "Hippies lived in town and down at Ozette," Ed Clapanhoo remembered, "and one of the hippies was a schoolteacher. So one Sunday afternoon I get a call from a hippie and he says, 'Hey, Mr. Clapanhoo, you've got to do something about those people. They're taking stuff out of your house.' Clapanhoo leaned back in his chair and smiled at me. "I guess I could be polite and say 'some teacher' but the story sounds better when I say 'some hippie,' which he was," Clapanhoo went on. "But anyway, I hung up the phone and I went through my mind and I was thinking, What house could he be talking about? And then I thought, You know, you're a hippie and you're probably just doing weird things. And so I kind of put it out of my mind. But then a little later, this guy called again. And I said, 'You know, I've searched the reservation—I've gone house-to-house and I can't figure out what house you're talking about,' and he said, 'I'm talking about Ozette. There are sandbanks as high as your house there and people are going through it with shovels.' So the next morning I went with Mr. Parker and Mr. Irving, who are now both deceased. The ocean's usually very rough in February, but on that day for some reason it wasn't, so we said, 'Let's take a boat.' And after I saw what was happening I went back and made a phone call."

The call was to Daugherty, who packed his car and drove ten hours from eastern Washington to the cape. He slept at the trailhead. The next morning, he hiked the four miles in and saw the planks of a longhouse spilling

[5] In the early days of my time in Neah Bay, I did not see any links between Melville's fictional whale hunt and the whale hunt that I was reporting on; as I delved into biographies of Melville, I considered the little details that jumped out at me to be coincidences. Like this one: when Melville wrote *Moby-Dick*, he lived on a farm in the Berkshires, in Massachusetts. Everywhere he dug on the farm, he found artifacts. He found so many artifacts, in fact, that he ended up calling the farm Arrowhead.

from a bank of vines and trees and clay with the ocean's encouragement. In a few days, the dig began, and a house emerged from the hill, a house that had been lived in for fifty years, that on one spring or perhaps summer morning a few years before Columbus arrived in the Caribbean had been covered in a slide of clay and perfectly preserved. Made of cedar planks, the house was fifty feet long and thirty feet wide. The floors were meticulously swept. The roof had been repaired with a whalebone. The storm drain ditches were made from whalebone. Stored away were wooden bowls filled with seal oil, mats, fishhooks, ropes, splitting wedges, cedar boxes, a bundle of cedar bark, conical rain hats woven from spruce root (adult's and children's sizes), fish clubs, seal harpoons, and whale harpoons. There were tools tipped with iron and copper, possibly from Japanese fishing boats that had drifted across the Pacific, possibly from ships wrecked all along the cape. There were containers of bright-red ocher ready to be applied as decoration. There were blades of grass and alder leaves, still green. There was the giant, carved-from-wood dorsal fin of a whale, decorated with some seven hundred otter teeth, the prize in the house of a whaler.

Daugherty immediately set up a dig. Students came to help. There was a thirty-five-person crew. The head of the field laboratory was Mary Flynn, a Makah. The crew hosed the clay off the uncovered artifacts with pumped-in seawater. They preserved wooden materials in polyethylene glycol, the same kind of fluid used to preserve unearthed Viking ships. Supplies were flown into the faraway roadless area by Coast Guard helicopters. Students in tie-dyed shirts built A-frame houses and covered them with plastic sheets; they built shacks made with spruce shingles. They grew their own vegetables, and ran a one-cylinder engine to power a laundry machine. They stacked thousands of sea mammal bones and eventually calculated that the inhabitants of the longhouse dined on ninety-seven varieties of shellfish. Five years into it, there were fourteen master's theses and four Ph.D. dissertations. "A student can find enough material in one morning to spend three days writing reports and making maps," Daugherty said at the time. In a year or so, funding ran out, but many student volunteers stayed on. The federal government granted more money. Senator Henry Jackson called the site "one of the ten most significant archaeological projects in the world." Ozette was America's Pompeii. Archaeologists came from all over the world. It became the most visited place in the Olympic National Forest. The digging went on for ten years. Sixty-five thousand artifacts were recovered. Then, in 1981, budget cuts forced Daugherty to stop. On June 15, the site was closed up and subsequently the bodies that had been recovered were quietly buried in Neah Bay.

In his living room, with the rain pouring down, Ed Clapanhoo offered me more fish and something to drink, and then he went on about the dig as if it all had happened yesterday. "Everybody went down there. It was so exciting," he said. "Everybody! Even the elders! Some that were eighty years old walked down there. And then a National Guard helicopter brought other elders down there. There were elders who had never been in a helicopter. They thought it would tip but they went. And the view!

"In the seventies," he continued, "we decided we had to have a museum to house all the artifacts, to display them, so we did. And when the museum was opened seniors went down to the rebuilt longhouse and then went in and sat down and started singing songs and they didn't come out." He said that young people discovered carving after the Ozette dig, that people looked again at the tools of the past. He leaned forward to describe an old fishhook, exactly like the kind found at Ozette. He said, "I look at some things and I marvel at the imagination of our forefathers with amazement."

Right after I spoke with Clapanhoo, I went back to the museum, walked around some more, and savored the exhibits and the dark quiet. I stepped inside the dark longhouse, which, through lighting and a trompe l'oeil painting on the wall outside the door, seemed kind of real. I sat beneath the hole in the cedar-planked ceiling and heard a silent discourse on life at the beach and imagined a night before a red glow of nonplastic coals, imagined the storms, the rain in the winter as it coursed down in sheets. Eventually, I walked out, and in the back of the museum, I wandered into a small side exhibit of the work of Young Doctor, a carver at the turn of the century, who was also a healer and an artist. There was an old photograph of Young Doctor standing beside his work, in which his eyes seemed either tired or foreboding, I couldn't decide. A sign said this: "Young Doctor kept singing, kept carving, kept his heart and mind alive with traditions, kept his family alive with selected business activities. Young Doctor helped to keep the Makah culture alive by simply inviting his friends and relatives to dinner to sing and keep straight the ancient wisdom. Through companionship and the love of fellowship, he launched his dreams and songs into the future of the Makah people. Now is the future. We keep up the struggle started long ago. We stock our streams with salmon. We run our own museum. We attempt to strengthen our families' tradition. We continue to live with dreams in our hands, with songs on our lips, with our children before us. The desire to hunt whales returns."

6 / The Crew

Naturally, having traveled to the cape with the matter of whaling in mind, I was hoping to meet the prospective whalers, but during my first visits to Neah Bay, there were no whalers for me to officially meet, and nothing, as far as whale hunting went, seemed to me to be happening. The whale hunters were only just being chosen. The Makah Whaling Commission, which included representatives from all the families on the reservation, was also just working out how the hunt would be executed, drawing up physical and spiritual guidelines for the crew. The commissioners were working with an eye to the past and an eye to the present: decisions were discussed among commission members and families and tribal elders and then vetted by the tribe's attorneys in Seattle. I was getting the idea that the Makah hoped for a Colonial Williamsburg–style hunt, a historical re-creation with a cedar canoe and a harpoon as well as a few modern additions, like a motorized support boat and a high-powered whaling gun. The hunt was going to be a modern traditional whale hunt; it was going to be ceremonial *and* insured.

Then toward the end of the winter, I was directed to John McCarty, a retired fisherman who had just been appointed executive director of the whaling commission; he was—in the very beginning, that is—the man in charge of the whale hunt.

I met John at the tribal center in the whaling commission's little office on the second floor of the Fisheries Building. He was huddled over a phone with a blinking message-waiting indicator. In the spare office, on the wall before him, was a poster illustrating the various species of whales of the world as well as a map of western Europe that had Monaco marked on it—McCarty and other members of the whaling commission had recently visited Monaco for a meeting of the International Whaling Commission.

John McCarty was a former fisherman who had once worked as a drafts-man in Detroit: as he sat talking on the phone he doodled meticulously. When he hung up, he spoke with excitement about the planning and preparations for the hunt and about the whale hunting permits required by the whaling commission's management plan, as well as where a new har-poon might come from and what was going on with the development of a whale hunting gun. He said he hoped to find funding—a grant, or monies from the federal government or the Bureau of Indian Affairs—to sponsor full-time training for the crew of young men. "We know how we need to go about our business," John said.

When I asked him about his family, he was effusive. He told me that he was the son of Jerry McCarty. He said that his father was given his name by a white boarding school teacher who did not allow McCarty or any of the children to speak Makah. He said that his father was then sent away to Idaho, where he went to school with members of the Nez Percé tribe, including people who were later massacred alongside Chief Joseph. John's father became a Presbyterian minister and married John's mother, Matilda, who was from Ozette, and whose two uncles, the Weiberhard brothers, were some of the last Ozettes to live at Cape Alava. As it happened, John's father grew up in the cedar longhouse of *his* father, Hishka, a name which means "plenty of things." Hishka, according to John, was one of the last of the great old-time Makah chiefs. He lived at Waatch, and, John informed me, he was a whale hunter.

At sixty-three, John was too young to have ever seen a whale hunt but he remembered his family's whaling equipment: the harpoons, the lines, the painted floats. He recalled that when his father moved his family to Seattle to work during the Depression, all the whaling gear was in the attic of the house. When they returned it was gone. John insisted that the right to hunt was not something that the tribe should have to negotiate for with the federal government or with the International Whaling Commission. "We did that as a concession," he said. He added, "Many of us on the commission consider it a birthright. We don't feel we have to ask a com-mission to hunt. We feel we have to ask the fathers."

John and I headed out for hamburgers downtown. We left the whaling commission office and walked down the back stairs of the abandoned Air Force building. Outside, as he squinted in the sun that filled the Waatch prairie, John explained that while he was sometimes frustrated by all the red tape—with the minutiae, for example, involved in buying insurance for a

Makah whale hunting canoe—he sometimes felt as if everything were the same as in the old days. "We have to do all this paperwork," he said, "but when it came time to choose the crew, I picked my son the way the old guys did!"

A little while later, John McCarty invited me to his office and introduced me to a few of the newly chosen whalers. Leaning back in his chair with his hands behind his head, he pointed to three guys sitting on chairs and leaning against the wall. "So this is the crew," he said. The men he pointed to were Micah McCarty, Donnie Swan, and the one person who, as things went over the course of the next two years, I ended up spending more time with than anyone else on the reservation. This last man was Wayne Johnson, the captain of the whaling crew.

7 / A Descendant of Kings

Micah McCarty was John McCarty's son. Micah was twenty-seven when I first met him in the whaling commission office, and he was wearing black jeans and a black hooded sweatshirt, black hiking boots, and a black beret, beneath which his long black hair was tied in a ponytail. He had the look of a bohemian whale hunter. He was eloquent about the whale hunt, and he seemed to enjoy talking not so much about the procedures of the proposed whale hunt as about what it all meant—at least to him. "I think there's a strong sense of consciousness, of knowing what I'm confronting," he told me once. "To me, I'm the last living will and testament of my ancestors, as opposed to dying in the job in some industrial reality." He was a kind of Save the Whales whaler, who saw environmentalism and whaling as compatible if conducted on ancient Native American terms. Activists who were against the Makah whale hunt oftentimes seemed to relate to Micah's version of the whale hunt, especially when he talked about being in harmony with nature—he used their vocabulary. One of the people who protested the whale hunt, a man who worked to save whales and dolphins for a conservation group, talked to Micah for a long time one day and when Micah walked away, the protestor turned to me and said, "He's very cool."

When plans for the first whale hunt were just beginning, I drove over to where Micah was living, in a little cluster of houses on the beach near Waatch. Micah had just moved to the reservation from the Olympia area, where he had gone to high school and lived with his mother, John McCarty's ex-wife. Micah was making his living as a carver at the time. Some of the masks and paddles and other pieces that he carved were showing up in small galleries in Seattle and Victoria. He was dating a Coast Salish woman from Canada. She lived just across the Strait of Juan de Fuca, in a village near Victoria. Outside Micah's window, beyond the beat-up cars and rusty fences, you could see Makah Bay and the coast and the low evergreen hills as they ran south through the mist of the crashing ocean waves. The tired, one-level buildings were once housing for the Air Force base personnel. Before that there was a Makah village on the site. It was in the village called Waatch, Micah explained to me, that Hishka, his great-grandfather, would have lived. Micah relished this coincidence. "I am living near the stream where my grandfather bathed and prayed," he said.

Micah's living room smelled of freshly shaved cedar and was littered with paperbacks; the decor was coastal dorm room. The walls were thin; the wind off the ocean seemed as if it would burst into the room any second, a raid. Micah was sitting in a rocking chair and carving. He was talking about going to college after the whale hunt; he was enrolled for the spring. He planned to become a lawyer; he said he hoped to fight one day to retain the rights granted in Native American treaties. As he spoke he carved a mask. "I grew up as a minority kid and I knew I was the descendant of these people who were like kings, and I was like, Why?"[b]

Micah said that in preparation for the whale hunt, he had been eating foods that he had gathered in his daily walks from his home. "Some mornings, I walk on the beach at low tide and pick sea urchins. It's part of my

---

[b] Both Melville's grandfathers were Revolutionary War heroes—though Melville always seemed to have wondered exactly what kind of heroes they were. His maternal grandfather, Colonel Peter Gansevoort, commanded Fort Schuyler, and he was involved in massacring a group of Tory and Native American forces that attacked the fort (including Joseph Brant, a white man who translated the Bible into Mohawk and then renounced white civilization to become a Mohawk himself). A painting of Colonel Gansevoort shows up in Melville's novel *Pierre*. Melville's paternal grandfather, Major Thomas Melville, was one of the organizers of the Boston Tea Party, in which Major Melville and his compatriots dressed in buckskins, headdresses, and war paint and marched through the streets of Boston chanting, "Rally, Mohawks. Bring your axes and tell King George we'll pay no taxes." Melville grew up hearing both sides of the family tell of conquering savages. Mayor Thomas showed his grandchildren a handful of tea leaves he claimed to have saved from the tea party, a kind of relic in the family museum.

own subsistence pathway," he said. "It's how I keep my skills on living on the land, my traditional sanctuary. I pick mussels too. I haven't found mussels big enough to make a traditional harpoon yet. But I've already learned to make traditional two-strand cedar bark rope."

After a while, Micah took a break from carving and we went for a walk out on the beach.

Before the whale hunt happened, Micah was the model student. "I've been doing a lot of spiritual preparation on my own. That's been an ongoing deal. That's the mind, body, soul-edification process. And I've started gathering things that are relevant to the position my grandfather had. You know, the harpooner. Once the harpoon is thrown, he ducks down like this . . ."

Micah ducked. "Down to the floor of the canoe," he said. "That's just to keep me out of the way of the lines when the whales start running or diving."

Most days, Micah woke and said a water prayer, thanking the Creator for the gift of water. He stretched out, practiced some breathing exercises, put on his Nike Air cross-trainers and ran. From his home, he walked away from the little cluster of thinly built barracks and across the stream where his grandfather would have bathed. He might climb the creek to the little reservoir pond and then run back down and across Waatch Creek and down Makah Bay to Hobuck Beach and the beach called Sooes. He was pushing himself. "There's an old saying that the whale chooses the whaler," he said, "and I want to be honorable enough to be chosen by the whale."

On one hike up the coast, he found himself imagining the whale hunt. "I was visualizing the scenario of the final approach," he was saying. "With the whale blowing its stack. I was visualizing plunging the harpoon. And I was wondering would it be an electrical charge from the animal to me? What will the animal feel in its heart? What would it be like? What would it be like to be there with the whale?"

In the beginning, he had great hopes for the crew. "We have to love each other like brothers," he said. "We have to trust each other. Because we are all going to have our lives in each other's hands. It's like, you know, we'll all be in the same canoe."

8 / Squire

Donnie Swan was the de facto assistant to the captain of the whaling crew, a kind of whale hunt squire, and on the day he was introduced to me, he was on his motorcycle, which was red and white and low to the ground. I watched him bank it hard as he made the turn into the Waatch Valley, racing the river to the sea. He was twenty-two years old at the time and wearing camouflage pants and a white T-shirt and wraparound Oakley sunglasses; a hunting knife was strapped to his belt. Donnie is strong and thick-boned. In the small house he was living in at the time, he and his brother Randall kept a weight machine in the unkempt and undecorated living room. Donnie played on the football team in high school. His nickname was "The Neck." The football team sometimes trained by swimming up the rivers from the ocean. Since high school he had worked on the reservation, except for the time he lived nearby, in Forks, where he worked in the woods, and when he went down to California to work on a construction job, staying at the house of a man his mom was seeing. "The floors were marble and you could slide on 'em forever in your socks!" he recalled.

Donnie's mother thinks of him as somebody you can always count on, as somebody who comes through in a pinch, who never gives up. She told me that once, when Donnie was younger, a baby fell unconscious in downtown Neah Bay, and Donnie stopped and attempted to revive the child using CPR. He worked and worked until the ambulance came and the child was finally pronounced dead. When I first met Donnie, he was training for a position on the volunteer fire crew and he was thinking of joining the ambulance squad: he was putting down roots. Donnie has been married for a few years to a woman in Neah Bay, but they separated recently. He has a daughter, who is three, and when he rides around with her in his lap in the front seat of his pickup truck, his tough exterior melts; he wears a big crooked grin. Around the time that crew training first began, he said, "My daughter's always saying, 'My daddy's gonna catch the whale.'"

There aren't many full-time jobs in Neah Bay. The unemployment rate is 50 percent in the summer and 75 percent in the winter, and most of the jobs come from the sport fishing trade. In 1995, the per capita income was estimated to be $5,200. There is no casino in Neah Bay—partly because the tribe has chosen not to build one there, and partly because Neah Bay is so far away from a big city and the interstate that in all probability no one would ever visit a casino if there was one there. And yet, despite the abysmal economy, Donnie has always managed to find work in the woods and on the water. In the woods, he has gathered fir boughs and other plants to sell in Forks (he learned which plants to pick from some Mexican friends he made in Forks). "If you know what to look for you can always make money in the woods," he said. He has also cut cedar shakes, as many men in Neah Bay have done.

To cut cedar, a man carries a chainsaw and a day's supply of gasoline out into an area of the woods where the cedar trees have previously been logged. Then he cuts the wood left over from the large logging operation into blocks. The blocks are stacked and, if he is just a few miles in, then the cutter carries the wood out on his back or in a truck. Otherwise, the cutter contracts a helicopter to fly the wood out to one of the various local mills that manufactures cedar shingles. The helicopter costs about three hundred dollars an hour so a cedar cutter will typically share the rental cost with other shake cutters. When Donnie cuts shakes out in the backwoods on the reservation, he generally carries a gun. "A lot of times you'll be cutting shakes and all of a sudden you'll feel like somebody's watching you, but it's usually just a bear," he says.

Donnie also works on the Neah Bay fishing boats from time to time, though he prefers not to—he gets seasick, which is something his brother, Randall, a fisherman, is always teasing him about. Mostly Donnie is a diver. He dives for sea urchins. Boats from Port Angeles hire young men to walk along the bottom of the Strait of Juan de Fuca to pluck sea urchins and sometimes abalone and put them in a bag. Donnie learned diving from the most successful commercial diver in Neah Bay, a man who makes his living by diving in septic tanks. Diving is a dangerous job. The currents in the strait are notorious. Divers are paid between fifteen and twenty cents a pound. Sometimes, seals kill divers when they get tangled in the divers' oxygen lines. While diving and picking urchins, Donnie sometimes sees even bigger creatures underwater. "Once, I was walking along pickin'," Donnie said, "and all of a sudden I see this huge shadow on the ground, and I looked up and it was a whale."

9 / The Captain

Wayne Johnson is five foot eleven and wiry, with a chin that he holds high in unconvincing defiance whenever he gets a little nervous. He slouches when he stands. I remember that when I first met him I didn't think he looked so much like the captain of a Native American whaling crew as a stuntman, semiretired at the age of forty-five: his skin was worn and his eyes seemed tired; he drew smoke from his cigarette in a manner that gave me the idea he had seen a lot, not all of it so good.

For a long time, I wasn't entirely certain what Wayne's job was on the whaling crew, and I often got the feeling that he wasn't either. Sometimes, it semed to me he ended up as captain because it was a post akin to vice president in that it was assumed he would never actually be in charge. In the beginning of the planning for the whale hunt, he was a kind of lame-duck captain. He was a member of the whaling commission but he wasn't on the crew per se; he wasn't planning on being in the canoe during the hunt. According to his job description, he was in charge of preparing the crew physically and spiritually. That spring, he did have some idea of what crew preparations would entail—paddling practices and maybe some hikes and so forth—but there were a lot of issues he still hadn't worked out—in particular, those concerning spiritual training. Spiritual training was something most people on the commission preferred not to discuss, especially Wayne. Wayne seemed hampered in his role as whaling captain in that he didn't engender the greatest amount of respect in Neah Bay. "Sometimes, he's kind of wishy-washy," one of the crew members told me early on.

Despite his lack of public stature, Wayne was one of a small number of people in Neah Bay who, before the whale hunt began, could say they had already caught a whale, even if it was by mistake. He had done so when he was in his thirties. He was out fishing in Makah Bay, at the mouth of the Waatch River, and a gray whale accidentally got caught in his net. He and the other fishermen he was with towed the whale to shore. The whale was dead. Wayne considered butchering it; people in town were interested in eating the whale, the way they used to. But the federal government prohibited anyone from doing so. An armed guard was posted near the whale. A helicopter flew the whale across town and dropped it in a hole, where it was buried. Wayne was going to be fined $10,000 for catching an endangered species, even though he didn't have $10,000. The charges were eventually dropped. The next day another whale got caught in his net. Wayne just cut the net. The net itself was very expensive but less expensive than catching a whale. "I couldn't afford to catch another whale," he said.

Except for a couple of years living in Portland, Oregon, and a few brief stays in places like Tacoma, Boise, and Spokane, Wayne had lived most of his life on the reservation. He was born there, and his father left home when he was very young—Wayne never really knew him.[5] In his twenties and thirties, Wayne fished, mostly for salmon, before the commercial salmon runs were all but depleted in the Northwest. After that, he spent a short time in Tacoma doing stuff he told me he'd rather not talk about. "You don't want to know," he said to me once, although on other occasions he indicated that whatever it was had to do with spending a lot of time in bars. Wayne has never been out of the Northwest except for the time he went to Monaco. The tribe flew him there to attend the annual meeting of the International Whaling Commission in 1997. At the time, the California gray whale had just been taken off the Endangered Species List and the United States was trying to get permission from the IWC for a Makah hunt. Wayne and Micah McCarty went, along with several other tribal whaling commission members, to state their case for the revival of the hunt, arguing that it was imperative for the survival of Makah culture. Just before his flight, Wayne decided he should be wearing something dressier than work boots. He bought a pair of off-white leather loafers at the department store near the Seattle airport, the Bon Marché. He and Micah stayed in a hotel just outside of Monaco on the French Riviera, which he

---

[5] As I keep saying, it seems to me a good idea to know a little about Melville when you get aboard *Moby-Dick*. (This point was confirmed for me by the editor of this very book, who happened to study *Moby-Dick* in college and preserved her notebooks and read to me this line: "Biography as literature. Literature as biography.") And so I am compelled at this point in the story of the Makah whale hunt to note that Melville's father, Alan Melville, died when Melville was twelve. Alan Melville was an "importer of French Goods and Commission Merchant," in Albany, where the family had migrated to from New York City. When Alan's business failed during a recession, he experienced a mental collapse, which many biographers of course say haunted Herman his entire life—madness being a major theme in *Moby-Dick*. Herman was forced to leave school and go to work as a bank clerk. He ended up educating himself and he roamed from job to job—working in the family fur business and teaching from time to time—until he finally went to sea, which he liked; it seemed to get him away from his problems at home. When he came back and was expected to go into business he wasn't really certain what to do for a while; he hung out, basically, until he finally went back to sea at the age of twenty-one. In 1841, he set sail from New Bedford, not to return for four years. He went aboard the *Acushnet*, a whaling ship named after an Indian tribe.

found to be very different from Neah Bay. It was a little bit of a culture shock for everyone involved, in fact. The French couldn't get over the fact that most of the Makah were unemployed and living in poverty. "They thought we were all rich from casinos," Wayne recalled. Wayne, meanwhile, couldn't get over the price of French beer. "We were drinking six-dollar beers," he told me. And he couldn't get over the coffee. The coffee seemed so strong to him that to this day when he sits down in the Makah Maiden in Neah Bay and the coffee is too strong, he leans back, puts down the cup, grimaces, and says, "Oooh, *France* coffee."

As captain, Wayne's responsibilities were theoretically similar to those of a coach. Over the course of the crew's training, there were to be tests with guns and harpoons, swimming tests, and drug tests—the whaling commission members were adamant that the hunt was to be drug and alcohol free. Wayne was responsible for making certain that everyone on the crew passed his drug test and for administering swimming tests and the like. (In the time leading up to the hunt, the size of the crew roster would rise and fall.) Wayne's strength in this position lay in the fact that as much as he loved Neah Bay, he had often wanted to leave the reservation. He understood the downside of the place and thus could relate to the potential young crew member who said the hunt might make no difference, that there wasn't any hope for a partying-free life in Neah Bay, that a whale hunt was no replacement for what everyone in town really needed—jobs. Wayne had been through some difficult times growing up there; aside from drugs and drinking, he had witnessed suicide attempts, for instance. Even he thought it was a little ironic that he would be in charge of preparing a crew physically and spiritually. First of all, he was not much of an athlete—not like Donnie, his younger cousin. Second of all, he didn't think of himself as very ceremonial, much less religious. Before the hunt, if people merely talked about things like God in his vicinity, it made him anxious. "I'm not too good with the spiritual stuff," he was always saying to me.

In fact, Wayne never seemed certain about how he fit in, in town. He told me as much one day in early spring when we went out in a boat in Neah Bay. There was a wisp of a cloud in the bright blue sky over Bahokus Peak; the trees around the clear-cuts seemed preternaturally green; seals moved silently in the glassy water. We were in a harbormaster's boat, and it was long and gray and shaped like a bathtub. Wayne had picked up the boat at Fort Lewis on behalf of the whaling crew. It was surplus military material. "We get it for free from the government," Wayne said, showing

it off. "The tribes are considered kind of like wards of the state or something. It's not very fast but it'll be good for following along with the crew
in the canoe while they're training."

The engine coughed into action. We putted slowly out into Neah Bay.
Wayne was wearing a Los Angeles Raiders jacket and jeans and a T-shirt.
As he steered, he leaned back on the side of the boat and lit a cigarette,
squinting in the bright sun. We cruised out toward Waadah Island, a little
island in the bay that is covered with trees. Wayne reflected on his current
situation in Neah Bay.

"I was gonna get out of here until this whole whale thing started,"
Wayne said to me. "I just got my trucking license when this started and I
was thinking of getting a truck and driving across the country, seeing the
whole country, you know? Getting out of here, anyway. But then this
whale thing came up and I thought I'd stick around."

After we docked, Wayne went home. He lived back by the high school,
in a small, neat house. For a long time, I only saw him downtown or talked
to him on the phone, and when I telephoned him at home, a woman, who
was very nice, always answered, and I just assumed the woman was Wayne's
wife. Once I said so to Wayne, and he sighed with exasperation. Then he
looked at me to see if I was trying to tease him, which I wasn't. Finally, he
shook his head at me and rolled his eyes and said, "That's my mom."

10 / The Whaler—An Ancient View

And who, I began to wonder early on in my time spent out in Neah Bay,
were those great whalers of the past? Who were the Makah men who got
into the canoe and risked their lives to hunt the great whale? And how did
they go about it? What were the procedures? What mortal Makah man
dared to re-create the act of Thunderbird, the great and powerful god-like
bird, or bird-like god, or, in some stories, the giant god-like man who
dons the garment of a bird, and spreads his great, broad wings and flies
from the mountains and dives down to the ocean and carries off a whale?
How, in the past, did a mortal man go about such a godly thing?

For insight into this and other matters, I turned to the ethnographers, to the diaries of early visitors to Neah Bay, who, even if they refer to the Makah as savages, as pagans, even if they looked at the people of the cape as people in need of Christianizing and other civilizing effects of late-nineteenth-century America, were invariably impressed by the hunters of the whale. There were men such as James Swan, who lived among the Makah for many years. He befriended many tribal members, and—more than most visitors, perhaps—sought to understand the ways of the tribe; he even adopted a child (who, as it happens, was the great-grandfather of Donnie and Wayne). Swan wrote of the Makah: "I have seen them occasionally run foot-races on the beach, climb poles set up for the purpose, and swim and dive in the bay, but they do not excel in any of these athletic exercises. They do excel . . . in the management of canoes, and are more venturesome, hardy, and ardent in their pursuit of whales, and in going long distances from the land for fish, than any of the neighboring tribes. They are, in fact, to the Indian population what the inhabitants of Nantucket are to the people of the Atlantic coast, being the most expert and successful in the whale fishery of all the coast tribes."

As I read through the notes of the old ethnographers, the great whaler eventually stepped out of the mists of time, so that I could sort of imagine him emerging from his cedar longhouse on a misty morning—the wash of the Northwest ocean tide in his ears, the gnarled, summer-bleached fir trees behind him, the low gray clouds out to sea. He was preparing to hunt a whale.

There is his whaling canoe pulled up on the beach. It is nearly forty feet long, and carved from one tree. The prow of the boat is carved separately and attached, and as it juts out ahead of the great craft, it cuts like a knife through the waves. The canoe's wide interior is a deep red; its exterior is black and painted with a solution of burnt alder and fish oil or sometimes with a special mud from a swamp. It is simple, almost stark.

In the canoe are the paddles—black and shaped like a human tear about to fall and carved from strong, hard yew wood—and the bailers, also painted red, which are ingenious, triangularly shaped devices made of alder and equipped with cedar rope handles: they scoop the cold ocean water from the boat.

And there is the huge harpoon, a device crafted with an eye to thousands of years of technology, an awesome tool. It is comprised of two lengths of yew, lashed together in the middle to make an eighteen-foot shaft. The harpoon has grips made of braided cedar bark and then covered with cherry bark. In order to make it straight, the shaft of the harpoon has been wrapped in kelp and held over a fire and rolled between the harpooner's knees. The yew wood of the harpoon was carefully selected, generally in secret, and two pieces were always used.

There is the tip on the harpoon. It turns as the hand of the whaler turns it, so that it may be inspected, so that it can be seen to have been made with large, sharp mussel shells, or—if the whaler is a less ancient whaler, a whaler who was whaling after the time of the first contact with Europeans, whose boats were wrecked at the shore of the Makah villages, and were subsequently used by the Makah as *plein air* whaling, fishing, and hunting supply stores—the tip of the harpoon might also be made with sheet copper or sheet iron or a piece of the blade of a saw. The point itself is attached to barbs of elk or deer horn and is in turn fastened to a thirty-foot-long line made from whale sinew and covered in cherry bark. The harpoon head is covered with gum from spruce trees and kept in a case made of two pieces of cedar bark folded and decorated with grass.

There, perhaps, is the long steel lance that some later reports speak of, the instrument that the whale hunters used to kill the whale after it had been repeatedly harpooned.

There are floats in the whaler's canoe, handmade buoys that were crafted from the skin of a male hair seal's inflated torso. The floats were soaked in a creek the night before and then inflated, corked with yew wood, and attached to the line at the end of the harpoon. They are intended to slow the progress of the harpooned whale, and when the whale dies, they keep the huge creature afloat. On the beach in the past (or in my imagination at this moment) the floats are decorated with drawings of Thunderbird or perhaps with lightning fish, and the whaler who is standing on the beach today, inspecting his equipment as it is loaded in the canoe, is likely to believe that these paintings on the floats will make them more deadly to the whale.

In the mist rising from the surf, the harpooner's eight crewmen work to load the canoe, their long hair tied up for the task. Each crewman has a particular job. The man in the bow throws the harpoon; he is the owner of the whaling equipment; he is the captain, the one in charge. The man behind him and to his right stands ready to cast out the floats should a whale be struck. One man keeps the ropes clear after the whale run. The man in the stern steers and shouts signals.

To say that the crew is skilled in the water is an understatement.

T. T. Waterman, an ethnologist who studied the Makah in the early 1900s, said, "Better canoemen than the Makah probably never existed."

Each of the crewmen has been training since youth, when he raced around in a miniature canoe and threw toy harpoons on the beach. His life is built around the hunt for the whale. Even the ancient Makah marriage ceremony resembled a whale hunt. Eight men carried a canoe on their shoulders, while a man sitting in the back of the canoe pretended to steer, a man in the center prepared to cast off a float, and a man in the bow launched a harpoon toward the woman's door.

At last, on this misty morning in my mind's eye, the crew pushes off. They are wearing conical cedar caps that repel the rain. They are wearing rain capes fashioned from cedar that is carved and stripped and woven in cloth. If it is the evening, the crew uses the stars as a guide. At daybreak, they are several miles out near the halibut banks, ready to hunt. They sing songs: songs to ask the whale to surrender itself peacefully; songs to persuade the whale to swim toward and not away from their shore; songs to convince the whale that it would be welcome back at the whalers' village.

And when they spot a whale, they paddle as fast as they can, the canoe breaking through the water behind the great creature's soundings, the harpooner rising, timing the breaths of the whale, watching its tail come up and curve down into the dark depths, preparing to throw.

The crewmen on the hunt all knew the risks. "I once speared a whale near the tail, when the tail was under the front of the canoe," one Makah said long ago. "The tail came up and splintered the canoe. Some other canoes were watching and came to help us, but we lost the whale." Sometimes the whales tow the canoe out to sea. Towing could go on for three or four days, unless a lance was at hand to kill the whale more quickly, as in later years. The whalers carried dried fish and water for such situations, and in a box filled partly with sand, they built small fires, using coals carried inside a shell. Sometimes the whale raced ahead and the canoe began to submerge, to fill with water, so that the crew had to bail ferociously for their lives.

But in addition to the dangers, each crewman also knew the tradition of persistence, of courageous relentlessness for which the Makah whaler was admired, for which he is still admired, especially in Neah Bay, especially among his ancestors. One whaler was known to jump on the whale with a butcher knife, following the whale down into the dark, clinging to its back until it came up for air.

When the whalers caught the whale, when the harpoon was thrown and the crew began paddling backward ferociously, when the whale dragged them and dragged them and finally gave up, one man dived into the cold gray ocean, and to prevent the whale from sinking, sewed the mouth of the whale shut.

And then the canoe would tow the whale back—a task that could take several days, or, if in later years they ran into a tugboat, could take a few hours. (In one report, from the early 1900s, a tug towed four whales in one day.) On shore, the whalers would pray and then celebrate, and then they would have a feast, a huge celebration. When European settlers came, the Makah traded their oil in what was eventually Seattle and in what became known as Canada and made good money. In Neah Bay it is said that Victoria, British Columbia, was once lit with the whale oil of the Makah.

11 / The Whaler—A Modern View

One morning in the winter, Wayne Johnson invited me to come to a meeting down at J.J.'s Pizza, a little pizza place/coffee shop that was next to the fish storage dock in Neah Bay, where I could meet some of the first guys to join the crew. Darrell Markishtum, a paddler, was there. Darrell was in his early thirties and was an extremely nice guy, almost gentle. He talked about working to learn the Makah language at the museum; he said he was very interested in the stories and songs associated with the whale hunt. He ordered a latte. Donnie Swan had a Pepsi. Micah was supposed to be there but he drove out of town at the last minute and took the ferry from Port Angeles across the strait to visit his girlfriend in Canada. Wayne had coffee, black. Wayne is a big coffee drinker.

The crewmen talked about the possibility of taking hikes and maybe some sweats together in the future. They all seemed eager to get started. Darrell was thinking about getting back into tai chi. Wayne was needling Donnie about Donnie having given up smoking in preparation for the hunt. Wayne said that he and Micah had been out on the water with the National Marine Fisheries Service gray whale biologists the year before. Wayne had brought the whaling commission's new video camera, the idea being that the crew could study the best manner in which to approach a gray whale in a whaling canoe by watching the tape. Wayne said he had been filming a whale as it came up out of the water to breathe and that he didn't back up when the whale decided to blow. A wash of mucus-laden breath nearly ruined the commission's new camera. "You should see it," Wayne said. "It came right up in my face. I said, '*Jeez!* That *stinks!*'"

They were talking about what they'd heard of the old days, the time when whalers would go through long periods of quiet and fasting, of deprivation and prayer before the hunt. They talked about how men would beat themselves with stinging nettle plants, the nettles raising red welts on the whalers' backs, causing them to bleed.

Donnie said that he'd heard that the nettles raised the whalers' body temperatures so that they were better able to withstand the cold ocean water.

Wayne said that men would purify themselves by living alone in the woods and bathing in ponds and streams in the hills; they would abstain from sex, he said.

"If they hunted a whale," Wayne said, "and the whale got away, the first thing they would do is look around the canoe and say, 'Okay, who slept with his wife?'"

At this, everyone solemnly nodded his head and looked down into his caffeinated drink.

After coffee, the crewmen wandered down to the beach to inspect their canoe, the *Hummingbird*.[5] The canoe was kept in a shed alongside the senior citizens center and, as opposed to the whaling canoe of historic times, which was owned and maintained by the wealthy and powerful whaling captain, this canoe was communally owned. Then again, the crew did not intend to use the *Hummingbird* as the whaling canoe—it was just a practice canoe for now, until a traditional whaling canoe could be made.

Inside the Hummingbird were a few paddles the crew members had carved from planks of wood milled from timber on the reservation or else

5 In *Moby-Dick*, Melville writes that the whaling ship, the *Pequod*, is named after an Indian tribe from Massachusetts. But according to the commentary in my edition of *Moby-Dick*, this tribe was from Connecticut—specifically the area around Mystic, where, in a surprise attack just before dawn on May 26, 1637, between five hundred and eight hundred Pequot braves were killed by white settlers. Descendants of the survivors of the massacre still live in New England within several branches of the Pequots, including the Mashautucket Pequot. In 1935, forty-two members of the Mashautucket Pequot lived on the reservation. In the 1970s, the tribe began to make money selling firewood and maple syrup. In the 1980s, the tribe started a bingo game. In 1992, the tribe opened a casino, Foxwoods Resort. Also in that year, when the tribe was building a new museum, the site of the 1637 massacre was rediscovered.

just bought at a convenient lumberyard· and then decorated with black and red paint. There were also empty bleach bottles cut off at the top, which were used as bailers. The crew hadn't decided yet how they were gong to go about making the floats that they would attach to the harpooned whale, nor for that matter had they decided on exactly what type of harpoon they were going to use. There was a lot to do.

That morning, Wayne had talked about paddling around in the bay in the canoe, but now it was cold and rainy—the sky wore the gnarled, gray face of winter—and paddling didn't seem like a good idea anymore. Instead, they all stood around the canoe and made plans to train hard and then just talked. Darrell told a story about a whaler from long ago who got caught in the harpoon line and was carried to the bottom of the ocean and presumed dead until he came up a long time later—after he had, according to the story, seen the sunrise seven times. Donnie shared some modern whaling stories he had picked up, like the one about Russian whalers, indigenous inhabitants of the Chukotka region of Russia, who the Makah whalers had met at an indigenous people's whaling event. The Russian whalers described being tossed from their canoe and dangling in the freezing water as the whale came back and studied them as if it were pricing cheap jewels.

"When we met the Russian chief," Wayne added, "he said that not everyone's going to come home all of the time. The gray whale, if he gets mad, he'll attack you."

They all nodded their heads and were quiet for a while and then Wayne compared the length of a fifty-foot-long gray whale with the length of their thirty-foot-long canoe.

12 / The Canoe

One of the first tasks on John McCarty's agenda as executive director of the whaling commission was to see about getting a proper whaling canoe, but before the execution of this particular whale hunt task is considered, let me digress for just a moment with a brief report on the nature of the Northwest coast canoe, a report which may in itself seem tangential but is in fact significant to the story of the whale hunt as attempted by the

Makah. For a canoe may be a canoe to some people, but to the executive director of the Makah Whaling Commission or to most any Makah or to any of the people of the self-described Canoe Nations of the Northwest coast, the canoe is what a car would be to a twenty-first-century American if a car were not just a way to travel hundreds of miles for personal or business matters but also a piece of art—stylized and beautiful and designed for prominent display. The canoe is a tool that also happens to be the symbol of an entire culture, or, in the words of one contemporary canoe maker, "a spiritual vessel that was an object of great respect, from its life as a tree in the forest to its falling to earth as a log and finally landing on the beach as a finished craft." The canoe has been called "the single most important aspect of the Northwest coast culture."

It is only in the past twenty years that a Makah could pick up the phone in Neah Bay and readily talk to a canoe builder about building a canoe. Canoes were nearly extinct all along the coast in the 1950s, at around the time that many tribal members began purchasing gas-powered boats. In Neah Bay in the fifties, canoes were still used for fishing, though they were often towed out by powerboats to the halibut banks. Eventually canoes began showing up wrecked and rotting on the beach at Makah Bay and the beach at Sooes. A few people still remembered how to carve canoes, but the reservations all along the coast were being logged, and the big cedar trees necessary for carving canoes were more and more being sold off to timber companies.

The canoe was reborn in the early 1980s, thanks in part to the work of a tribe called the Haida, whose traditional land is north of Vancouver Island, along the coast of British Columbia, in the bays and rivers that now surround the borders of Canada and the United States. At the time, Bill Reid, a carver who lived in Vancouver, British Columbia, and was part Haida, began studying canoes in museums. He discovered much of what was written by anthropologists about canoes was wrong. The canoe in the Museum of Natural History in New York City is built backward, for example; the bow is carved from the butt of the log. Eventually, Reid built small models, and from those models he carved a fifty-foot-long canoe, using new and old tools. He named the canoe *Loo Taas,* which is Haida for "Wave Eater," and it wasn't the only Northwest Coast canoe on the water at the time, but it was certainly the most well known. With other Haida, Reid paddled from Haida Gwaii, in British Columbia, to Hydaburg, Alaska, to protest the division of a Haida land cut through by the international border. At one point, the *Loo Taas* traveled up the Seine River in France to Paris.

Different tribes soon began making their own canoes, which were expensive: a twenty-five-foot-canoe cost $35,000. Paddling events were organized, at which tribes along the Northwest coast met and paddled together. In 1989, at the Paddle to Seattle, on the one hundredth anniversary of the founding of the state of Washington, canoe tribes such as the Hoh, the Quileute, the Squamish, Tulalip, and Lummi convened. They delivered a message to the residents of the state of Washington that quoted the Duwamish leader Chief Seattle: "We lived and died here for hundreds of generations, and we offer our assistance in your coming to balance as an adult." *The Forum*, the newspaper in Forks, reported that people stood on the beach waiting for the canoes to return. The trip took fourteen days on the water. *The Forum* carried the headline: PADDLE TO SEATTLE BEGINNING, NOT END.

At the Paddle to Seattle, a member of the Heiltsuk tribe challenged all the other tribes to meet in Bella Bella in 1993. Tribes all along the Northwest coast that had not had canoes for a generation began building them and assembling crews. Soon, elders were taking young people out in canoes, teaching paddling, telling stories. In *The Great Canoes: Reviving a Northwest Coast Tradition* by David Kneel, one Northwest coast tribal member says: "We took a lot of sacrifices money-wise, which really didn't matter to us at the time, because we had young people involved, trying to find themselves, trying to keep away from the drugs and alcohol. No matter where we go we stress that because we believe it's important." The man added, "Myself, I'm an alcoholic and I haven't used the alcohol for quite a few years, since 1980. And I've been really happy doing what I'm doing, helping the young people. . . ."

When it came time to paddle to Bella Bella, in the summer of 1993, the canoes of the Northwest coast traveled for weeks on the Pacific. Support teams followed on land carrying supplies. Tribal elders went along and taught people the canoe etiquette that had nearly been lost. They told the young people the way, in the old days, paddlers prayed upon entering a village and showed respect for its people. The paddlers thanked the water for its help, thanked the tree that made the canoe.

The Makah crew paddled to Bella Bella, which is approximately 340 miles from Neah Bay, in the *Hummingbird*, a canoe that had been built on Vancouver Island for the Makah. It was summer. The Makah canoe traveled along the west coast of Vancouver Island, along the edge of the Pacific.

The U.S. Coast Guard had protested the Makah paddlers' itinerary; the other canoes went on the eastern shore, through the Inside Passage between Vancouver Island and the British Columbia mainland, which, in comparison, was a calm waterway. The Coast Guard advised the Makah to do the same. But the Makah paddled their traditional route, visiting the villages of their ancestors and relatives, the Nuuchahnulth. The seas were rough. The winds were clocked at thirty miles an hour. When they arrived in the little villages—Port Renfrew, Ahousat, Tofino—their canoe was carried in on the shoulders of the host villagers. The villagers greeted them with songs and celebrations and food—so much food that the men who paddled on that trip still remember feeling full and tired the next morning as they got into the *Hummingbird* again. To this day, the people who were on the paddling trip describe the event as a milestone for the tribe. It was as if a piece of the culture had been replaced, filled in, discovered again after being missing a long time. They recalled being tired and excited and overjoyed. One person remembered that in the last village on the last day of the trip someone had said, "Now we can go whaling."

Once I went out in the *Hummingbird*. It was a warm winter day and a couple of whaling crew members rolled it down to the beach on small logs and into the water. As they did, young Makah boys darted around the canoe like excited shorebirds. Micah paddled, along with Darrell and some other guys. The *Hummingbird* felt solid and imperturbable as it effortlessly cut through the water. It slipped past the tiny whitecaps in silence, almost secretly, as if it weren't a canoe at all. It sliced. In the distance ahead, the windblown blue water turned from bay to strait to infinite ocean.

13 / Details

As I continued to visit Neah Bay over the winter, as I became more comfortable with the winding and sometimes icy road into town, as I was forced repeatedly to convince the magazine editor to whom I had promised a short, concise report on Makah whale hunt preparations that, yes, training would most likely begin in earnest soon, that, at the very least, there would be a new canoe that I could write about or that the magazine might be able to photograph or something—as I stalled, basically—the details surrounding the whale hunt seemed to me to get even more complicated.

There were lots of problems.

With regards to the canoe, for example, John McCarty wanted it to be carved in Canada while other whaling commissioners wanted the canoe to be carved on site, by local carvers. John was having trouble getting money for the crew to train full-time, and was toying with the idea of getting the crew members jobs making roofs for hot dog stands—though this plan wasn't going over well with the crew. John was also frustrated about the rules for the hunt that had been negotiated between the tribe and the federal government. He had been on the phone with the National Oceanic and Atmospheric Administration, and officials there were saying that they wanted the Makah to hunt whales in November, when a gray whale migration was certain to be in full swing. "I told them that it was ridiculous to send the crew out there in November," John said. "There could be twenty-, twenty-five-foot waves." Micah commiserated with his father. "Our sacred tradition is so wrapped up in red tape that we're incarcerated," he said.

Some of the things that seemed to be going well for John were the interviews that he helped arrange. Newspaper reporters who came out to see the whalers were almost invariably impressed with Micah, and pictures of him began appearing prominently in the local papers.

But the single feature of the hunt that could actually be seen rather than visualized was the element that was to deliver the whale hunt's final detail: the whaling gun.

The gun that the Makah initially planned to use to kill a gray whale, after landing a harpoon, was a .50-caliber rifle. It had been recommended and developed for the tribe's use by a veterinarian from Maryland named Al Ingling. Tall and lanky, and in his late sixties, with gray hair and beard and mustache trimmed short, Ingling was a retired professor of veterinary medicine at the University of Maryland, where he was known, among other things, for perfecting ways of slaughtering cattle by electrocution. Aside from being a veterinarian, Ingling was a man of diverse engineering-related interests who always seemed to be on the verge of solving a complicated mechanical puzzle that was vexing him. He was an electrical engineer, a licensed master electrician, and a certified truck mechanic. He enjoyed welding in his spare time. When I ran into him on the reservation, he struck me immediately as a man of acute practicality. "I have a fascination with tools," he told me as he lay back on his bed in the tribal motel back behind the tribal offices. His long arms were folded behind his pillow. "I probably have more tools than anyone you know," he said.

Ingling ended up working in Neah Bay by accident. He had recently finished studying camel husbandry in Africa, and, shortly after he returned to the United States, he wound up in Barrow, Alaska, where he assisted an Inuit tribe. Alaskan tribal officials had contacted the University of Maryland for help with their bowhead whale hunts on the Arctic Ocean (the Inuit bowhead hunt is also sanctioned by the IWC). For many years, the Inuits used a bomb lance, which is not a lance, in fact, but a bomb that explodes upon penetrating the whale. (The term *lance* is used because a lance was the instrument traditionally used to kill a whale after harpooning it.) But the bomb lance had mixed success for the Inuits. In the seventies and up through the mid-eighties, many of the whales targeted on these whale hunts were wounded and not killed or killed but not captured. In 1977, according to a report on aboriginal and subsistence whaling issued by the IWC, seventy-nine bowhead whales were struck but then lost. Around that time, a Norwegian veterinarian who also had an interest in weaponry, Egil Öen, worked with the Inuit to develop a penthrite bomb lance, the charge of which was meant to be less hazardous to the whalers and more effective in killing whales. (Alaskan whalers often lost their unexploded bombs in unkilled whales, and the bombs would only be recovered years later when the whales were successfully killed.) Öen's recommendations didn't immediately help the Inuit. It was in an attempt to remedy this situation that Ingling was contacted by a scientist in Alaska. "At that point, a friend up there called and said, 'I know you're a vet and I know you're interested in crazy things. Could you come up and help with this problem?' So I went up there and I resolved the problem with the gun," Ingling said. It had all been a matter of miscommunication—the Inuits and the Norwegians used different weaponry measurements, Ingling pointed out. "It's a basic law of ballistics that the ammunition has to fit the gun," Ingling told me. Shortly thereafter, the percentage of whales wounded and not captured by the Alaskan whalers dropped by 60 percent.

Ingling happened to be in Alaska on the day in 1997 when the Makah tribe called for advice on how to go about hunting a whale. "Basically, the Makahs' problem was they didn't know where to start," Al remembered. "They couldn't just use the technology their ancestors used because they would basically just be putting a whale on a stick and waiting until it died. And they knew that was no good. So they called the American Eskimos.

On the phone, they said, 'Can you come down on your way home?' I said, 'Let me go home and repack my suitcase.' Then I went home and I brought a gun back to Neah Bay with me, and I said, 'Look, this is the way I think you should do it. You can do your hunt in the canoe. You can follow your traditions. The only thing that's different is you won't have to chase the thing around for hours. You can use this damn thing.'"

He pointed to the gun in the case at his bedside. "Basically, when you look at the tradition here," he said, "the Makahs' ancestors never used the darting gun and the U.S. government said you have to use the darting gun the way the Eskimos did. So I said to these guys, 'Look, your ancestors saw the darting gun and they didn't use it. For about forty years, from 1870 to 1910, they had access to it. So you have to ask why. Why didn't they use it? And I think it's because the gray whale is too small. So I recommended that they go harpoon the whale and then just shoot it with a big rifle."

Ingling thought of the ancient hunt without sentimentality, and he seemed to me to have developed his own very clear vision of how it had gone, especially for the whale. "Oh, the old whaling, it was terrible," he said. "You stick a harpoon in it and you chase the whale until it tires out— for hours. Then you'd take a lance and you'd stick it in the heart. Quite often you'd miss the heart but you'd hit the lungs and, you know, it would drown in blood or something." He shook his head, as if confounded by the inefficiency of it all. "There was no way that you could drive a lance through the brain by hand," he said.

It was Al Ingling who presented a paper on the humane killing of whales to the International Whaling Commission on behalf of the Makah. As a result, he was attacked by people opposed to the whale hunt, especially animal rights activists, but he saw his work with the Makah as a service to the whales.

"With humane killing," he told me, "what you want to hit is what you call the brain stem. That's the primitive point of a brain. That's what the animals developed first. That's what controls breathing and simple actions. Or you can hit the spinal cord. So in a whale, that's probably an area that's two feet long and probably about a foot wide. That's where we get a lot of criticism. They say it's such a small target. The whole brain is only about this big"—he stretched out his arms—"which isn't very big. Kind of like a chicken, relatively speaking. People are always talking about how intelligent whales are, but if whales were so intelligent—well, I mean, go up and look at the Eskimos. They whale in skin boats. If whales were so intelligent, then the

Eskimos would all be dead. But going back to the gun, if you hit anywhere near the spinal cord, the brain's pretty much going to be liquefied jelly."

14 / The Protestors

Each time I arrived in Neah Bay early in my whale hunting observation adventures, I scanned the marina for any sign of the armada of antiwhaling vessels that were rumored to be on their way. After a while the thought of their arrival, or, more specifically, the thought of any potential clash between these protestors and members of the Makah tribe made me agitated, in part because it was taking them so long to show up. Several well-known environmental groups had decided not to get into the public debate over the hunt. (Greenpeace did not officially oppose the hunt, for instance, nor did the Sierra Club.) But there was one group that had already sailed into the harbor at Neah Bay and asked the Makah not to whale. That was the group I was always on the lookout for, the group I'd already heard so much about. That group was called the Sea Shepherd Conservation Society. By the time the Makah were first poised to hunt, on October 1, 1998, there would be many individuals and groups who would come by boat and car and try to stop the Makah whale hunt, but the Sea Shepherd Conservation Society was the de facto lead protestor, the first among equals, and the leader of Sea Shepherd was Captain Paul Watson.

Watson, the founder of Sea Shepherd and the group's president, came to Neah Bay as a legend among radical oceangoing conservationists. A founding member of Greenpeace, he had been a part of some of the most famous antiwhaling protests of all time. In 1975, Watson was on board the *Phyllis Cormack,* a converted halibut seiner, when it encountered a pirate whaling ship, the *Dal'nii Vostok*. The *Dal'nii Vostok* was a 750-foot-long, ten-story-high factory ship; it took in whales from a fleet of smaller whaling boats that followed it through the ocean, and it slaughtered and processed the whales on board for eventual use in such products as shoe polish and lipstick. Watson hoped for an encounter between the *Dal'nii Vostok* and the *Phyllis Cormack*, and the *Phyllis Cormack* set off on an anti-whaling mission, flying flags from the United Nations, Greenpeace, British Columbia, and a Buddhist monastery. The Soviet ship was at sea for fifty-eight days; along the way, its food stores had become contaminated with diesel fuel. The activists finally discovered the whaling ship three hundred miles off the coast of California. The stench of the floating slaughterhouse hovered over a bloody sea of whale appendages. On board the Soviet vessel, there was a woman playing volleyball in a bikini; she waved at the activists, not knowing their intention, as blood dripped from the decks of the ship. Watson and his fellow activists watched the whaling ship pull whales up through a giant door in its stern. Later, in his memoir, *Sea Shepherd: My Fight for Whales and Seals,* Watson sounded like an old-time sea captain, when he recounted standing on the deck and soliloquizing: "What manner of beast it is that feeds through its anus!"

When they arrived on the scene, the activists immediately came upon a young sperm whale. "My God!" one of the crew members shouted. "It's only a baby!" Watson got out of his boat to stand on the whale as it died. He felt the whale's skin, still warm and oily, and the warm blood running from its body. Watson calculated that the whale was only twenty-three feet long, seven feet short of the IWC regulations. "I felt lost and lonely upon the ocean with that dead whale child," he later wrote. Then, Watson and his crewmates set out to get in between the whalers and the whales. They used inflatable boats, called Zodiacs, a model recently developed by Jacques Cousteau that would soon become stock-in-trade in the whale protest movement. When riding in the Zodiacs, the activists wore white banzai scarves and referred to themselves as kamikazes. At one point, Watson got between the 250-pound explosive harpoon and a pod of sperm whales. The harpoon fired over his and his fellow protestor's heads. It hit a female sperm whale with what Watson described as a *thwap!* The harpoon immediately exploded within the whale, killing it. "We heard her scream," Watson said. At that point, according to Watson, the male sperm whale that was swimming beside the female whale turned and headed toward the Soviet whaling ship and slammed into the steel bow. The whale was then harpooned. It bled from its head. "His eye fell on Fred and me," Watson wrote, "two tiny men in a little rubber raft, and he looked at us. It was a gaze, a gentle, knowing, forgiving gaze. Slowly, slowly, as if he did not want to disturb the water unduly, as if taking care that his great tail did not scrape us from our little perch, he settled into the quiet lapping waves."

On that expedition, the Greenpeace crew filmed the death of the sperm whale that had been harpooned. They also filmed their relatively diminutive Zodiacs standing before the harpoon guns of the whaling ships. A few weeks later, Walter Cronkite introduced their film on TV and helped make Americans aware of pirate whaling. The *Phyllis Cormack*'s expedition was considered a milestone in the battle to enforce the worldwide ban on commercial whaling.

After its battle with the *Dal'nii Vostok,* Greenpeace continued on, but eventually Watson left the group. He became known for the use of violence to accomplish his conservation goals—he had become too radical for the radicals. He founded Sea Shepherd Conservation Society in 1978 with the support of Cleveland Amory, an animal rights activist. He bought a 779-ton trawler, rechristened it *Sea Shepherd,* and reinforced its bow with eighteen tons of concrete. In 1979, he rammed the *Sierra,* a pirate whaling ship, in the waters off Portugal. He rode into the *Sierra* as if he were riding a mad whale. After hitting the *Sierra,* the *Sea Shepherd* made a run for England but was apprehended by a Portuguese destroyer. Watson's passport was confiscated but he escaped to England. In 1980, Watson went to jail in Canada for interfering with a seal hunt. He ends his memoir like this: ". . . I must die some day. And when I do, an epitaph that said I fought to save the whales and the seals and all the creatures of the earth would not be too bad a thing. That is what I will be doing—fighting for the whales until there are either no more whalers or no more whales. I will be doing that and I will be continuing to worry about this: We know what killing the whales is doing to whales. But what is it doing to us?"[b]

---

[b] In "What's Your Archetype?" an article published in the July 1997 edition of *Writer's Digest,* a magazine for writers, Nancy Kress, the author of the piece, analyzed four classic plots for fiction writing, including the chase, the competition, the romance, and the quest plots, using examples from literature, including *Moby-Dick.* She offered the plots to be used by writers "as a skeleton over which to fashion your individual characters and incidents." *Moby-Dick,* Kress wrote, has at its core a subspecies of the quest plot, called an object-quest plot. "In some object-quest novels, the object being sought may not even be that important in and of itself. How much was a white whale really worth to Ahab . . . ? But as Herman Melville well knew, objects take on symbolic significance to the human mind. *Moby-Dick* isn't really about the quest for just a white whale. It's about the quest for mastery of nature, for imposing one's will on the enormous Other. . . ." Some questions that Kress suggests writers ask themselves before they undertake a novel with an object-quest archetype are: What is being sought? Why? What are the obstacles to finding it? How many different groups are looking for it? Who are they? Is the object going to be found? Where? Is it found where it was expected to be? Who's going to triumph in the quest? How will other groups react? Where does the object end up at the conclusion of the story? Alfred Kazin, another writer who wrote about writers and writing, wrote this about Melville's object-quest novel, in an introduction to *Moby-Dick:* "The book is not only a great moral skin of language stretched to fit the world of man's philosophical wandering; it is also a world of moral tyranny and violent action, in which the principal actor is Ahab. With the entry of Ahab a harsh new rhythm enters the book. . . ."

One day, I called up Paul Watson and spoke to him on his ship-to-shore phone about the Makah whale hunt. He was on his way to Neah Bay via Coast Rica where he was tentatively planning to protest shark and dolphin poaching. He said, "This is the most important whale hunt of the past twenty-five years."

15 / Whalers of the World

Early in the spring, when the snow began to fade from the clear-cuts across the strait on Vancouver Island, when salmon ran up into the rivers and the whales began migrating past Cape Flattery on their way to Alaska, when the start date for the whale hunt was nearer and hopes were running high among the Makah whaling crew, a contingent of whalers from around the world arrived in Neah Bay. The whalers were members of the World Council of Whalers, a group of aboriginal and nonaboriginal whalers who are interested in reviving whaling around the world. The world whalers took the ferry to the Olympic Peninsula from Victoria, British Columbia, on Vancouver Island, where they had just wrapped up their second annual world meeting. (Victoria is a few hours' drive south from their one-room world headquarters in Port Alberni, British Columbia.) The Makah, who consider it a matter of pride to be good hosts, immediately set about welcoming the group, which included Chief Happynook, a Nuuchahnulth whaling chief from Port Alberni, who was the president of the council, and representatives of the World Council of Whalers, who had traveled from such places as Antigua and Barbuda, Canada, Dominica, the Faroe Islands, Greenland, Grenada, Iceland, Indonesia, Japan, New Zealand, Norway, the Philippines, Russia, St. Kitts and Nevis, St. Lucia, St. Vincent, the Grenadines, Australia, and Tonga.[5] The arrival of the world whaling rep-

---

[5] Melville himself traveled in the vicinity of Tonga. In between the time that he was at sea as a whaler, and before he returned to the United States as a sailor aboard a U.S. naval frigate, the *United States,* Melville jumped ship in the South Pacific. He spent a few months living in the Marquesas, among a tribe that was thought to be cannibalistic. He left when he thought that he might be eaten. He got aboard a passing whaling ship, and became involved in that ship's mutiny, for which he was jailed in Tahiti for a short period of time. When he finally made it

resentatives gave Neah Bay a global feel. But at the same time—given that the politics of whaling are such that pro-whaling nations are considered to be practicing a philosophy counter to what is considered good for the continued existence of the whale species and given that whaling is deemed disreputable and is despised in so many parts of the planet—all the delegates, as much fun as they seemed to be having, also seemed to be glancing nervously over their shoulders the entire time.

To look at the faces on the visiting whalers as they stood around on the main street in Neah Bay was to see a mini-history of humanity's nearly expired hunt for the whale. There were the Icelandic whalers, who had whaled since medieval times, when they called their prey horse whales, red whales, and pig whales. They also hunted what today are known as the killer whale, the narwhale, and the right whale. There were the Greenland whalers, who have long hunted the minke and traditionally eaten its blubber as a snack, called *muktuk*. There were the Tongan whalers, who began to hunt whale just after 1888, when a man named Albert Cook was left behind by a New Zealand whaling ship and married a local woman named Liangiangi and then built a whale boat and began whaling and selling the whale meat to the islanders, who eventually whaled. There were Maori whalers and the whalers from New Zealand and the whalers from Indonesia, who do not generally eat the meat of the whales but trade it instead for vegetables. There were the whalers from the Faroe Islands, who are known among people who are philosophically opposed to whale hunting as the most ferocious whalers because of their custom (documented annually since the time of the Vikings) of herding pilot whales into bays and then up onto the beaches, where the Faroe Islanders wade into the shallow water and kill the beached whales with knives. Also in Neah Bay with the World Council of Whalers, standing in back, were the most reviled of the world's

---

back to America, sailing stories were all the rage and he decided to write up his adventures, first in *Typee: A Peep at Polynesian Life*, and then in its sequel, *Omoo: A Narrative of Adventures in the South Seas*. Both were big hits, even if they were decidedly antimissionary, an unpopular bent at the time. After this success, Melville decided to become a professional author, which was a pretty difficult thing to do in the mid-1800s. (Only two American authors—Washington Irving and James Fenimore Cooper—were making a living as writers.) He became known as "the man who lived among the cannibals." Henning Cohen, of the University of Pennsylvania, wrote: "*Typee* also shows tendencies which Melville would continue to develop: the suspicion that things are not quite what they appear to be, that values and behavior differ from place to place—though in any place people have a capacity for evil, even when their life seems idyllic or their avowed aim is to do good—and that objects and events are meaningful though one can never be sure *what* they mean. These things lay beneath the surface, and this, too, was characteristic."

reviled whalers, at least among nonwhalers and the people who fight to save the whales: the Japanese.

On the morning of the second day of the world whalers' visit, there was a demonstration of the whaling gun. Everyone carpooled out of town to a little clearing out toward Sooes Beach.

I drove with Darrell Markishtum, one of the members of the Makah whaling crew. Also in Darrell's car were two Japanese whalers. I was interested to hear what the Japanese whalers had to say because opponents of the Makah whale hunt often argued that the Makah hunt was being funded by the Japanese and that the Makah were just being used by the Japanese to reestablish worldwide commercial whaling. These particular Japanese whalers did not speak much English, however, and I do not speak Japanese. On the way to the gun demonstration, we passed the old village site near where Darrell's family is from. Darrell pointed to a spit of land. "The other day I was down there with my nephews and I said 'This is where you are from,'" Darrell said.

At this point, the Japanese whalers asked Darrell and me something but we weren't certain what they were saying, so we all ended up smiling and nodding at each other.

Then Darrell talked to me about being prepared for protestors. He said that he had served in the military in Germany and in the Korean demilitarized zone and that he expected to put his military training to good use. "One of my specialties, I guess you could call it, is terrorism," he said. "I'll be able to use some of my skills here."

We got to the clearing, which was within sight of the beach and the river, and we waited around with other whalers of the world. There were a lot of jokes about stringent antiwhaling regulations and about environmentalists. The tone of all the conversations was *anti*-antiwhaling. A man in his thirties from New Zealand, who described himself as a policy guy and not as an actual whaler, said that environmentalists in New Zealand sometimes played music into the blowholes of beached whales to ease their pain in dying. Everyone within earshot of this story shook his head and laughed.

Pretty soon, Wayne arrived with the .50-caliber rifle that Al Ingling had been testing for the humane-kill portion of the hunt. Wayne carried the gun in its aluminum case and he was wearing mirrored aviator sunglasses and cowboy boots so that when he stepped out of the car he looked like some kind of hit man from the seventies, as if he'd just stepped out of an old Clint Eastwood movie. Micah, who was his usual hip looking self, was assisting Wayne, and everyone watched as they prepared to fire the whaling rifle into a big cedar stump.

Wayne knelt down with the gun in his hand and peered slowly through the gun sight and then looked up and warned everyone about the sound. He explained that when he had tried to shoot it in the canoe before it was adjusted for kickback, the rifle had knocked him down. The world whalers all held their fingers in their ears for a while until nothing happened and they unplugged them. Wayne stood up and said there was some kind of problem. Micah tried to shoot the rifle and the same thing happened, so everyone stood around making more inside jokes about international whaling regulations. Finally, Wayne knelt down again and shot the gun. The blast hurt my ears, which were plugged. The bullet went through the stump and Wayne went flying back. The stump barely moved. Then Micah shot the gun and a chunk of red cedar rose high up into the air. The whalers took their fingers out of their ears and broke into applause.

After the gun demonstration, all the world whalers drove down to the beach to take a ride in the Makah canoe, the *Hummingbird*.

John McCarty was there, talking to a Tongan whaler, a heavyset man with a windbreaker that said TONGA. John McCarty introduced him to Micah. John was talking about the spiritual importance of the hunt, about his family and his son. He told the Tongan whaler about all the logistical details, the management plan. The Tongan whaler listened. John recalled the tribe's trip to Monaco, to the International Whaling Commission meeting there. "At Monaco we were told, 'You better do it right,'" John said.

"It's like being on a stage," Micah added.

I stood with a whaler from Iceland and a whaler from the Faroe Islands. The whaler from Iceland said that their languages were related enough so that they could understand each other fairly well. The whaler from the Faroe Islands introduced himself to me in his thick Scandinavian-sounding accent and exaggeratedly rolled his eyes, as if to say he had heard all the criticisms of his style of whaling before. "I am the bloody pilot whaler," he said.

"Everyone in the business is interested in this," the Icelandic whaler told me. "In Iceland, we do the whaling, well, like we are running a paper mill. Not this religious way."

At one point, the Faroe Islands whaler questioned John McCarty, saying, "What are you going out there in the canoe for? Have you gone Hollywood?"

"Well, it's how we said we'd do it to the International Whaling Commission," John replied.

Eventually, the canoe was carried down from the senior center, as children and dogs watched. A few whale hunting crew members got into the canoe. The Icelandic whaler turned to me and shook his head. "I hope they are careful," he said. "In Iceland, we hunt for whales much smaller than the gray whale and we use a boat that is much bigger than this one. I hope they are careful because with a whale, you know, it's not a game."

The Icelandic whaler and then the Faroe Islands whaler and then a Japanese whaler stepped carefully into the *Hummingbird* for a trip out into the bay. At one point, Micah rose up in the canoe and pretended to launch a harpoon. One of the Japanese whalers standing on the shore snapped a picture.

16 / Potlach

On the second evening of the visit of the World Council of Whalers, the Makah held a big dinner that was intended to welcome the visitors and introduce them to the ways of the Makah, their culture, their music, the way that they whaled. It was like a potlach, which is a kind of feast particular to the people of the Northwest coast. In the tradition of the coast people, the potlach is more than just a party. It is a party and a community meeting and a family celebration and a state dinner and even a kind of religious service all in one.

The word "potlach" is rooted in a Nuuchahnulth word meaning "gift" or "to give"; sometimes it is translated as meaning "Indian business." A potlach might be held for a marriage or a birth, to dismiss the shame associated with the escape of a slave, or to celebrate the coming of puberty for a chief's child. A potlach could last for days. People canoed in from all over the coast. Potlaches were great ceremonial events during which chiefs stood and gave speeches that stressed the lineage of their power. They could go on into the night in the cedar longhouses on the beach, with dancers wearing elaborate costumes with giant flapping wings, masks carved from cedar, jaws that opened and shut. There was singing and speech giving and dancing—dances with masks made from cedar and decorated like the faces of wolves, like the head of Thunderbird—but potlaches were mostly an occasion in which to distribute gifts: otter skins, the skins of fur seals, seal oil, baskets, blankets, and whale oil, which was highly prized. A chief's greatness was demonstrated by the greatness of his gifts, by the wealth he distributed. Wealth was everything, though a person was known not so much for his private wealth as the wealth he distributed, and some of the names of long-ago Northwest Coast individuals reflect this tradition. Some translations are He-Buries-Them-with-His-Gifts and What-You-Get-You-Can't-Store-Up-Because-It-Is-So-Much.

When European sailing ships came to the Northwest coast, the potlach changed, as did Northwest coast society in general. Russian fur traders were the first to come, trading with the Tlingit in Alaska around 1760. In the 1770s, British and Spanish ships arrived. In the beginning, change was not so much imposed on the tribes; it was more the result of trade. Most obviously, goods such as muskets upset the balance of power among coastal tribes; raids became more deadly than they might have been otherwise. But the fabric of society was also transforming. The economy switched from one based on hunting and gathering to one based on trade. Very quickly there was a frenzy of acquisition. Suddenly, a mere commoner who was adept at trading had the wherewithal to hold a potlach ceremony rivaling that of a great hereditary chief. A chief, meanwhile, had access to incredible amounts of new wealth such that, in the years after the first contact with whites, chiefs all along the coast commissioned totem poles and carvings and all kinds of objects that were executed gloriously and expertly, not just in the customary materials—in wood, in stone—but in new kinds of material that were not traditional per se but were handled by traditional carvers in traditional ways. The Tlingit carved chess pieces and cigar cases that were sold to visitors but also used at home. In a Haida village in Alaska, there is a totem pole crowned with a non-Indian, a sailor. It was a chaotic bull market.

While the economy was changing and villages along the coast were being introduced to guns and alcohol and Christianity, people everywhere were dying. Thanks to smallpox, influenza, tuberculosis, and venereal diseases the Northwest coast population went from fifty thousand to thirteen thousand between 1835 and 1843, according to rough surveys of officers of the Hudson Bay Company. (The population is thought to have been as high as seventy thousand before the arrival of the boats that coastal residents referred to as the Houses on the Water.) The end result was a simultaneous Golden Age and expiration of Northwest coast culture. Thanks to the influx of wealth that came from trade with Europeans and Americans, potlaches could be bigger and more grand than anything seen before; chiefs had more to give away. However, both the lineage and the very culture that a potlach could now so enthusiastically celebrate were nearly gone.

When the coastal land became of value to the early white settlers of Canada and what eventually became the United States, the influence of whites went beyond trade and disease, and both governments set out to contain and then destroy the culture of the coastal tribes. The Nuuchahnulth and the other coastal groups were confined to small areas of land. They watched as canneries ate up their salmon or—in the case of the Makah—as commercial whaling made their hunt untenable. All over the coast, the tribes were prohibited from speaking their languages. Christianity was forced on them. And beginning in 1886, potlaches were banned. One Canadian government official at the time described the potlach as a "foolish, wasteful and demoralizing custom."

And yet, at the turn of the century, around the time that the Makah were embarking on their last whale hunts, when they were using canoes and harpoons and being towed back by steamboats, the potlach was still alive, though undercover. The tribes did not call them potlaches. They called them Christmas celebrations or Thanksgiving celebrations; they said that they were merely giving out gifts the way the white man did. They said they were just dropping by in their canoe to deliver some birthday gifts or anniversary gifts or whatever. They said this because if they were caught giving a potlach or playing old Indian games or dancing old dances, then they would be arrested. In order to host their non-potlach potlaches, tribes built great buildings and disguised them as gymnasiums and then cleared out the gymnastics equipment and, when the Indian agent wasn't looking, danced and sang for days. Older people in Neah Bay still talk about how their parents used to paddle out to the back of Tatoosh Island, out of sight of the Indian agent. There, as the surf pounded onto the sandy beach, they would dance and sing and tell stories and shower one another with gifts. On the side of the island that faces the sea, a whaling captain basked in the glory that the whale brought.

And customarily, at that time and in earlier times, the setting at which plans were announced for a potlach, or for any great undertaking of a village or a tribe, was a feast.

So it was that the Makah held a feast for the visiting world whalers.

The feast was held in the community hall, which is a white one-room building on the edge of town. Long folding tables were set up with lots of folding chairs. Women came out of a small kitchen with paper plate after paper plate heaped with smoked fish and boiled potatoes. Plastic drinking cups were filled with seal oil, which people used for dipping fish and potatoes. There was fruit punch donated by the local market. And a guest of the World Council of Whalers, a Japanese woman named Mrs. Ohnishi, served raw halibut. The raw halibut was unusual for a Makah potlach. Generally, the Makah don't eat raw fish at their community meals—it is not considered a traditional dish. But this particular dish of raw halibut was prepared by Mrs. Ohnishi on behalf of the Japanese whaling delegation, who, through translators, had expressed some dissatisfaction with the afternoon meal of fish chowder. Mrs. Ohnishi did not speak English but I learned from New Zealand's whaling delegate that she had a whale restaurant in Japan and had written a whale cookbook, the title of which was translated for me as *Mrs. Ohnishi's Whale Cuisine*. Out of respect for the Makah, Mrs. Ohnishi was dressed in a traditional Japanese kimono. When the Makah women approached her in the kitchen, where a group of Japanese whaling delegates were huddled, she smiled and bowed. When Mrs. Ohnishi's raw halibut dish was distributed throughout the hall, it was eyed tentatively by the Makah.

At the dinner, I sat next to a man interested in supporting Scandinavian whalers in traditional-style whale hunts, and as I sipped my fruit punch I couldn't stop thinking that he looked like a Viking: he had a strong chin, steel blue eyes, and white hair that looked permanently blown in an invisible wind. Across from me and to my left were two men and a woman from England; they spoke furtively about the taste of whale meat and said they were working on some sort of pro-whaling publication. One of the guys in this group was making jokes he didn't explain, which began to bug me—there was something that seemed sinister about him—and after dinner was over I moved across the room and waited for the festivities, while the tables were cleared away by the Makah teenagers.

As the sky faded to black, six or so men stood in a circle and began to drum. The drums were made of strips of cedar bent in circles that were covered with elk skin. All the men wore caps and jeans and T-shirts and flannel shirts and were dressed like anyone living on the west end of the Olympic Peninsula except that they were also wearing headbands woven from cedar and their vests were decorated with white buttons in the old style. The men sang to the high ceiling of the community hall in tones that sounded like a cross between a moan and a cry. They sang songs that were so old that even those among them who spoke the Makah language did not understand all the words.

Then came the dancers. A long line of women and children danced the Paddle Dance. They wore button blankets—red and black blankets decorated with white buttons arranged in the shape of birds or animals, such as eagles or whales—over jeans or skirts or sweatpants. They carried paddles, and danced as if they were in a long canoe, paddling, turning, singing, as if repeating the lines of a poem over and over.

Suddenly a man came out of the kitchen area in back. He wore a red and black button blanket that almost completely covered him as he crouched ominously in nothing but gym shorts. I learned later that it was Arnie Hunter, one of the whaling commissioners. Arnie danced The Mask-Changing Dance, which was accompanied by a song that originally came from Clayquot, a settlement on Vancouver Island, and was given to Charlie Swan, an old chief and relative of Arnie Hunter's. (The song was *given* to Charlie Swan because to the Makah songs are like property. There are some songs that are owned by the tribe, songs that anyone can sing or even record, and then there are songs that are owned only by a particular family, in this case the Swans.) Arnie danced slowly, theatrically, with bursts of hypnotizing movement. He danced low to the ground, like a wolf, his face painted black.

I watched senior citizens mouth the words to the old songs. I watched some of the tribal council sitting in front. I saw Micah watching the proceedings and talking to the world whalers as they approached him—the visitors seemed to like Micah, seemed caught in his natural charisma.

Wayne Johnson was off to the side of the hall. He was neither drumming nor singing; he rarely stood to sing the tribal songs or the songs of his family. In fact, he never really drummed—that wasn't his thing. He was sitting there during the potlach trying to get the whaling commission's video camera going, which he finally did with help from a Scandinavian whaler.

The World Council of Whalers delegates bounced their heads to the music. Mrs. Ohnishi sat down in a chair in the front, her hands in her lap; she sat on the very edge of her folding chair in her kimono. She was the picture of courtesy and politeness, of respect.

The drummers sang *Wa' nu nukwinay ke su o' ye,* which is part of a song that can be translated like this:

> *I am singing because of the seasons.*
> *That is why I am singing.*

They sang the song over and over, the drums beating, Arnie Hunter dancing, covering his face with a blanket from time to time, as if he were an animal hiding behind some brush. And then suddenly, as he continued dancing, he put on a mask that he'd hidden beneath the blanket. He did it so smoothly that you barely noticed the change, you barely noticed the metamorphosis that is often part of the old Makah stories and art—the transformation, in this case from man to wolf.

And then, after more drumming and more singing, a speaker stood before the small crowd and began to speak as if he were in a hall even larger than the one he was in. He spoke ceremonially. "We thank you for coming to our nation today," he said. His voice filled the hall, like water in a tide pool. He waved an eagle feather, pointed around the room, and then said, "We know that all of you are here because of this great creature, the whale. You know we are here under a microscope, and everybody is waiting for us to do something we are not supposed to do, but we are a proud people, and we will do what we are here to do."

With his feather, the speaker pointed to the whalers sitting behind him in their chairs—to Donnie, who sat there looking typically strong and confident, a sly smile on his face; to Micah, who was his charismatic self; to Wayne, who had the video camera turned off now, resting in his lap, and was looking uncomfortable.

After a while representatives of different families stood with small wads of dollar bills and made speeches of thanks and gratitude and then passed out bills to the visitors, to friends, to council members, and to elders, as a sign of welcome, as a sign of power. The last thing I heard the speaker say was this: "It's time for us to forget about all those disagreements among families. It's time for us to think about all these great men who have come so far to see us. Once again, our ancestors have taken care of us. And so our

ancestors take care of us and next we'll have whales on our shores again."
The room erupted in cheers.

The singing and dancing went on into the night. I stayed as late as I
could. Somewhere around midnight I realized I was falling asleep in my
chair against the back wall, along with a couple of other people who were
dozing off. When I left, everyone was still dancing and singing, and Mrs.
Ohnishi was sitting on the edge of her chair, smiling a tired but exquisitely
perfect smile—a picture of respect.

In the whaling office the next day, John McCarty was talking to Darrell
Markishtum, Donnie Swan, and Wayne Johnson. All of them were jazzed
up about the night before, especially John, who was talking about how the
crew qualification process was about to begin. More crew members had
been chosen and now just about all of the twenty-three families in the village were represented on the canoe.

Micah said he'd talked to other whalers about the timing of the harpoon throw. Donnie said he had also been talking to some whalers about
harpooning and had spoken to a Japanese whaler about an electric lance.
"What really got me was that everybody was in there hearing about our
culture," Donnie said.

Darrell mentioned that he felt a little queasy after eating the raw fish
that the Japanese contingent had prepared. Everyone grimaced in unison.
A few minutes later, Donnie said his stomach felt funny too—although
no one actually got sick.

The following week, the Humane Society got wind of the fact that the
World Council of Whalers had been to Neah Bay, and representatives of the
Humane Society complained to the U.S. Commerce Department; they said
it was proof that the Makah were at the heart of an international conspir-
acy, that the tribe was part of a cabal intent on overturning the worldwide
ban on commercial whaling. The newspapers reported the Humane Society's complaint. The Commerce Department then called the Makah and
asked them not to associate with the World Council of Whalers anymore.

"Showing hospitality is our way," John McCarty told a newspaper
reporter. "And we felt an instant comfort with these people because they
were fellow whalers. But we didn't invite them. We've been told not to get
involved in any way with these guys."

A few days after that, John told me that he was sorry the world whalers
had come.

17 / Whales

At the center of the controversy over the whale hunt that was about to begin in Neah Bay was a particular species of whale.

Of the dozens of species of whales, the whale at the center of the controversy was *not* the great sperm whale. The sperm whale is, of course, the whale that most people imagine when they are imagining whales. It is the whale in *Moby-Dick*. It is the whale whose head is filled not with sperm, as people believed thousands of years ago, but with a clear liquid, the purpose of which scientists are not entirely certain about. (I recently read an article that speculated on the role of the liquid in buoyancy control.)

The whale at the center of the Makah whale hunt controversy was also not the humpback whale. The humpback is the whale with the long wing-like flippers that many of the people who paint whales enjoy painting. It is the favorite whale of whale watchers everywhere, the celebrity whale. It is the whale that makes a sound while swimming underwater that people record and put into popular music, sometimes with jazz saxophonists playing along. The humpback is the whale that, despite its name, doesn't actually have a hump but a small dorsal fin.

The whale on behalf of which the protestors were protesting in Neah Bay was also not the orca, which is known as the killer whale and is actually not a kind of whale but a kind of dolphin. The killer whale is the small but formidable predator that roams through the bays of the Great Pacific Northwest in packs, like wolves, which is what the Northwest coast people believed these whales turned into when they magically transformed and took to the land. The killer whale is the movie star whale, the whale in *Free Willy*, a movie about a boy who makes friends with a whale in an aquarium and frees it into the open ocean. In real life, killer whales hunt all kinds of underwater mammals, even the largest whales. In fact, some experts believe that the name "killer whale" may been a mistaken reversal of the Basque term for the orca, which was "whale killer."

Likewise, it was not the blue whale that the Makah would be hunting. The blue whale is the largest animal that has ever lived on the earth— dinosaurs weighed less. The blue whale takes in as many calories in krill in one day as the average human being eats in a lifetime. It has arteries large enough for a child to crawl through. The blue whale cannot be measured precisely, given that it can never be put on a scale all at once. The blue whale is thought to have the most powerful voice of any animal if the sounds that blue whales make can be called voices. Its sounds can travel fifteen hundred miles underwater—a blue whale could conceivably talk across an entire ocean—though what the blue whales actually use their voices for, no one can say with certainty.

Most if not all of the above-mentioned whales have been hunted, of course, by various tribes and nations and corporations in various places around the world at various times in history. For example, the ancient Persians hunted whales, as did the Phoenicians. The Basque hunted whales and kept whaling ships on the shores of North America in the 1500s, long before Columbus explored the West Indies; the Basque were the first great commercial whalers. Another great commercial whaler was the United States. At the height of American whale fishery at the end of the 1800s, America had more whaling boats out to sea than all other nations combined, many of them sailing from Nantucket. The Pilgrims learned whaling from the Nauset Indians. Before they even landed in the New World, early on the Pilgrims proved that they needed whaling lessons. It is sometimes said that the first shot fired in the New World by one of the Pilgrims was fired at a whale as it passed by the *Mayflower.* The gun exploded and the Pilgrim who fired it was nearly killed.

American whalers followed the same general procedure that whalers followed throughout time and throughout the world. They sought out and subsequently discovered whales in a new area that had not previously been whaled. They then whaled there until very few whales remained. Then they looked for a new place to whale. One of the most extreme examples of this pattern occurred in Antarctica. In 1904, the first whaling ship to visit Antarctica was like a kid in a candy store. There was, according to one whale expert, "a slaughter unparalleled in the history of human hunting. . . ." The whalers brought huge factory ships, which dragged the whales up a slipway and onto the deck, where men worked with winches and huge flensing knives and giant pots and cut up the whale and boiled and rendered it—a fifty-ton whale could be processed this way in forty-five minutes. In later years, people in airplanes watched from the sky for more whales to hunt and kill and process.

In Antarctica, 750,000 fin whales were killed, in addition to 360,000 blue whales, and then hundreds of thousands more sei whales and humpbacks and sperm whales. The slaughter was so complete, so maniacally efficient that even the whalers became worried about saving whales. In 1948, the International Convention for the Regulation of Whaling formed the International Whaling Commission. In 1972, the United Nations passed a resolution that called for the end of worldwide whaling. In the same year, the United States passed the Marine Mammal Protection Act. And then, finally, in 1982, the IWC approved a moratorium on all commercial whaling. The Soviet Union stopped whaling in 1987, the Japanese in 1988. (There are still nations that engage in quasi-legal whaling under the auspices of science.) In some cases, the moratoriums were too late. Some whale populations are today reduced to the point where they may not ever come back—whales like right whales, bowheads, and humpbacks. At the moment, no one knows how many blue whales exist.

But—and it should be stressed again—blue whales were not the species of whale that the Makah were planning to hunt. The whale the Makah were planning to hunt was the gray whale.

18 / The Grayness of the Whale

The gray whale is gray. The skin of an adult gray whale is a dark gray—it looks like wet rubber. The skin is mottled, with barnacles and scars and parasitic creatures that altogether make for a texture that causes the gray whale to appear even more gray. The gray whale is so gray, in fact, so visually at one with the cold, slate-colored ocean it swims in when it swims in the Great Pacific Northwest, that as it rises slowly from the waters off Cape Flattery, it seems geologic, like an underwater outcropping, like a part of the earth itself that's coming up to look at you, a great gray cognizant rock. The gray whale is so gray that sometimes, when you see a gray whale, it is unclear at first what exactly it is, if anything. Sometimes, it seems like a natural ripple in nature's own gray matter, a small swatch of the ocean's vast-textured fabric.*

---

* In his introduction to the Modern Critical Interpretations edition of *Herman Melville's Moby-Dick,* Harold Bloom writes: "The visionary center of *Moby-Dick,* and so of all Melville, as critics always have recognized, is Chapter 42, 'The Whiteness of the Whale.'"

Other names for the gray whale are the hard-head whale, the mussel digger, the gray-back, the rip-sack, and the scrag whale. In Japan it is known as *kukujira,* which means "the small whale," though the gray whale is considered a relatively large whale in Japan. The scientific name of the California gray whale is *Eschrichtius robustus,* a name which was given to it in 1864 to honor Danish zoologist Daniel Eschricht. Its first scientific name was *Balaena gibbosa,* which means "humped whale" in Latin, possibly because of the series of knuckle-like humps that run along its back where a dorsal fin might otherwise be. That name was later changed to *Rhachianectes glaucus,* which means "the gray swimmer along rocky shores." Early whalers along the Pacific Coast referred to the gray whale as the devil fish, because of the fierceness with which it avoided being hunted—gray whales routinely smashed boats.

Some facts that are more or less certain about the gray whale are as follows:

The gray whale grows to between thirty-five and forty-five feet in length. It weighs between twenty and thirty-five tons. It is long and narrow; in aerial photographs, it is shaped like a bold-faced exclamation point, with a fluke at the bottom instead of a dot. The tail of a fish is vertical but the tail of a whale is horizontal, and the two flukes of the gray whale's tail generally measure about ten feet across and weigh in the neighborhood of four hundred pounds. The long head of a gray whale has a small amount of bristly hairs, possible proof that the gray whale evolved from fur-covered land animals—most likely artiodactyls, which are hoofed, even-toed animals like pigs, cows, and hippopotamuses. The skeleton of a gray whale resembles that of a hippopotamus; its six-and-a-half-feet-long flippers look amazingly like hands. The eye is brown and the size of a softball.

The gray whale has grooves in its throat that expand as it feeds. It sometimes feeds on the ocean floor; on the bottom, it rolls, sticks its head in the muck, and sucks the mud into its mouth. Gray whales almost always put the right side of their heads into the mud, leading gray whale biologists to believe that gray whales are right-handed, in a sense. With its giant tongue, it pushes the mud through the baleen that lines its mouth, straining out the food. The baleen is nearly white and resembles the whisks of a broom. The baleen plates are made of keratin, which is the same substance that makes up human fingernails. In 1874, Charles Scammon, an early expert on California gray whales, observed the following about gray whales with regard to their eating habits: "When returning to the surface, they have been seen with head and lips besmeared with the dark ooze from the depth below . . ."

When a gray whale finishes eating, the ocean floor is dimpled with ten-foot pits. In the Bering Sea, the average gray whale sifts 156 tons of sand every year. Much of the food that they eat off the ocean floor consists of tiny amphipods, which look like very small shrimp. They also eat ghost shrimp, opposum shrimp, and tube-dwelling worms called *Diopatra*. When they eat food that lives closer to the surface they eat things such as plankton, krill, crab larvae, and herring roe. They will suck eelgrass for small crustaceans. They eat kelp. They eat a ton of food a day but what is most notable about their eating habits is the variety of food they eat. Gray whales are not picky. They eat almost anything.

Gray whales carry more lice and barnacles than any other whale, so that as the gray whale spends its life eating its way along the West Coast, things are constantly eating gray whales. Gray whales are covered with tens of thousands of barnacles. The barnacles sit in their limestone shells and group in clusters on the gray whale's back; they filter plankton from the water as the gray whale swims. Gray whales can carry up to a ton of barnacles on their bodies. They also carry little creatures that are called whale lice but are not lice at all. They are amphipods, and they feed on the gray whale's damaged skin. They settle in scars and cuts. They are about the size of a quarter. They cling to your hand with a sharp pinch, and if you look at them closely they look like something made by a special effects team for a science fiction movie about a scary creature from deep space that attacks the world and can't be stopped. Of the three types of whale lice commonly found on gray whales, the most common is *Cyamus scammoni*. (*Cyamus scammoni* is named after Charles Scammon, the previously mentioned gray whale expert.) One hundred thousand *Cyamus scammoni* were once counted on a gray whale's body. When gray whales are born they are a pure and smooth gray, but they begin accumulating barnacles and lice as they scrape the ocean floor, developing patterns that are distinctive, so much so that whale biologists are able to identify particular whales. The total effect is to give the creature a sad, tormented palette, which, if the gray whale weren't thought of as beautiful, might be considered ugly. Then again, the gray whale isn't always gray. In 1957, a Russian biologist reported seeing a partially albino whale in the Bering Sea. His front half was completely white.

The gray whale is the buffalo of the sea. In giant herds, most California gray whales migrate every year from the Bering, Chukchi, and Beaufort seas to the Baja Peninsula, a trip that can be as long as five thousand miles; it is the longest migration undertaken by any mammal. Gray whales feed off the coast of Alaska in the summer and then they swim down the coast of British Columbia and Oregon and Washington and California and stop in the coastal lagoons of Baja, where the females give birth. In the spring they swim back up again and wait for the next migration. During the three-month-long trip, the whales eat nothing. They worry about killer whales attacking them, which Scammon described: "The attacks of these wolves of the ocean upon their gigantic prey may be likened to a pack of hounds holding the stricken deer at bay. They cluster about the animal's head, some of their number breaching over it, while others seize it by the lips and haul the bleeding monster under waters; and when captured, should the mouth be open, they eat out its tongue." The Makah, in addition to other Nuuchahnulth tribes, hunted gray whales as the whales migrated past Cape Flattery, and the tribes of Alaska hunted gray whales as well, but the aboriginal hunt is thought to have had little effect on the whale population. The numbers are estimated to have been close to twenty thousand before commercial whaling began on the West Coast. Commercial whaling brought the California gray whale close to extinction in the mid-1870s. Today the gray whale population is thought to be near twenty-four thousand. That the gray whale has come back so successfully from near extinction is considered a great conservation success story.

As is the case with whales in general, there are gaps in man's understanding of the gray whale's physiology. For example, the gray whale's taxonomic classification is disputed, as is its evolutionary standing. Some scientists say it is highly developed and others say that because it feeds close to shore and breeds in lagoons it is in fact the most primitive whale of the species. Scientists know very little about the level of intelligence of the gray whale. (Scammon saw intelligence in the manner in which they ran from harpoons: "Numerous contests with them have proved that, after the loss of their cherished off spring, the enraged animals have given chase to boats, which only found security by escaping to the shoal water or to shore.") Gray whales' social behavior is not well understood. It is still unclear why gray whales travel to Mexico to breed and give birth or why some migrating whales do not go all the way to

Alaska, but live in the bays off the coast of Washington and Vancouver Island—the whales in this latter category are referred to as resident whales. It is not understood why some male resident gray whales lie side by side with their sexual organs intertwined. Jim Darling, a gray whale expert who reported such an incident, has said: "What their mating system is, how they communicate, which is part of social behavior—all of this is still a mystery."

There are also gray areas in the area of human relations with gray whales. For example, why have humans sometimes become enamored of gray whales and sometimes slaughtered them? One of the most famous instances of human compassion for gray whales happened in 1988. An Inuit hunter off the coast of Point Barrow, Alaska, discovered three young gray whales. Traditionally, an Inuit hunter would have used the whales to feed his village. But on October 15, this particular individual used a chain saw to cut square patches in the ice that led to open water. Other villagers helped. They used water-circulating pumps to keep the ice from freezing at night, and a hover barge blasted warm air on the water. A giant crane pounded holes through the ice with a giant hammer. New teams from all over America and the world arrived to see if the whales would escape. President Ronald Reagan announced that the gray whales were in the nation's prayers. The National Oceanic and Atmospheric Administration was there, with whale biologists. The U.S. State Department contacted two Soviet icebreakers in the area. The whales were surrounded by pack ice. It is thought that they had been feeding and forgot to migrate. For a while, the whales were hesitant to leave the area. At one point it looked as if the whales were going to go but when the reporters all ran across the ice to watch, the whales swam back. The edges of the ice cut the whales and made the snow bloody. While they sat there, the whales were given Inuit names and English names (Putu, Siku, and Kanik, and Bonnet, Crossbeak, and Bone, respectively). At one point, when polar bears threatened the whales, there was talk of shooting the polar bears. Eventually, the smallest whale, a nine-month-old baby, died on October 21. On October 28, one of the Soviet icebreakers broke the ice and led the two remaining whales to open water. The rescue cost a million dollars. The headline in *Time* magazine read in part: FREE AT LAST! One of the biologists on the rescue commented: "This is completely out of proportion." But a whale expert expressed the sentiments of many people in retrospect when he wrote: "Although the rescue of the gray whales trapped in the Alaskan ice involved huge expense to reverse a common and natural event, it underscored the changing attitudes of humans toward whales."

To many people, especially those on the protest boats that would soon arrive in Neah Bay, it was clear that a gray whale should not be hunted and killed, let alone any other whale. But for a lot of other people, there were considerations that gave the situation an ambiguity. The gray whale was no longer considered to be on the verge of extinction—in fact, the gray whale's population had rebounded incredibly; the Makah promised to take a small number of whales—five in two years; the Makah said that they would not whale commercially. In some people's minds, my own included, the effect that the hunt would have on the gray whale population, not to mention whale-human relations—wasn't clear. It was gray.

19 / Donnie Doesn't Kill a Seal

As the spring progressed, I thought I noticed that Wayne was becoming more and more exasperated with the progress of the hunt preparations. There were protests in Seattle and the continued threats of protests in Neah Bay, but a lot of John McCarty's plans were fizzling out, due to lack of funding and a general loss of political momentum. Eventually, the whale hunt preparations stalled. On the positive side, the crew took a trip to Alaska to meet with Inuit bowhead hunters. There had been plans to go out with the Inuit on one of their traditional hunts in April, but when the Makah flew to Barrow, Alaska, and met with the aboriginal whale hunters, it was too cold to hunt: ice covered the Arctic Ocean. The trip was still exciting for the crew. Micah danced for the Arctic whalers, and Wayne saw the skin boats that the Inuit hunted in and talked with Alaskan whaling captains about their crews. Donnie got to know some of the women in the Inuit village. But then, when the crew returned to Neah Bay, hunt preparations came to a standstill. The crew ended up just killing time as the excitement of the trip to Alaska evaporated. There wasn't much to do besides wonder about the protestors, whose planning seemed to be going a lot better than the whale hunters'. Around this time, a made-for-cable-TV version of *Moby-Dick* came in over the satellite dishes that sprout up around the reservation. Some of the guys watched it.[5] "The crew is falling apart," Wayne said to me. "It's like we're losing community now."

As captain, Wayne was trying to keep some momentum going on the hunt, if only for himself and Donnie. So one day, Wayne and Donnie went out and tried to hunt a seal.

I met the two of them outside the market. They had just chopped some wood for an elderly woman in town. They were in a white pickup truck, reading the local paper, *The Peninsula Daily News*. The headline said, SHERIFF PREDICTS WHALE OF A PROBLEM, and it cited the increase in Web sites that were critical of the Makah. Neither Wayne nor Donnie had jobs at the time, although the tribal council put them to work from time to time cleaning up around town. They picked up fallen tree branches, raked the three cemeteries, or cut the grass in the park that commemorates all the people who died in the smallpox epidemic at the end of the 1800s. In Neah Bay, working in this capacity is referred to as working for the Beautification Committee. They drove over to Donnie's house, the white double-wide trailer where he was living with his brother Randall, the fisherman. They picked up a thick, seven-foot-long dowel that Donnie had bought at the market. He put a barbed seal hunting tip on the end, one that he'd been given by a whaler in Alaska, and attached a strong nylon line. Randall watched Donnie and teased him.

"Watch out for them big seals," Randall said.

Donnie rolled his eyes at Randall and then showed him the seal hunt-

---

[5] According to *Broadcast & Cable*, an industry trade magazine, *Moby-Dick* scored the second-highest viewership ratings in what is referred to in the cable television industry as "basic cable history." Only USA Networks' original movie *China Lake Murders* received a higher rating, in 1990. The chairman of USA Networks, Kay Koplovitz, stated that she was pleased the mini-series "drew such a highly diversified audience, many of whom where exposed to this significant American classic for the first time." The other top scorers that week were *South Park*, a cartoon show; *Rugrats*, a cartoon show; and TNT's *World Championship Wrestling*. I didn't get a chance to watch that version of *Moby-Dick*, but in Hoquiam, which is south of Neah Bay on the Olympic Peninsula, I discovered an old copy of *Moby-Dick* in an antiques store. It is a shorter, happy-ending version of the story, in which Ahab, the monomaniacal whaling captain, manages his anger and ends up making it home to his wife, whose name is Faith. I later discovered that this book is the novelization of the 1930 film version of *Moby Dick*, in which the whale loses and Ahab (John Barrymore) hobbles home to his wife (Joan Bennett), even though Ahab's wife only appears offstage in Melville's version of *Moby-Dick*. In the novel, Ahab doesn't make it home. The little book ends like this: "He came to the familiar gate, and was about to enter, when suddenly a figure flashed out of the house and ran down the path. 'Ahab!' Faith called. 'Ahab, it's you! I knew you'd come. Oh, Ahab, dear Ahab, I've waited so long.' No more words were necessary. Ahab knew he was forgiven. Life was full and golden—it had been given him to have his revenge, and to receive his reward."

ing permit in his wallet. The permit had significance for him. "These are probably the first seal tags pulled by a Makah in maybe decades," Donnie said. Then he announced, "This is definitely a kind of mock whale hunt."

Before he went sealing, Donnie ate a late breakfast over at the VFW hall, while Wayne watched him. Arnie Hunter was there.

Arnie Hunter is the whaling commissioner who danced at the potlach-like feast held for the whalers. He runs the local VFW hall. It is the only all–Native American VFW post in the country, according to Arnie. Once in a while, I've seen him out jogging in the morning, or at least I've seen the light from his big-screen TV flickering in his front window as I passed by. In addition to exercising, Arnie also stays in shape by eating healthily. He buys powders and extracts at the health food store in Port Angeles, two hours away, and takes a handful of vitamins every morning. He drinks only herbal teas; he eschews caffeine and alcohol.

Part of the reason he takes good care of himself is his role as a tradi-tional dancer. Arnie learned the dances from his grandfather. Arnie once told me that he thought his grandfather would pass on the dances to someone besides him—one of his older male relatives, perhaps. But one day, out of the blue, his grandfather began teaching him. Arnie doesn't restrict his interest in music and dance to traditional Makah music. He is also the DJ on Friday nights at the Clallam Bay Inn, one of the two tav-erns half an hour down the road; the first time I saw him there he was playing a lot of funky stuff from the 1970s, like the Bee Gees. And yet, despite his extensive involvement in traditional and contemporary ritu-als, Arnie is basically a quiet guy. One time I was standing down by the marina and watching the sunset. Arnie was standing there too, and he mentioned that his family is a member of the bear clan. I asked him if there are any personality traits that characterize the members of the bear clan, to which he responded with a long silence. He was still looking out into the sunset and I was thinking that he had perhaps not heard me and that I should just forget the question, when at last, Arnie said, "Kind of shy, I guess."

The inside of Arnie's trailer is huge. There is a kitchen, an office for Arnie, a few bedrooms for visiting veterans, and a bathroom. There is an eating area that doubles as a meeting room; there is a large-screen TV and people come to sit before it and drink coffee and talk for hours. On the walls are pictures of some veterans in town—Bill Tyler, Frank Smith, Clifton Greene—and a sign that reads:

GREAT SPIRIT

GRANT THAT I MAY NOT CRITICIZE MY NEIGHBOR

UNTIL I HAVE WALKED A MILE IN HIS MOCCASINS

The VFW hall doubles as a small restaurant, and a woman named Joan Carol is the cook. On this morning she made Donnie a big breakfast: eggs and pancakes and sausages. I had pancakes. Wayne had coffee and cigarettes. Arnie's mother, Helma, was there. (Helma is also Donnie's and Wayne's aunt.) Helma was often at the VFW hall around breakfast time. She works at the museum as a language teacher, among other things. Once I watched her as she was copying over the weather diary of James Swan: pages and pages of careful and ornate nineteenth-century script that repeated over and over the word *rain*. Helma is in her eighties, and she is her family's matriarch.

We all sat quietly for a while and watched TV as Martha Stewart made lampshades.

As he ate, Donnie mentioned to Helma that he was going sealing that morning. Helma became especially animated at this news, and she immediately began reminiscing about a relative of hers who had hunted seals in the sea caves in and around Cape Flattery. She said that the caves were dark and this old seal hunter would sometimes enter with a torch. The thunder of the waves as he entered a cave was deafening but he had an advantage in that respect because he was deaf. He would swim into the cave and surprise the seals, sometimes clubbing them to death. She said that occasionally men would get lost in the cave as the tide came up and then would be rescued at the next low tide.

Donnie and Wayne and Arnie listened to Helma while they watched TV, and then Wayne and Donnie got up and went to the marina. On the way out the door, Donnie said, "The traditional stuff—it's all starting to come back to me now."

At the docks, Donnie got into a polyethylene canoe he had borrowed from a fisherman. A friend of Donnie's paddled. (I don't remember his name but I do remember that when Donnie picked his friend up at his house, the friend's wife was with their newborn baby and she was complaining that it had been a week since she had asked the clinic for antibiotics for the child's ear infection.) I was with Wayne as he followed Donnie in the harbor boat, putting along as quietly as we could. We passed fishing boats and little racing canoes made by the high school:

sometimes I saw a few of the women in town using the canoes for paddling practice out on the bay late in the day, keeping in shape. Donnie and
Wayne moved slowly around the marina in tandem. It was a perfectly
clear day. A wisp of a white cloud stretched out over Bahokus Peak, which
stood against the steel-blue sky like a 3-D illustration. Inside the breakwater, where Donnie was poised now in the bow of the canoe, the water
was as smooth as glass. Ahead, the whiskered noses of seals broke the surface over by the fish dock, where they ate discarded fish guts.

Donnie was ready. He had his Oakley sunglasses down and a cigarette
dangling from his lips—he was smoking again but he planned to give it up
again soon, in time for the final spiritual and physical preparation period
before the hunt.

In a few minutes, Donnie moved toward a seal in the open water and
threw his harpoon. The shiny brass tip of the harpoon slipped into the
water. Simultaneously, the seal disappeared into the brownish-green darkness. Four or five seconds passed slowly and the seal did not appear.
Finally, the harpoon floated up to the surface, a miss. Donnie looked back
and shook his head. "As soon as they see me stand up they're gone," he
said. Wayne joked that the seals seemed to be relearning aspects of traditional seal hunting faster than Donnie was.

Wayne and Donnie changed tactics and Donnie got into the harbor
boat with the harpoon. Wayne moved the boat very slowly under the fish-
processing dock. In a minute, we spotted a harbor seal. It was huge—
about three hundred pounds. It was lolling in the water, maybe dozing,
impersonating a log. We inched toward it. Donnie launched the harpoon.
It was a long and difficult throw, but the harpoon arced perfectly. "You *got*
him!" Wayne said. The thick nylon line attached to the harpoon ran from
the boat for a second. "You *got* him!" Wayne said again. Donnie grabbed
the line and pulled quickly. When he got the harpoon into the boat, he
saw that it was attached to nothing.

They spent the remainder of the morning cruising for seals out in back
of Waadah Island, but they didn't see any. Donnie was not discouraged.
"We'll be going out all the time now," he said.

Wayne docked the boat early and went over to Arnie's house, where he
helped him make a fire on the ground in his backyard. When the fire got
hot, they threw a bunch of rounded black stones into the coals. The stones
were for a sweat that evening, when Wayne and Donnie were going to
come over and sit in Arnie's sweat lodge. The lodge was a circle of plywood

covered with insulation, the kind traditionally used to wrap water heaters. Inside, the floor was covered with a brown shag carpet. In the center of the carpet a circle had been cut around a small hole in the earth, which was lined with the metal tire rim of a car. The tire rim held the hot rocks.

That night, when the rocks were hot enough, everyone stripped down to gym shorts and went inside the sweat lodge. The rocks seemed to glow for a moment as Donnie carried them inside in a wire crate, and then they were dark. When we'd all found our places on the ground, Arnie poured water from a coffeepot onto the stones. The stones protested with sizzles and sputterings and steam. Wayne and Donnie and Arnie were mostly quiet, except for sighs and exaggerated gasps for hot air.

After a while, Wayne spoke up. "Pretty soon, everybody on the crew is going to start taking sweats three, four times a week," he said, "when the training really gets going."

Donnie nodded. Arnie remained silent.

Wayne continued, "And we're gonna start getting out there in the canoe." Wayne was curled up low in the lodge, the heat almost unbearable. "The women are out there every night canoeing," he said, "and if the women can do it, we can too."

Things got worse before they got better because it was around this time that Wayne went in to see about whale hunting supplies and ended up in jail.

He had driven into Port Angeles with Donnie and some other crew members. He brought one of the Alaskan whalers' harpoon points with him. He wanted to get them copied by a machinist—ideally, the crew wanted to have five or six of them.

Wayne got out of his car to talk to the machinist, a guy he knew. "How much would it cost to get one of these made?" Wayne asked.

The machinist told him the price.

According to the police report that was eventually filed, the machinist said that Wayne then proceded to ask him for money for liquor, which he refused, and then Wayne "sucker-punched" him in the mouth as he turned away. According to Wayne, it wasn't like that at all. "If we bought three of them, would you give us a discount?" Wayne asked.

The machinist looked at him and began grumbling. Then according to Wayne, the machinist said, "Oh, yeah, you fucking Indians. You always want a deal."

Wayne got mad. "You better stop saying that or I'm gonna hit you," he said.

The man supposedly then repeated himself: "You fucking Indians. You always want a fucking deal."

Wayne could feel his blood boiling, his temper taking over. He slugged the machinist, who went down. As the man was getting up, Wayne got back into the car and started driving back to Neah Bay. On the way, a police officer stopped them.

"Is Wayne Johnson in this car?" the policeman asked.

"Maybe." Wayne responded.

The police officer noticed that Wayne's hand was bleeding. Wayne was put into the patrol car and later convicted of fourth-degree assault. The sentence was $250 in fines and a year in jail. He didn't have the money to pay bail or get a lawyer. The jail time was suspended after he'd been in jail for two days. He didn't have any money left from his unemployment check. "I pleaded guilty because I couldn't afford to come back," he said later. When he filled out the paperwork in court and he came to a form that asked his occupation, he wrote, "whale hunter."

When he showed up at court several days later, he was ordered to get a psychological analysis and subsequently to attend an anger management class in Port Angeles. Attending the anger management class was going to be difficult for Wayne. He had no car and no job. "I don't know how I'm gonna get there," he said. "It makes me mad."

20 / All Riled Up

And now for a little bit of the big picture, for a view from above of the state of the hunt, from a satellite, let's say, with which we can discern the overall progression of the whale hunt machinations in Neah Bay and environs. Now for an end-of-the-summer whale hunt wrap-up on the crew, the protestors, and the news media representatives, starting with the latter, who were, as a group, an inspiration to themselves, a kind of self-stirring pot, a crew all astir. As the news that the tribe was planning to hunt some time after the first of October made its way through phones and computer

screens to Seattle and elsewhere, newspaper editors and television producers and news professionals of all kinds grew increasingly interested in the
whale hunt. This was followed by a commensurate growth of interest in
the whale hunt on the part of the antiwhale-hunt activists, the end result
being that the hunt began to develop a momentum of its own, with more
unforeseeable outcomes, more controversies within the already existing
ones. The hunt became—in the chaotically formal and semiliturgical
manner of the postmodern news coverage that tends to surround such
controversial public happenings—an event.

In other news, various groups of protestors made several attempts over
the summer to stop the tribe in court, all of which failed. Judges ruled
that the Makah had gone through proper channels and, furthermore,
had the right to hunt whales, as stated in their treaty. There was a rally in
Seattle against the whale hunt. And in August, calls went out for protestors to turn up at Makah Days, the annual summer festival in Neah Bay,
in which members of tribes from all over the Northwest and Canada
come to race in canoes and dance and sing and enjoy games and carnival
rides in remembrance of the day in 1924 when Makah tribal members
became citizens of the United States. With threats of violence in the air,
the governor of Washington sent truckloads of National Guardsmen to
Neah Bay to stand guard over Makah Days. An FBI SWAT team was also
reportedly on call, though in the end Makah Days went off without incident. During Makah Days, Sea Shepherd was barred by court order from
entering the harbor. Captain Watson sat offshore and broadcast whale
calls from the loudspeakers on his boat, the *Edward Abbey*. In the sky, an
airplane towed a banner that said SEA SHEPHERD OPPOSES MAKAH COM-
MERCIAL WHALING. Small groups of picketers lurked along the edge of
the reservation, but hoards of protestors did not appear. In the absence
of conflict, one of the most notable events of the weekend came during
the canoe races, when for the first time in many years a Makah canoe
won.

Taken together, the newspaper and television reports were like a growing wind that the modern traditional whaler would be forced to forecast
and monitor, to maneuver with or against before the crew was to hunt, and
this wind had already picked up over the summer. The reporters began to
assign the participants in the whale hunt various roles. The gray whale was
cast as the representative of nature. Whales were shown migrating, viewed
from the air, in pods of two or three as they cruised through the clear blue

water, resembling oversized dolphins. Captain Paul Watson appeared as the defender of those whales, as the dauntless commander of the small fleet of ships that would perhaps stop the hunt, or at least get in the way—a often-noted possible turn of events that only added to the potential drama. As for the Makah, they were generally shown in the canoe. Sometimes, the video footage featured Micah—bare-chested, looking as if he could have stepped out of the Makah museum, looking like a symbol. One television station repeatedly featured him throwing the harpoon at a life vest that stood in meekly for a gray whale. This video was broadcast over and over, and each time Micah missed. Another television station showed Wayne—in a T-shirt and aviator glasses, looking unceremonial in comparison—holding what was deemed modern and thus impure: the gun.

The news reports also mentioned those tribal members who were against the hunt. Over the summer, a group of tribal elders who were representatives of this last group took out a half-page ad in the local paper, *The Peninsula Daily News*. The ad said that the current tribal council's decision to hunt whales did not reflect the opinion of the majority of the tribal members and that tribal bylaws had been disregarded. "The whale hunt issue has never been brought to the people to inform them and there is no spiritual training going on. We believe they, the council, will just shoot the whale," the ad said, adding, "For these reasons we believe the hunt is only for the money. They can't say 'Traditional, Spiritual and for Subsistence' in the same breath when no training is going on, just talk. Whale watching is an alternative we support." One of the elders who signed the ad was Alberta Thompson, who was the self-proclaimed spokesperson for those Makah who were against the hunt. She had allied herself with the protestors, and the protestors welcomed her—especially Sea Shepherd, and a less-well-known group called In the Path of Giants.

Thompson spoke regularly at whale hunt protest events. She appeared in the video produced by such groups as the Progressive Animal Welfare Society, or PAWS; she was filmed on her trip to Baja, California, to see gray whales in the lagoons where they bred. On its Web site, Sea Shepherd offered a video of her speaking out against the hunt. Thompson lived on the reservation and worked in the senior center, where she had an office and helped with the food program. Short but heavyset, Alberta Thompson had black hair with a beautiful streak of silver in it that reminded me of the streak of white that characterizes an orca. After she saw the whales in Baja and touched a mother and her calf, she told the Associated Press, "I'm in it to save the whales." Alberta Thompson had a long history of speaking up on the reservation on various topics. Some people called her a gadfly; some people called her a hero. (Once Wayne said, "If I was against whaling, she'd be for it.") At the end of the summer, it was reported that Alberta Thompson had lost her job at the senior center—she was ostensibly fired for making a long distance phone call. This enraged the protestors.

The protestors did not deter the crew—even if they made some of the men on the expanding roster of whale hunters anxious. There were some personnel adjustments—John McCarty was replaced with a new executive director, Denise Dailey. She was a Makah fisheries biologist, a woman in her thirties who had previously worked over at the hatchery. She was not a member of the whaling commission; by appointing Denise the whaling commission had put a fisheries bureaucrat in charge, someone who could keep the paperwork moving, issue a whaling permit, and perhaps even apply for grants. She moved into John's office and papered the wall behind her desk with editorial cartoons that were against the whale hunt and tried to get things rolling, to execute the whaling commission's commands more efficiently. Because she was a woman, the commission insisted that she not speak for the crew, so Keith Johnson, the president of the whaling commission, was dubbed the spokesman for the hunt. Denise debated for a couple of days before she took the job. "I'll never hunt a whale because I'm a woman and I'm okay with that," she told me one day. She was in her office. She was wearing a flannel shirt and jeans, and we were talking about hunting and bird-watching, two of her hobbies. "A year ago, I wouldn't have imagined that I'd be sitting here," she said.

John McCarty wouldn't have imagined it either. John had lost his job. He told me that he had only found out secondhand. He said that when he confronted the council members, he was told the council was planning on shutting his office down. John had seen his own plans fall apart: there was no funding for full-time training and the federal government was still asking the crew to hunt during the time of year when the water could be rough. In the end, he was so upset that he left town for a while. He went to work with a relative who was a roofer over on the other side of the peninsula.

By August, Wayne was still the captain of the crew, but now there was a new, higher-ranked captain, a captain *in* the canoe, who outranked Wayne. That was Eric Johnson. Eric was the son of Marcy Parker, the Makah councilwoman who had served as the tribe's delegate to the International Whaling Commission. (Keep in mind that many people are named Johnson in Neah Bay, and keep in mind further that all of the Anglo-Saxon names were handed out arbitrarily by the Indian agents who administered the Makah reservation early on: sometimes brothers were given the same Anglo-Saxon name to replace their Indian names, sometimes different ones. That said, Eric was not directly related to Keith Johnson. As a matter of fact, he happened to be very close to Wayne's mother.) Initially, Eric had not been involved in the hunt. His instatement as captain was a kind of coup de crew imposed by the council, against the will of at least a few whaling commission members. He joined the crew just as the contingent of whalers left for Alaska. Although he had not previously trained with the team, Eric was an experienced paddler. He had paddled from Neah Bay to Bella Bella years before. Since then he had been in the Navy and now he taught preschool at the Head Start program in town. He was a muscular guy of medium height, with a gentle face and a soft voice. This personnel change was a shock to some of the paddlers on the crew—to Micah, for instance, who was still officially on the crew even if his father was without portfolio in the whaling operations. And yet despite all the political ripples, Eric Johnson had the crew out practicing nearly every day.

When John McCarty returned—he'd quit the roofing job when he hurt his back—he was a disgruntled member of the whaling commission. He had had plans to take the crew off for a spiritual retreat, to enable Micah to harpoon the whale in what he envisioned as perfect spiritual purity. But he had been, in his estimation, ignored, beaten back. As a result, when he got back to town, he became the sacred whale-hunter-in-exile, the loyal opposition.

On a hot day, toward the end of the summer, I ran into Micah in the parking lot of the market. The dirt road back by his house was dry and dusty. The water in the ocean and in the bay sparkled in the breezy sun. Micah was still carving but he had also gotten married to his girlfriend, and he and his wife showed me a sonogram of their baby, a girl. The outline of the fetus looked like a carved Northwest coast symbol for *child*. Micah said he was still hoping to hunt whale, though he added he was also planning on attending college and moving off the reservation—I didn't understand how he could do both. He seemed to have some reservations about the hunt and the way the hunt was being run, because when a whaling crew member passed in an old sedan out of which music was blasting, Micah nodded toward the guy driving. "There goes one of our sacred crewmen," he said ironically.

Then he said, "I'm really interested in a traditional bowhead hunt." He was referring to the bowhead whale.

I went looking for Wayne, and when I found him in the market with Donnie, he immediately pointed to the Sea Shepherd boat, which could be seen from behind the comic book racks in the deli area. Wayne and Donnie were talking about the protestors who were on their way to Neah Bay. They both seemed really riled up.

They were taking a break from their work with the Beautification Committee. Wayne was wearing some surplus green fatigues that he had picked up at another surplus auction at Fort Lewis and Donnie was wearing his camouflage pants and a Michigan sweatshirt. Donnie was getting lunch—fried chicken. They told me that we had to leave the store to discuss things. They said we had to go outside.

"We can't talk here," Wayne said.

Donnie was looking around suspiciously.

"We've got spies," Wayne went on. He pointed toward the ship again. "Sea Shepherd," he continued. "They say we're under surveillance. I'm sure someone's watching every move we make."

We drove over to the longhouse by the museum. I looked through a crack in the padlocked door and saw a huge semi-hollowed-out log. Wayne said that they had decided to make the canoe in town, with a Makah carver. A forty-foot-long log was being carved out with new and old hand tools. It sat in a nest of curled red shavings. You could smell the sweet fragrance of cedar.

I was confused about the politics of the hunt so I asked Wayne if the hunt was still going to happen, what with John McCarty having been kicked out and all. "We're still gonna go," Wayne said.

We were admiring the unfinished canoe, taking turns peeking through the crack in the door. "This one's not gonna be done for a while, but we can use the *Hummingbird* for the hunt."

I asked about John McCarty again. Wayne frowned. "Forget John," he said.

Donnie said, "John couldn't get us any money."

Wayne praised the new executive director, Denise Dailey. "She might be able to get us a grant," he said. Wayne said that even though John was out, Micah was still on the hunt, though he probably wouldn't throw the harpoon. Wayne said, "Maybe him," and he pointed to Donnie. Donnie smiled.

I asked about the management plan and if the tribe had worked out the problems they were having with the federal government over rules and regulations. Wayne summed up his feelings on the matter by saying, "We just have to go out there on fucking outboards pretty soon and tear up the management plan."

Wayne wasn't very concerned about the harpoon. He was more interested in the gun—it seemed as if the gun was all he could think about, as if he thought the harpoon was just an unnecessary detail.

"Forget the harpoon," Wayne said. "We can just go out there and shoot one." Wayne simulated the firing of a rifle.

Donnie nodded. "Yeah," he said. And then he made a kind of motion with his hands that indicated he too was also firing an imaginary rifle at a whale.

Around this time Wayne started telling people that it was just a matter of time. "We're ready now," he would say. "We could go out there tomorrow." He also said, "The whales are almost here."

21 / The Experiment

Television stations and documentary film production teams around the Northwest and in New York and Los Angeles weren't the only ones hoping to film the hunt. The Makah hoped to film the hunt too. They planned to document the hunt for their own sake, for the sake of their museum and cultural resource center's archives, where, tribal officials hoped, the hunt could be preserved forever in its once-in-a-lifetime, singular exactness. And so, with the help of the tribal attorney, the tribe chose a documentary film production team from Germany. Aside from the film crew chosen, there had been several other filmmakers interested in filming the whale hunt. One had even presented a script. But the chosen film crew had been to Neah Bay before, to produce a film entitled *Daniel und die Geister der Makah*, which translates as "Daniel and the Spirits of the Makah." As a result, they had an edge in the tribe's film crew selection process. The German crew who flew to Seattle and rented a minivan and drove to Neah Bay for the filming included a cameraman, a soundman, and a director. The director was a tall, artistic-looking man, with strawberry blond hair that was thinning on top but long on the sides, which he often tied back in a red bandanna. His name was Ralph Marschalleck. The Makah whalers called him Ralph.

I first met Ralph and the German film crew at the Burke Museum on the campus of the University of Washington in Seattle. He was simultaneously filming, attending, and speaking at a reception being held to raise money for the filming of the Makah whale hunt—the tribe needed to raise about $60,000. I drove from Neah Bay along the strait and took a ferry across Puget Sound. After a few minutes on Interstate 5, I pulled into the University of Washington, where I parked next to a car with a bumper sticker that said, PEOPLE WHO ABUSE ANIMALS RARELY STOP THERE. I went inside and saw Wayne and Donnie and a lot of other people from Neah Bay, including Arnie Hunter and his mother, Helma. Marcy Parker was there too, with her son, Eric, the head of the whaling crew. Together we looked at the Alaskan bowhead whale hunting exhibit downstairs. I had not previously talked with Marcy Parker very much, having found her daunting. But that day I talked easily with her about the various film deals that the tribe had entertained. Marcy expressed doubts about the German film crew. In fact, several people said that they had seen scripts that they had preferred to the Germans'.

Upstairs in the lobby of the museum, people were chatting and eating cheese and crackers when Ralph and the German film crew walked in. They were immediately identifiable as the film crew from Germany. The cameraman was wearing a lime-colored shirt and green pants, and Ralph himself was wearing orange corduroys. Just after he entered, Ralph made a square with his thumbs and index fingers, through which he scanned the room. He folded his arms and pondered something for a long time. Then he pointed out camera angles to the cameraman.

Ralph filmed the next portion of the reception, which consisted of several tribal members singing and dancing. Arnie Hunter danced The Mask-Changing Dance, and his mother, Helma, sang, as did Marcy Parker and several other people. Off to the side, Wayne and Donnie watched quietly with their hands folded, soldiers at ease. Midway into the event, Greg Arnold, a whaling commission member who was drumming and singing that day, asked the film crew to stop filming, explaining that certain songs are not considered recordable, given that they are privately owned by families who had inherited them centuries ago. Ralph dutifully gave the signal for his crew to stop filming, though he looked slightly perturbed. After the singing, I spoke with one of the Germans on Ralph's crew. He explained to me that people in Germany knew very little about the Indians of the Northwest coast. "The Germans," he said, "they think America is New York on the one side and on the other side is Los Angeles and then of course Las Vegas. And they think that all in the middle is rodeo. This is what the German people think of America."

The crowd was invited into the auditorium of the Burke Museum, to see some of Ralph's previously collected film footage of the Makah and Cape Flattery. A fact sheet was handed out. It was titled, "The Story of the Cooperation Between the Makah Nation and German Filmmakers," and it read like a treatment of a soon-to-be-released major motion picture. Under the heading "How It All Began," the fact sheet said: "It was a foggy day when we arrived at Cape Flattery, the most northwestern tip of the U.S.A. We knew that we had reached the end of the Western world . . ." Under the heading "Intercultural Dialogue," the fact sheet continued: "In Germany, there traditionally has been a vast amount of interest in American Indian culture. However, in order to get the right understanding and the proper picture of a different culture, authenticity is required." Under the heading "What Makes This Project Unique," it said: "A partnership commencing with the conception of a script to the sharing of the rights of a cinema-length film, to be used in theaters, for television broadcast, and in video form."

Ralph and his partner, Detley Ziegert, then spoke. Detley Ziegert went first and he spoke in German, so Ralph translated for him. Speaking for Detley, Ralph said, "As filmmakers we start with a dream." Detley began talking about a German author named Karl May, who, he explained, wrote extensively about American Indians. He went on to say that today many Germans are interested in Native Americans thanks to Karl May. Next, the audience of potential donors learned that the production companies of Detley and Ralph were East and West German teams, respectively, and that they considered themselves to be a partnership of East and West Germany, or so Ralph translated. I found this particular part of the presentation difficult to follow, but Ralph said that Detley said something along the lines of "We are partners. We are sharing your experiment and you are sharing ours."

Ralph, speaking for himself now, went on to talk about how much he respected the Makah. "We have learned respect," he said, adding, "and I would like you to know also that we are aware of the respect." Finally, Ralph motioned for his assistant to roll the film, and he began pacing back and forth in the back of the room. The film showed beautiful shots of bald eagles and golden eagles and Makah canoe paddlers and cormorants that clung to the rocks on Cape Flattery as the waves crashed—lush images of nature at the cape that looked like one still life after another except that there were winds and tides and triceps and biceps muscling through them. The film ended with whales blowing breath through the surface of the water, and Makah drummers drumming. It was an ominous touch.

When the film was over, people applauded. Ralph stepped forward and nodded his head just slightly. Then the head of the German consulate in Seattle stood up and, in another apparent reference to the combined East and West German origins of the production team, made a statement: "In my heart I think I am an Indian. I think it is wonderful that the united German teamwork will help preserve your history and traditions." Meanwhile, Ralph was instructing his cameraman to take shots of Darrell and Wayne and Eric and everyone sitting in the front rows.

Toward the end of the presentation, Al Ziontz, a Seattle attorney who has represented the tribe since the sixties, gave a short speech and said, "Makah culture is truly a diamond, a gem in American culture that we should work to preserve." There was a short pause, an accidental moment of silence into which an elder in one of the front rows stood up and looked back at the crowd and said beseechingly, "Please bear with us." Later people explained to me that the Makah are not comfortable with asking for help, for being so public about a need. They are used to perpetuating their image as a generous people. The elder went on to say that he had retired from the Army in 1986 and that he had been stationed in Germany and that he had loved the German people. He thanked them for their help and then he said, "This is kind of a last-ditch effort to save Makah culture."

Though the night was fun for everyone there, and though a lot of the Makah, including Wayne and Donnie, went out to a local seafood restaurant and had a good time on the town, from a fund-raising standpoint the event ended up being nearly a wash on the books. I was told it raised only $700.

22 / Enter the Protestors

The fleet of antiwhale-hunt ships slowly assembled in the final days before October 1. Sea Shepherd brought two boats. There was the *Edward Abbey*, a 173-foot-long converted buoy tender painted sky blue and decorated with pictures of whales. It carried a thirty-six-foot-long submarine painted to resemble an orca and equipped with underwater speakers that broadcasted orca sounds which would, it was hoped, scare away gray whales. (A judge ended up banning the use of the underwater orca sounds, on the grounds that they would harass the whales.) And there was the *Sirenian,* a former Coast Guard cutter, painted black and named for the zoological order of aquatic mammals: it flew a pirate-esque black-and-white Sea Shepherd flag. Both boats anchored in the bay just off Waadah Island, where everyone in downtown Neah Bay could see them. Like most of the protestors, Sea Shepherd personnel rarely went into town. Captain Watson slept aboard the *Sirenian,* which people in town referred to as the Black Boat. The Black Boat floated quietly, almost solemnly, day and night, as if it had taken its place on a stage and was waiting for the action to begin. But at last, one morning, after months and months of dramatic buildup, I saw a protestor set foot on Makah land—only he didn't initially present himself as a protestor. His name was Steph Dutton.

Steph Dutton is a record-setting ocean kayaker. In 1993, he kayaked solo from Victoria, British Columbia, across the Strait of Juan de Fuca, and down the West Coast to Baja, Mexico, in two months. In the winter of 1995, he kayaked down the Oregon coast. In the wintertime, the Oregon coast is a savage, wave-racked route, and in making the journey Steph crashed and was nearly lost on several occasions; he tore both his shoulders up en route. On his trip to Mexico, during a storm at sea, he came upon an area of heaving water, which he soon realized was a pod of gray whales. That was an important moment in Dutton's life, for he has worked with gray whales ever since—strapping video cameras to his head to film them on their migration route in the sea off the coast of California and carrying biologists in his kayak to tag the whales with radio transmitters and then to track the gray whale pods. Steph Dutton has written this of a gray whale passing his canoe: "As it passes, mere feet away, it turns on one side to look up at me. Its powerful flipper almost touches my kayak as it glides by below. I know that my life will never be the same." He once told *Paddler*, a paddle-sports magazine: "My fascination with the grays is not anthropomorphic. It's not all cuddly-feely. I don't have a single, stuffed whale toy on my couch, and I never will. The bond that I sense with them comes from something deeper. These animals have withstood the ravages of greedy humans for more than a century. Yet, somehow they have found a way to endure. . . ." Dutton founded In the Path of Giants in 1996. At the moment he landed in Neah Bay, In the Path of Giants was in the midst of a documentary project on the gray whales' migration from Alaska to Mexico and back.

As he stood on the docks of the Makah marina on this clear, crisp, late September morning in Neah Bay, he was wearing part of his waterproof kayaking outfit, which was donated to him by one of his sponsors. He was tan, with thick curly hair and a big mustache and looked younger than his age, which was forty-seven. He has the smile of a movie star.

Nearby on that same morning was Heidi Tiura, a woman from California, who was described in the heretofore-mentioned *Paddler* article as "a strong-bodied woman who grew up with the glow of ocean sunsets in her eyes and the salt wave spume in her strawberry hair." Heidi is in her forties. In Neah Bay that day, she was wearing a blue water-repellent jumpsuit and sunglasses. She is a self-described veteran offshore marine operator, which is her way of saying that she has worked on fishing boats for many years, as well as on tugboats; she is a Coast Guard–licensed one-hundred-ton-vessel master. She runs a school for children out of her home port in Monterey, California, called Sea Dog School, in which she teaches children about boats and sea life. Heidi is married to Steph Dutton. They met in Sitka, Alaska, where she was the captain of a tourist boat and he was a visiting kayaker. She once told me that she had heard about Steph's solo West Coast kayak trip from her sister, long before she ever met Steph; Heidi's sister read her an article about Steph from a newspaper, and in the moment that she heard about Steph, Heidi said, "I want that man in my life." Of her initial encounter with Steph at the airport in Sitka, Heidi said: "Our eyes met. My stomach flipped and . . . three days later we were planning our life together. It's the fairy tale of all time."

When Heidi introduced me to Steph on the docks of the Makah marina, she said: "You have to meet Steph. I don't have many heroes, but Steph is my hero."

Steph and Heidi told me that they were against the hunting of gray whales, but that they were presenting themselves to the tribe as observers, as a neutral party documenting the hunt. Heidi told me that she and Steph would be making a slide presentation to the tribal council within the next twenty-four hours and that they planned to convince the Makah to start a whale watching operation. Heidi was confident of the power of their slide presentation. (The kayak manufacturer sponsoring Steph once said that the slide presentation did not just promote kayaking products. "[T]he presentation also is magical," he said. "It creates an expanded awareness of the importance of studying and protecting these giants.") Heidi was also confident of her own ability to help the Makah. She hoped to have an opportunity to prepare the Makah for work on the ocean. She said she wanted to train prospective Makah captains and get them ready for their Coast Guard–license examinations. Heidi was confident not only that the Makah would buy their plan but that, between the two of them, she and Steph had the expertise to train the Makah and establish a moneymaking whale watching operation that would also preserve the Makah's heritage, as the In the Path of Giants team saw it. "We can help them," she said.

Heidi was telling me all about how she and Steph could educate tribal members in the ways of the sea around the time that the whaling crew was paddling into the marina, after a long practice out in the bay. Upon landing, the crew stood in a circle on the docks and said a prayer. Then they bailed the canoe. The water they bailed was bloody: there was a dead seal in the bottom of the canoe. The blood-red of the water matched the red of the canoe's interior. They removed a rifle from the canoe. They threw the dead seal into a cart. It landed with a thump. A woman came to the dock and, with two crew members, carried it away to have it rendered for the seal oil that would be served with dried fish and potatoes at the next community feast.

Steph—who smiled in the face of this gore, who beamed confidently, who, like Captain Paul Watson, I had heard so much about and yet never actually seen—approached the canoe.

As opposed to Steph and Heidi, who were buoyant and in high spirits, the whaling crew was upset. It wasn't a matter of environmental politics per se. Basically, the whaling crew was upset that some of the kayakers had just kayaked so close to them in the bay a few minutes before. There had been a lot of talk about protestors doing whatever it took to stop the hunt and the situation was already very tense. And the kayakers in question happened to have been Steph and his In the Path of Giants kayaking companions.

It should be noted that as Steph approached the whalers' canoe he limped. Steph walks with a limp, though the limp is barely perceptible—he is so fit, so athletic, so sure of his step. And it should further be noted that the reason he walks with a limp is related to why he identifies personally with gray whales, especially in their triumphant comeback as a species. Heidi explained to me that Steph had been forced to come back himself. Before he was a kayaker, before he paddled on behalf of gray whales, Steph was a fireman in southern California. He was driving home from work when he came to an accident scene. There was a man lying in the road and covered with a blanket. At first, Steph thought that the man might be dead, but the man was still alive. Steph was examining the man when he heard a car coming. The story goes that Steph was just able to push the man away when the car hit Steph. As a result of the accident, Steph has only one leg. Although Heidi is usually the one to tell this story, Steph does often mention that the recovery of the California gray whale population, which was nearly extinct but managed to rebound, inspired him in his recovery from his injury: the whale was his strength, the symbol of his own personal courage, of his worth and goodness.[5] Both he and Heidi, for that matter, seem to see the gray whale as the sum of all goodness, as a note of peace in a harsh and violence-filled world. Once, at one of his gray whale slide presentations, I watched Steph show a slide of a gray whale and then he said, "Maybe you can get a sense of the magic that you can feel when you are out there with these creatures."

That is some of the background behind the first meeting of protestors and the whaling crew, behind the first time that an antiwhale-hunt group introduced itself to the whaling crew as the whaling crew stood alongside its boat, after the protestors had been isolated, in effect, from the native whaling crew. And this, in part, is what was said at that first meeting between Steph and the whaling crew:

[5] Patrick Stewart was the actor who played Ahab in the aforementioned made-for-cable-TV movie version of *Moby-Dick*, the version that aired earlier that spring. *People* magazine reported that the director of the film isolated Stewart from the rest of the cast of the movie—a touch of Method directing intended to contribute to the theatrical terrorization of the crew by the fabled captain. "That first week, I was sitting on a beach in Fiji while [the crew members] were being sent up mastheads and throwing up over the side of the training ship," Stewart said. *People* reported that Stewart had difficulties walking as Ahab with only one leg. "[T]he two times I fell over, there was always a pair of hands to catch me," Stewart said. When asked how he concealed his real leg, Stewart replied, "That is more information than [the audience] would want to have."

STEPH: (*with his head held high as he walks to the Makah canoe, with an air that said,* Big plans.) Hi, my name is Steph Dutton and I just want to introduce myself. You guys look good out there.

A BIG GUY ON THE WHALING CREW: Fuck off.

23 / Prophets

With the hunt seemingly imminent, and as the press arrived in the final days before October 1, questions kept popping into my head as I drove around Neah Bay and the cape—questions such as: How do you measure the success of a traditional subsistence whale hunt? How do you know if the protestors are right and a whale hunt is no longer necessary? How can you tell if a tribal whale hunt is no longer important or that a Northwest coast whaling tribe is going about Northwest coast whaling all wrong? How can you possibly know, for that matter, what it's like to live in Neah Bay if you are just staying in a motel room and cruising around in a car?

In pondering these and other matters, I went to visit with George Bowechop and Gary Ray, the first people I'd met in Neah Bay the year before. George lived at the western edge of the village, just up from the beach. His home has a big picture window from which he can see clear across the strait. I had seen him up early that day, as I did most days: he sits in a chair that looks out on the bay and Vancouver Island. I knocked on his door and his wife sent me to see him in the workshop in his garage. He offered me tea and we sat down and talked for a while. At one point, he said, "You can have a good life here."

George also told me that once, many years before, a small group of men used to sit on the beach in Neah Bay. I asked some questions about these men and he said that they sat down by the water and watched the sky and the fishermen as they walked off their boats. They could tell by the puff of the cloud over Bahokus Peak that the fleet had better turn toward home soon. They had an idea, after watching a man from afar, that he might get involved in the tribal government, that he would make a good leader. These men took councilmen aside, discussed things privately. They were an unofficial government body, a quasi-spiritual advisory board. One of those men was named Lance Kallappa, who lived at the turn of the nineteenth century and was considered by many people to be a prophet. According to people who believe in his prophecies, he predicted that man would one day walk on the moon. He predicted the invention of submarines. He predicted that every Makah would return safely from any war that they might fight in, which, to this day, they have. He also predicted that one day the hills would move and protect the boats in Neah Bay and the village itself, which is susceptible to waves that roll off the ocean and into the strait. In the forties a breakwater was built. It was built with rock from the peaks, and this is often viewed as the fulfillment of the prophecy of Lance Kallapa. A newspaper columnist from Seattle used to visit Neah Bay. Once, he asked the men on the beach about an upcoming winter. The men said that it would be long and hard. The columnist asked how the men knew this information. They said they had ways of knowing. The columnist pressed them. They said they could tell the upcoming winter was going to be long and hard because the white man who lived across the street had cut and stacked a lot of firewood.

When I was asking about who might be in the circle of men on the beach if that circle of men sat on the beach today, George mentioned Gary Ray. I hadn't seen Gary Ray in weeks and I'd heard he'd been cutting cedar shakes in Alaska. I'd heard that at one point he'd been trapped under a log and was alone and couldn't get help but finally managed to wrestle himself out alive, which, having met him, I could believe. A campaign poster left over from when he ran for tribal council read, HARDWORKING. RESPONSIBLE. COMMITTED. HONEST, and it featured a quote from Theodore Roosevelt: "The work we do for ourselves follows us to the grave. The work we do for others lives on forever." I went over to his farm on the Sooes River a few days later when I was looking for a raven—the creature who, one Northwest coast legend had it, brought light to the people of the Northwest coast, who was crafty and wise and married to the crow, and who was called *klookshood* in Makah. Gary was checking the fish smoker in his barn, and he was wearing a T-shirt and a pair of orange waterproof fisherman's pants and a felt fedora that was dotted with tiny drops of rain. He came out and shook my hand firmly, as if he were gripping an ax. He looked hard into my eyes and took me in back of his house, down by the river, where we watched for a while until a raven appeared, the flap of its huge wings beating against the winds like a sail filling suddenly. Gary was acquainted with this particular raven and I tried to be quiet while Gary called to it and the raven called back.

Gary was on his way back upriver to his parents' property to check on his nets in the river and he invited me to drive with him. We hopped into his big pickup truck, he offered me a Pepsi, and ripped two from the plastic holder. We bounced over the rutted road and back into woods I hadn't seen before, into the Sooes Valley, below Waatch and Cheeka and Sooes peaks. "I've been about every place that you can be on this land. When I was a kid I used to go exploring."

I asked if he ever got lost.

"You can never get lost. You've got the ocean on one side and the strait on the other. You can't get lost," he said.

Gary said that his father had come to Neah Bay with the military and that his father had married a Makah woman. His paternal grandparents had come to Ohio and Indiana from Germany as missionaries, and Gary recalled the time his German grandparents came to Neah Bay to teach him German. "Worst summer of my life," he said.

Eventually, Gary talked about the state of the Makah Nation, as he saw it.

"I think we're on a kind of a teeter-totter right now," he said. "A kind of crossroads. People are coming back from the cities and they're bringing their values. I see kind of a red light flashing." He talked about his work at the museum, where he is on the board of trustees. "We were trying to come up with a mission statement for the tribe," he said. "They asked everybody what it means to be a Makah and the younger people had no idea. The people in their forties and fifties, they said they knew, and the elders, they were angry because they hadn't ever been asked. That's when I knew something was happening. So I went to the elders and I asked, 'Why are you so angry?' It was just my own personal project. I said, 'If those young people out there don't have a grandma or a grandpa then who is going to teach them? Who is going to talk to them? Your voice will die when you die.' And I think they began to understand."

I was sipping my Pepsi and trying to keep it from spilling all over the truck as we drove through muddy ruts and pond-sized puddles when Gary began to talk about the whale hunt. First, he mentioned the protestors who had begun to arrive in the area. "I think it's good," he offered. "It gives us an enemy. It brings us together. The only thing is, I was taught, we never talk about it. It's the younger people who are talking. They don't know. But, anyway, I think it brings us together." Then he mentioned whaling specifically. "I think we're whaling about five years too soon," he said. "We're being forced to draw blood is how I like to put it. But my thinking is, that's okay. It's bringing us all together. I mean, those guys on the crew . . ."

He looked over at me. As his truck hit each bump in the road, his head nearly touched the roof of the truck's cab.

"I mean, putting Wayne Johnson in a leadership position—well, it's making them strong," he said. "It's making them know what it's like to be a Makah."

When we arrived at the place where Gary's nets were in the river, the rain was falling in soft, lush sheets. He pushed a little dinghy into the water and paddled out to the middle of the small stream, which was swelled by the rains that were changing this cool end of summer into fall. He got down on his knees in the boat and leaned over into the water to work the net.

"You know," Gary said, as he grabbed panicked fish from the river, "there's a lot of work to be done on this reservation, and that's what gets me. A lot of the kids are doing nothing. In the old days everybody had a purpose. Everybody had a job and if you didn't then you had to leave. You were just put in a canoe without a paddle, so to speak. And if another tribe found you then they'd know you were banished."

I was thinking about how harsh this sounded to me, when Gary pulled back up on shore. He knocked each fish unconscious with a quick, deft blow. He laid them neatly out on the grass—a coho, a chinook, a steelhead, the mascots of the Great Pacific Northwest: their silver scales glistened like jewelry in the green grass. Then Gary kneeled on the ground. He cut each fish open with his knife and ripped out the guts with his hand. Blood splattered on his face, in the just-gray stubble of his beard.

"If the market was to close down today," he said, "we'd miss the butter and the eggs but we could live off what we've got in our waters. Our own people lived a good life here during the Depression."

With that he turned to me and looked up and asked me to hold out my hand, which I did. He placed in it the heart of a salmon. It was small and a deep rich red and it pumped desperately.

24 / The Media Arrive

And then the media came to Neah Bay—they blew into town like a great howling Aeolian force, armed with walkie-talkies and expense accounts and cellular phones.

The media came in giant trucks, in vehicles that were huge and unwieldy, and in vehicles that were small and nimble. They came by air. They came in rented boats. And the media were made flesh in the persons that were its accredited representatives. And these representatives came to tell stories, to transform the activities at hand into pictures and words. The stories they told were the stories they had always told, the stories they knew best: the story of the Native American, sacred keeper of the land; the story of the conservationist, warrior on behalf of the earth; the story of the whale, the huge and potentially picturesque sea mammal that could sometimes launch majestically, gloriously, dramatically from the dark depths of the unfilmable panorama and, if caught the right way on video, make incredible footage, a great shot. The stories that were not the stories that the media were used to telling were these: the story of the sacred keeper of the land killing a whale, which is, to the press and the public at large, the non-Indian symbol of the non-Indian sacred keepers of the seas; the story of the conservationist, lover of Native Americans' sacred earth values, saying unloving things about Native Americans; and the story of the whale being eaten.

The media came and set up their satellite trucks, the great wheeled news production facilities that were worth millions of dollars, and drove slowly around the curves on the treacherous road to Neah Bay. They beamed their stories into the heavens, sent off microwave signals that bounced off invisible objects far off in the sky. The media beamed out images of the whaling crew practicing in the bay, of the protest boats now waiting offshore, of the Coast Guard cutter that were attempting to keep the proceedings in line. Newspaper reporters installed fax machines in motel rooms, made sure their computers could transmit stories back to Seattle, across the strait to Victoria and Vancouver and to the world. The reporters checked their e-mail, browsed Web sites that insisted the hunt was not traditional, was not spiritual, was wrong.

The helicopters came last. The sky above the peaks was filled with the thunderous clapping, the beating of the rotors, until the news copters

hovered and set down on land. Each of them arrived with their own fan-
fare—over the peak of a hill, from around the edge of the bay—like a great
mythical bird from a mythical sky, with overhead-view omniscience. On
the first day of October, when the media were expecting the hunt to
begin, one of the TV news helicopters landed on the baseball field while a
team of eight-year-olds were up at bat. The eight-year-olds had to stop their
game.

The little speck of land that was Neah Bay was suddenly the encamp-
ment site of this huge and voracious visiting tribe, which the local residents all came out to see. The local residents drove downtown to check it
out and occasionally to play their part as men and women on the street,
and analyze the ways of their visitors. The technicians running the satellite
trucks let the kids inside to look around. In the market, at the checkout
counter, next to the beef jerky and the tide charts and the magazines and
the gum, a woman said, "Did you see the media out there?"

There were the so-called live shots at five o'clock, when a reporter with
a pad in hand would stand at the edge of the village, the water and the
mountains of Canada at his back, somewhere in between the ancient village
sites of Diah and Baada, and speak into the camera and describe the
weather, point toward the protest boats, talk about the migration of the gray
whales, speculate about the status of the hunt, and inevitably declare the
hunt imminent: *Stay tuned!* The reporters stood up again at eleven, the TV
lights reflecting across the quiet bay. The newspaper reporters seemed to be
working overtime to cover the event, given that the TV crews were working
so hard, and vice versa. The TV crews in particular had an institutional stake
in the hunt, for they had come during the month when TV stations across
the country compete fiercely among one another for viewership. The story
of the hunt had come during the month that stations use to set advertising
rates. The attempted revival of the ancient Makah whale hunt ritual had
come during what is called, to use the language of TV production, sweeps.

The hunt was on local news; it was on national news: one of the
anchors on the *Today* show mispronounced the tribe's name. For some of
them, especially the stations that had traveled from faraway, the longer
they stayed, the longer they *needed* the hunt to go on, given the invest-
ment in time and money that they had put into covering the hunt.

"The hunt is expected to begin at any time now," one of the TV
announcers said on the first day, standing in the rain, with the land of the
Makah behind him.

the mistaken impression that the hunt would be over shortly. When the wait for the whale hunt began, I told my wife I would probably only be there a couple of days—a week, tops.

Lodging was an issue. In the final hours before October 1, because I had no idea as to whether the hunt would happen in a day or a week, I was reluctant to take a motel room even if I could have managed to find one—the rooms at the Cape were all booked by TV stations and newspapers, as were the rooms in all the other motels. It seemed a good idea to keep my overhead low, given the unpredictability of it all. So I took my typewriter and a bunch of books out to the back of the Cape Motel's property, out to the camping area that is just a grassy field. I rented the little shack that fishermen sometimes stayed in. The shack was made of plywood. It had no insulation. It had no heat, except for a tiny portable heater that I was disinclined to use because I was convinced that the shack could very easily burn, with me in it. The shack had a window, a metal bunk, a table, and a chair. The people who ran the Cape Motel called it the shanty,⁵ and I was comfortable enough. In the shanty, with the foghorns blowing, with the roll of the tide, at the edge of the forest that led up into the hills behind the village of Neah Bay, I felt as if I were in a tiny old wooden ship, as if I had gone to sea. Looking out at

⁵ Melville followed up on his adventure writing successes with *Mardi*, a novel that starts out like a straightforward South Pacific adventure and then ends up becoming a wildly allegorical romance—a masterpiece, in Melville's mind, but a failed work according to critics then and even today. He lost money on it—a trend in his writing life—and with his wife pregnant and bills to be paid, in the middle of a New York City heat wave and a cholera epidemic, he quickly wrote two books, which he considered hackwork—*Redburn* and *White-Jacket*. "These are two *jobs*," he wrote his father-in-law, "which I have done for money—being forced to it as other men are to sawing wood." It killed him that the books did relatively well in comparison to *Mardi*. He wrote his father-in-law: "So far as I am individually concerned, & independent of my pocket, it is my earnest desire to write those sorts of books which are said to 'fail.'—Pardon the egoism." When he began writing his next book, *Moby-Dick*, he wrote his publisher in England to say that it too would be a straightforward adventure tale, this time about whaling. "The book is a romance of adventure founded upon certain wild legends in the Southern Whale Fisheries, and illustrated by the author's own experience," he wrote. But he was telling other friends that it was more. In a letter to Richard Henry Dana, author of *Two Years Before the Mast*, a popular nautical-adventure book, he wrote: "It will be a strange sort of book, tho', I fear; blubber is blubber you know; tho' you may get oil out of it, the poetry runs as hard as sap from a frozen maple tree;—& to cook the thing up, one must needs throw in a little fancy, which from the nature of the thing, must be ungainly as the gambols of the whales themselves. Yet I mean to give the truth of the thing, spite of this." While he was writing, he moved to a house in Massachusetts. The house was undergoing renovations, new additions, which he referred to as "shanties." "I have a sort of sea-feeling here in the country . . .," he wrote a friend in New York. "I almost fancy there is too much sail on the house, & I had better go on the roof & rig in the chimney."

the satellite trucks driven by the TV crews, watching the reporters run back to their motel rooms, where some of them had installed fax machines and coffeemakers, watching the news helicopters hover overhead as I arose each morning and set up my propane camping stove and made instant oatmeal, I felt a sympathetic feeling with all the media and felt a little apart from them all too, a little like I was out of my expense account league.

I didn't see much of Wayne and Donnie in the hours before people assumed that the hunt would begin. Wayne had offered to put me up at his house, as had Donnie, but they had a whale hunt to go on and I didn't want to get in the way. They thought I was nuts staying in the shanty. One day they came by to look inside; I was sitting in the chair, still trying to get through *Moby-Dick,* which was taking a long time, longer than I expected because I kept rereading chapters and looking up the allusions mentioned in the commentary.

Donnie said, "Oh, *man.* This is where you *stay?*"

Wayne took a drag on his cigarette. "It's like prison," he said.

I also rented a fancy four-wheel-drive car, which cost a lot more than what I would have normally rented and which ended up being a huge mistake but the guy at the rental-car office talked me into it. Then again, at that point, I didn't realize I was about to be trapped in Neah Bay, that I was in for a long and sometimes psychologically debilitating wait.

In the four-wheel-drive car, I went out to the beach and stood on big rocks to look for whales with my binoculars and didn't see any.

26 / Preparations

Preparing for the whale hunt: that was my self-imposed task. On the eve of the first day of October, with the winds of the press picking up, I was spending time in the shanty reading historical accounts of whale hunting preparations and drinking too much coffee. Neah Bay was generally packed with cars, the way it is in the spring and summer at the height of the fishing season, only none of the cars were carrying sport fishermen who came to take advantage of the halibut banks; they were pulling around men and women in expensive and out-of-place-looking outdoor-activity wear who were carrying cameras and notepads. The German film crew, meanwhile, had taken up residence in a house near the old village at Waatch; Ralph Marschalleck and his film crew could be seen coming to the market from time to time-stocking up on supplies. They did not associate with the press corps. For its part, the whaling crew had all but disappeared, and I didn't want to look for them because I was worried I would walk in on some kind of spiritual exercise that was private and would accidentally get everyone upset with me.

I grabbed my stuff from the shanty and drove out of town for the evening. As a result of my reading and thinking and wondering about spiritual preparations, I had it in my head that I should camp on the beach just south of the reservation, at the old Ozette village site where the archaeological dig in the seventies had unearthed examples of the old whaling life. I wanted to imagine what it was like to live in the old whaling village, what it was like to be a whaler just before a whale hunt.

The old reports from ethnographers working at the beginning of the 1900s described the Makah seeking out powers in the woods. I read that the powers that emanated from the ground were strong and that a person might be killed by such a power if he were to approach it unprepared or be hit by the wrong one. A Makah would roam the woods looking for a power that would, when he discovered it, describe his purpose in the village, whether that role be whaler or seal hunter or doctor.

In the particular matter of whaling preparations, the reports described the manner in which an ancient Makah whaler would pray and bathe in the woods. A whaler sought his power in the lakes and ponds in the twilight. He soaked in the quiet inland waters. He rubbed his body with hemlock twigs until it bled. Sometimes he scrubbed himself with plants he had seen in dreams—seaweed, for example. In the pond, the whaler dove beneath the water, staying under as long as possible. In 1920, in "The Whaling Equipment of the Makah Indians," T. T. Waterman wrote: "Mention is made of blood bursting from a bather's ears from long submergence." When he returned to the surface, the whaler blew water in the air, mimicking a whale. He moved quietly, slowly, in hopes that the whale he harpooned might mimic him and not take off out to sea. At night, in whispers, whalers prayed for success. They prayed to the whales. They waited for visions of successful whale hunts in dreams. Waterman wrote, "The hunting of the whale has for the white observer two distinct aspects. From our point of view the matter of greatest concern would be the arrangement of the tackle within the boat, and the methods of approaching and striking the quarry. From the Indian standpoint, however, the really important matter is the proper observance before and during the hunt of various ceremonial performances for procuring help from the spirits. . . . Secrecy in the religious preparations is very commonly observed."

One of the most secret aspects of the ancient whaling preparations and prayer was said to involve skeletons. Sometimes, whalers reportedly swam in prayer with a skeleton that was attached with ropes to their backs. Sometimes, they took skeletons from graves, strung them up in the woods, and prayed to them. Sometimes, they used fresh cadavers. Sometimes a slave was killed. According to Waterman, "One time a man put a corpse on his back in preparation for bathing, face forward, and it took a death grip on his throat, and killed him." Another report said, "On account of this need for human charms, the whaler and his family live in constant danger. They are at once under suspicion when any desecration of a burial place occurs." One whaler in Neah Bay was reported to have dug up a baby who had recently died. He disemboweled it and hung it in a smokehouse to dry. He then began dreaming that he was eating his own children, biting off their feet. This caused the whaler to fear for his children's safety, and after the birth of a son, he gave up whaling. The whaler buried the body of the child that he had dug up in the grave where he had originally found it in hopes of easing his conscience.

The protestors attempted to argue that the Makah might become involved in such necrotic acts again, but having spent some time with the crew members, I felt certain that Wayne and Donnie and Micah weren't out gathering cadavers. And yet the idea of preparing for a whale hunt did seem to force one to think about one's own mortality or at least what it would be like to try and kill a bus-sized mammal. That said, when I pulled my rented four-wheel-drive vehicle into the parking lot at Lake Ozette, the long, inland lake that is just a few miles from the Ozette village site, I was pretty keyed up.

I quickly decided that it was too late to hike to the beach and camp at the village site: I didn't want to hike in the dark. I went to look for a campsite at the lake and there were none left but two guys were nice enough to let me share theirs. Then, I took off alone into the woods on the shore of the lake, with the intention of simulating whale hunt preparation activities in a stream or a pond and ended up getting spooked by a low and ominous thumping sound, which I determined in my tent that evening to have been a perfectly harmless grouse. I spent a lot of time staring at the lake, which was flat and smooth. I contemplated diving in and swimming around in a manner that mimicked a whale but the best spot from which to do so was on a dock next to the park ranger's cabin, and I could imagine running into some difficulty if I told the ranger that I was only pretending to be a whale. In the end, it seemed ridiculous to try to experience a whaler's religious experience; it seemed absurd to attempt to simulate someone else's spiritual tradition. And, anyway, I was starved.

I went back to my tent and made dinner and chatted with the two guys I was sharing the campsite with. One man was from England, and he talked about being far from home and missing his family. The other man was from Seattle. He said he sold metal filaments to Boeing for a living. They offered me a beer, and we looked up at the sky from the campsite: it was thick with stars, spelling out something complicated and detailed that we tried to read. I pointed out the Big Dipper and the British man said that where he was from the Big Dipper was known as the Plough. I was amazed by that: it had never before occurred to me that people in England and people in the United States would refer to the stars differently.

I slept soundly in my tent and, the next morning, drove back to Neah Bay. When I got there, I discovered that the crew had camped down at Ozette the night before. I also heard from Donnie and Wayne that while I was off futzing around in the woods they had nearly caught a whale.

27 / The Crew Comes Upon a Whale and Decides Not to Hunt It

The whale hunt that ended up not being a whale hunt started in the evening, under the cloak of darkness. For despite the presence of all of the major news organizations in America, despite the watchful eye of a protest fleet that deplored the hunt and sought to stop it in whatever way possible, or at least to document the bloodiness of it all, the novice whaling crew had slipped out of Neah Bay, slipped past the protest boats that were patrolling the area, slipped past the assembled news media and into the Pacific Ocean.

Eric Johnson, the captain in the whaling canoe, had kept his plans secret, telling no one, not even the other crew members, not even Wayne. He called a meeting of the crew on the afternoon before the first day of October and announced to the crew that they would be leaving to hunt at 8 P.M., just after dark. When the time came, the crew prayed, got into the *Hummingbird,* and paddled out of the marina slowly. The Makah canoe slipped past the Sea Shepherd boats—the crew could see the whales painted on the side of the *Edward Abbey.* They paddled out of the bay, out past the breakwater. The canoe was pulled out of the water and put onto a fishing boat. The crew began a slow trip around the cape.

On the deck of the fishing boat, the crew tried to sleep, but they couldn't; they were too excited, it being their very first formal whale hunting excursion. At daybreak, the canoe was lowered back into the water from the fishing boat. And then the whaling crew found themselves offshore at Ozette.

The sun rose red in the clear coastal sky. Horsetails whisked across the bright blue ceiling. Shades of green kaleidoscoped through the fir trees that stood over the beach. Eric and the other paddlers—Darrell, Donnie, Andy, a teenager who had been training as steersman, and a tall, strong paddler named Theron, among others—gathered together the whaling equipment, put the lines and a harpoon in the canoe. They readied the gun. They prayed over the lines and the harpoon. They slathered their chests with seal oil, for warmth. Eric Johnson's two brothers were there, but he decided to take them out of the canoe. He didn't want to risk the lives of all the men in his family at once.

Because the crew was short a man in the canoe, Keith Johnson stood in as a paddler. Aside from being president of the whaling commission and a tribal council member, Keith had been an avid paddler in his twenties. But when the crew pulled away from the fishing boat, they pulled so hard that he fell back in the canoe.

Donnie was in the canoe and Wayne was on the fishing boat, and Arnie Hunter was on a big red powerboat operated by a Makah fisherman named Dan Greene. Dan Greene is tough and low-key. He was the can-do member of the whale hunt support crew. His boat is the fastest powerboat in the Makah marina, faster than almost any boat the protestors had. It was the official Makah support boat, the boat from which the crew would fire the .50-caliber whale hunting gun. As they started out the day, Dan and Arnie raced off past the canoe, to keep guard, to watch for the protestors and the press, neither of whom was around on this morning.

It was then that they spotted a large gray whale.

The whale was lolling in the kelp beds, diving and scrounging and sucking the muck from the ocean floor and then surfacing to breathe, to spray water in the plume of exhausted breath, to roll its great gray, barnacle-covered body over and back down into the water, which was shallow at seventeen feet or so.

As soon as Dan and Arnie saw the whale, they alerted the canoe, and all at once the hearts of the paddlers were racing. It was a magnificent day, and the magnificence vibrated through the charged, adrenaline-filled bodies of the crew members: they paddled in a dugout canoe, with Cape Alava to the south, the sea stacks of Point of Arches to the north, the very scenes and city-less sights of their ancestors, the whalers. And now, a whale was swimming before them in only seventeen feet of water. The German film crew was even there filming, recording, ready for action. The situation for a modern traditional whale hunt seemed ideal.

The crew was paddling and their hearts were pumping, and now almost pounding—the excitement turning to anxiety, the pace verging toward out of control. Keith Johnson sensed the crew's demeanor. He was sitting next to Darrell Markishtum, who was paddling and wondering how it was all going to go. Keith Johnson leaned over to Darrell and told him to sing a song, which he did. The song helped. It soothed Darrell and he could feel it soothe the crew. It allowed them to concentrate, made them think that they should hunt right then and there.

Eric Johnson wondered too. He debated. It was up to him, after all. He used a cell phone to talk to the tribal council. It was pointed out to Eric as they paddled in view of Ozette village that the Marine Fisheries Service whale biologist was not present and that nobody could get him on the phone. (The tribe had agreed to allow the federal government to observe the hunt.) It was also noted that the crew had only one harpoon. Because the water was so shallow, Eric considered shooting the whale first and then harpooning it. But in the end, he called it off. He decided the time was not right for a whale hunt. He decided not to rush it, not to take a chance.

In a few minutes, Sea Shepherd boats were in the area.

The crew spent the day paddling and singing and praying; they relaxed in the very last of the cape's summertime. Late that evening, they returned on the fishing boat—Donnie told me that he had lain on the dock and looked up at the sky, which was thick with stars, and noticed the Big Dipper. A TV cameraman greeted them at the docks not realizing that the hunt had almost happened: the next day's news reports showed the crew shivering and covered with blankets.

Also at the docks to greet the crew was a team of kayakers—the In the Path of Giants gray whale migration research team. The whale hunters complained that the kayakers had gotten too close to the canoe again. The next day the In the Path of Giants team was asked to leave the reservation.

Wayne was up at dawn the next morning and Donnie slept in, but they were both in front of the post office at lunchtime and talking as if the hunt were imminent, even if the weather, which had been so clear and beautiful for the past few days, was turning at that moment. Neah Bay was suddenly in a cloud.

"Everybody's pulling together," Donnie said.

Wayne was nodding. "The adrenaline was really pumping in us out there yesterday," he said.

"Everything's falling into place," Donnie said. He was opening a can of Diet Pepsi. "I don't know. I don't think the whale thought we were ready."

A man walked up, a protestor. He was wearing a fedora with a feather in it and faded blue jeans. He said he lived in Friday Harbor, in the San Juan Islands, just down the strait. His T-shirt said WHALE RESCUE, and he was driving around in a beat-up Volvo. He said he was from the Animal Welfare Institute. "I'm their whale and dolphin person," he said. He added that he had some experience in standoff situations. A former arborist in the Virginia area, he had campaigned extensively against the wearing of fur, having hung a sign that said NO FUR on a building in New York City. He said that he thought Sea Shepherd had made a mistake by bringing its boat into the harbor.

He greeted Donnie and Wayne kindly.

"Hey," Donnie said. He eyed the protestor, took a sip of his Diet Pepsi.

"Hey," Wayne said.

"Let me ask you something," the protestor said to Donnie and Wayne. "Do you think you guys are in touch with your traditions enough such that you could practice the whale hunt with nonlethal means?"

"What do you mean by that?" Donnie said.

"I mean, since you've adapted the hunt by adding a rifle, I mean, could you adapt it even more and come up to the whale and simply touch it?"

Wayne had his hands in the pockets of his Raiders jacket and he was watching the guy cautiously.

"No way," Donnie said. "I mean, how are we going to do our rituals and stuff? How are we going to bring the whale up on the beach?"

"Well, you can . . . ," the guy began to say.

"What would my grandfather say if I told him that?" Wayne blurted out.

"He'd say you . . ."

"He'd say, 'No way,' is what he'd say," Wayne said.

"Let me ask you something," Donnie said. "When you sit down and eat your turkey, do you ask that turkey for his life? Because that's the way it is around here. Around here we're hunters and we hunt for our families, and we ask for that whale, we don't just kill it."

The guy was just listening now.

"When you eat your turkey, do you just touch it and ask it to lie down on your table?" Donnie asked.

The conservationist said, "Hey, wait a minute. You don't see any leather on me. I'm no hypocrite."

They all talked for a while longer. The protestor wished Wayne and Donnie well—it had been a civil exchange—and he walked away. Donnie was calm. As Donnie finished his soda, I asked him what he thought of the conservationist. "He was okay, but I really told him with that thing about Thanksgiving."

Wayne, meanwhile, was practically erupting with excitement. "This thing has become so much more than we ever imagined," he said. He was having trouble keeping his arms at his sides. "Now, it's like we have to do it—I mean, for our kids and our grandkids. And some of us guys might get killed out there. But with all the media and all the people watching us, we have to do it."

28 / Exit the Protestors

In lieu of a photograph of a whale hunt on October 1, the front page of the *Seattle Post-Intelligencer* showed Heidi Tiura and Steph Dutton and the kayakers of In the Path of Giants in the midst of a heated discussion with the Makah tribal police. The Makah tribal police were upset because the kayakers had approached the whalers the night before, as they returned to town in the canoe. Heidi and Steph were upset because their offer to set the Makah up in a whale watching business had been turned down and because they were being reprimanded for approaching the canoe. (I was told that the tribal council had no idea that Steph and Heidi had been dissimulating. I had heard that the council members had enjoyed Steph and Heidi's slide presentation, especially the shots of the gray whales breaching: some of the council members were thinking they could use the presentation as a kind of training film for the whaling crew, which had to learn how to approach whales. But then Marcy Parker noticed the California license plates on one of the In the Path of Giants vehicles in the photographs, and she thought she had seen similar plates among a crowd of protestors and she began to have second thoughts.) That the In the Path of Giants team had approached the canoe so closely at night had made some of the tribal council people realize that In the Path of Giants was not just documenting the hunt, but that they also did not want it to happen, that they were bona fide protestors.

The next day Heidi and Steph—wounded, but not defeated—made a new base station east of town at a little boat ramp that sits at the mouth of a stream called Snow Creek. But just before they left, two of the kayakers who were on the In the Path of Giants team came back to see me at the shanty. They told how they had come upon the whaling crew in the *Hummingbird* as it returned to town. "We kind of freaked them out," one of the kayakers said. "We kind of stepped into a hornets' nest."

The other kayaker looked at me with beseeching eyes, as if he too was concerned about the tone that the whale hunt opposition had taken, about where the In the Path of Giants team had been led. "I just want you to know, I didn't come here to be hated," he said.

When I saw Heidi, as she was preparing to leave Neah Bay, she was furious, even raging. Steph was packing up the team's equipment.

Heidi walked over to me and said, "Have you been briefed yet?"

I didn't know what she was talking about. "No," I said.

"Come up to the room," Heidi said. She stormed away.

I followed her to a room on the second floor of the Cape Motel. There was equipment everywhere—computers, outdoor gear, cooking supplies. The door closed.

"We're getting kicked out of town," Heidi said. "And we didn't do anything illegal." She motioned to a chair. "Sit down," she said.

I sat down.

"You said in your article that they were hunting seals," she said. She had read the magazine article that I had written. I had mentioned that Donnie had gone out hunting seals. She spoke to me as if she were accusing me of something. She was making me feel pretty paranoid. "Who gave you that information?" she asked.

Steph wasn't around but I noticed the other kayakers in the room sheepishly looking my way.

I told her that I had seen Donnie's seal hunting permit and I told her that, anyway, I didn't want to get anybody in trouble—a response she didn't appreciate. Her face muscles tightened. She was seething. And she was angry with me now. "Maybe you'd better leave," she said.

I left.

Banned from the village of Neah Bay, prohibited from the Makah marina, excluded from the Makah Nation, the protestors protested their exclusion over and over and watched Neah Bay from the water, waiting just at the tip of the country, at the end of the world.

By now, the little fleet had grown to include various inflatable rubber boats, including the Zodiacs owned by whale watching companies in Vancouver and Victoria, who had volunteered their boats for the fight. There were a few pleasure craft, like the boat of the couple from Oregon who took a vacation to help save the gray whales, to stop the Makah. And there was a group called the Sea Defense Alliance or Sedna, for short, which, according to them, is the name of a mythic sea god in Alaskan aboriginal mythology. They were aligned with a few of the more militant animal rights groups.

Sitting in their police Jeeps, in their blue uniforms, the tribal police watched the boats from the marina and made certain the protestors stayed away. If the protestors touched reservation land they were arrested—they were considered trespassers. Once, a crew from the *Edward Abbey* rode a Zodiac up to the dock to deliver a message to the tribal council. The Sea Shepherd members leaned over the edge of the inflatable boat; the Makah tribal police officers leaned off the edge of the dock to receive an envelope, a final plea. The council read it over; they announced again that they were going to hunt a whale.

At night, the protestors took refuge at the docks in Seiku, a tiny fishing town just outside Clallam Bay, on the strait, where they rented motel rooms and did laundry and refueled their fleet. They sometimes ate dinner, had beers, played pool. And then in the morning the *Sirenian* and the

Edward Abbey and the tiny fleet of protest boats sat there, floating again on the periphery, harassing the Makah canoe if and when it paddled, waiting obsessively at the entrance to Neah Bay, zipping around in Zodiacs from one protest boat to another, on what looked—through binoculars on the shore—like urgent missions.

Steph Dutton and Heidi Tiura were there too. They were having engine trouble with *Sea Dog*, their research vessel, but they had made friends among the Sea Shepherd crew and they ran back and forth between the shore and the Sea Shepherd boats. Heidi believed that the Makah council had not presented the In the Path of Giants proposal to all the people of Neah Bay. She began to broadcast the In The Path of Giants whale watching proposal on the marine-band radio, along with other comments by other people against the hunt. She called the broadcasts Radio Free Neah Bay.

29 / On Watch

On the second day of the whale hunt watch, the waves swelled up in the strait, the winds blew hard off the ocean, and the sea crashed at the rocks off Cape Flattery, filling the rocky shore with white water that writhed and foamed hysterically as it rose in the sandstone cauldrons; and then sank back into the greenish dark; low cement-colored clouds herded in from the north and east and haunted the day. I hiked to the tip of Cape Flattery and it was as if I were hiking through a cloudy dream: along the marshy path, the overturned fir tree roots were rock-jeweled and mysterious, the gnarled branches of the bleached and branchless cedar writhed in the wind.

Back in town, at the market, I bought the papers, and returning to the shanty, I made tea and sat down to read a headline that dramatically announced the anticlimax: MAKAH DON'T TRY TO HUNT A WHALE ON THE FIRST DAY. The headlines also said FOES READY WITH AGGRESSIVE TACTICS TO THWART MAKAH'S EXPEDITION and DAY OF RECKONING AT HAND FOR WHALE HUNT. That evening, all the TV news programs in Seattle led with live reports from Neah Bay. I called my wife every hour or so on a pay phone. I called as many friends as I could think of. I told them where I was. They had all seen the whale hunt coverage on TV. They had all seen the live reports from Neah Bay.

The reporters pressed the crew for interviews, asked when the tribe would hunt, about spiritual preparations, about the whale hunters' spirits, about the readiness of their souls. The winds of the press howled and blew at the Makah and poked them with microphones and stared at them with cameras and lights. The tribe did not blink.

In that time, Ben Johnson, the tribal chairman, rolled into his office at the same hour he usually did, which was around eight-thirty, or he stepped out of his car the way he always did, which was slowly, or he leaned on the side of the doorway outside the council chambers, where he had a cigarette, his large frame against the doorjamb, his breath heavy, his voice slow, the smoke of the cigarette curling up in the damp air and dispersing like fog. Then he smiled at the reporters, and told them that the crew would go when the crew wanted to go, that the hunt was imminent though not necessarily about to happen. "No rush," he said. This, of course, was precisely the answer that the press corps did not want to hear.

Day Two, Day Three, Day Four: the newspeople sat late at night in the Makah Maiden, packed into the little booths in high-tech rain gear, staring at their cellular phones. Anxiety hung invisibly over the lazy little town like radioactive fallout. There was a constant feeling that the hunt could be happening at that precise moment, unbeknownst to anyone but the whale hunters—and for the reporters this was sometimes almost too much to bear. The reporters did everything they could think of to keep tabs on the crew, especially since the crew had slipped by them so effortlessly a few days before. Reporters and cameramen patrolled the beaches, roamed the hills, listened to marine-band radios, watched the canoe. The reporters watched the boats on the water. They telephoned the protestors' boats to see if they knew anything. They watched the weather and the tides and the sky. The reporters of Neah Bay were on watch like the crew of a ship on a sea they had never before traveled upon. The slightest disturbance, natural or otherwise, seemed preternatural, like an omen.

I am the first person to admit that I was not the greatest watch keeper. I was interested in the hunt, of course, and of what would become of the whale, but being without a news helicopter or a powerboat, being holed up in such a thought-engendering accommodation, and having gotten to know Wayne and even Donnie a little I was also interested in how people went about waiting for such a thing, how it affected us all. The way it was affecting me, I should mention, was that each whale hunt–free dawn made me want to leave a little bit more; then, by around noon, I would invariably realize that if I left then I would be throwing away all the whale hunt–waiting time that I had already put in. The way the wait for the whale hunt affected the reporters in general was that many of them seemed to be seeing Neah Bay in a completely different light. One night, for example, I was standing in the street talking to a photographer from Seattle. The sky had cleared and it was filled with stars. We were looking up. The moon was nearly full.

"Wow, look at that moon," I said.

"Yeah," the photographer replied. "Maybe it means something."

30 / A Prayer Closet

While the crew prepared (and waited), many of the protestors were telling the reporters that Wayne Johnson was gun happy, that he was an ego-maniac intent on getting his name in the newspapers. I wondered about that myself. But one morning at Arnie's VFW hall I got the idea that—in the heavy impendingness of the hunt—maybe Wayne was thinking about the hunt as more than just an opportunity to go out with a gun and shoot a whale. "We got everybody here," Wayne was saying as he was standing outside Arnie's place, in the street. He and Donnie were going to have breakfast. Wayne went on, amazed at what was happening: "We got CNN, CBS, *Seattle Times, New York Times,* the *Today* show. Can you *believe* it?"

As he was talking, Andy Noel drove up in his old sedan. Andy, the steersman in the canoe, has long dark hair and he is very cool, in a surfer kind of way. Andy told everyone about how a young woman had asked him what he did and how he had said that he was a whaler. "She said, 'Oh, my daddy told me about the whalers,'" Andy recalled. "She said, 'No sex for whalers.'" Everyone laughed. Andy waved and then drove off, and then we went in for breakfast.

Donnie had pancakes and Wayne had coffee. Arnie was across the street getting some wood ready for a salmon bake; he was going to bake some salmon for the lunchtime reporter crowd. We ordered and we all watched TV—some news and then Martha Stewart's show. Donnie talked about the various network news teams. "Money's no object with the *Today* show," Donnie said. He said that the show had bought the crew a big dinner. The crew had been very happy with the dinner and also with the *Today* show's coverage of the crew. The tribe had contracted a small public relations firm in Washington, D.C., that specialized in aboriginal issues, and Donnie had talked to one of the women working there. "She said that when she saw us on the *Today* show and we were in the canoe, she was shivering, it was so good," Donnie said.

Wayne cracked the trailer window open so he could smoke a cigarette. He mentioned that the day before he and Donnie had gone out looking for whales in Dan Greene's boat. They took along the German film crew but most of them got sick, so they let them off the boat. Then, they raced out of the bay. Protest boats pursued them for a while until they crossed the strait into Canadian waters. Then they boated, way offshore, where they saw dolphins and humpback whales around the boat. On the way back, they stopped on Vancouver Island, at Port Renfrew, which is a lot like Neah Bay, in that it is a tiny Indian village. They had lunch. Wayne had some coffee to warm up but he didn't have any money. He borrowed some and got a hamburger. He was freezing since he didn't have a great set of winter clothes or even any gloves.

As we sat there, a veteran, a man in his sixties, opened the door of the trailer. He sat down with Wayne and Donnie and ordered a bowl of oatmeal. Wayne was leaning back in his chair now, smoking his cigarette. Wayne and the veteran started talking about preparing for the hunt, about being spiritual. The veteran seemed as if he was trying to be delicate, as if he knew Wayne was reluctant to talk about this. Wayne was saying how difficult spiritual preparations were going to be. "I've got to start fasting soon," Wayne said. "Maybe I'll start tonight."

Donnie was still eating. Arnie's big-screen TV showed a report on the whale hunt, which concluded that while the hunt had yet to happen, it could happen any day.

"The thing is, it's gonna be a lot harder for me," Wayne said all of a sudden. He was talking about spiritual preparations. "I mean, these gray hairs aren't from hard work. They're from easy living. My grandfather, he raised me right, but he was too easy on me."

The TV went on for a while, and then the veteran interrupted. "You've just got to reach out to your creator," the man said. His hand was extended. "You've just got to reach out to him."

The veteran mentioned what the older Makah speak of as a prayer closet, a place where a person is alone and can pray. He mentioned an elder who had passed away and said that elder used to use a sweat lodge out in the woods as his prayer closet. He named a creek. "It's a good area because there are lots of nettles around there," the veteran said.

Wayne nodded, smoked, cast a wary glance. He said, "Mmm." He looked at the veteran skeptically. He smoked some more, turning to blow the smoke out the window. After a while he spoke. "The guys on the crew, they're already going into the creeks in the morning," Wayne said. And then he hurriedly changed the subject and smashed out his cigarette stub. "Yeah, the adrenaline was really pumpin' when we went out on the thirtieth, when we almost got that whale," he said. "The adrenaline was really pumping through us."

Donnie agreed as he ate.

At that point, I asked Wayne if, while the press could be distracting, it didn't make him think about the whole thing more.

"You got *that* right," he said, and he shook his head and looked terribly concerned.

31 / Q & A

The wait continued. And after a few days with the press waiting around, the tribe hosted what tribal members came to refer to as the Media Dinner. There was some hope within the press corps that the tribe would announce when the hunt would begin at the dinner but as the evening commenced it soon became clear the dinner was intended only as a dinner, or a feast, as some of the Makah called it, a gathering in which the tribe had other plans. There was food: the reporters ate salmon and potatoes and cautiously dipped their dried fish in seal oil. The walls of the community center were decorated with children's crayoned drawings of whales. After dinner there was dancing and singing and stories and speeches, and then, at the behest of the tribal emcee, newspeople stood up to introduce themselves.

Print reporters generally stood up to wave shyly, while locally famous news reporters said hello in booming voices that people in the hall recognized and cheered. The reporter from *The Seattle Times* said *tleko,* which means "hello" in Coast Salish. The crowd applauded, and all of a sudden a lot of reporters looked as if they wished they had said *tleko* too. The reporter representing *The Philadelphia Inquirer* stood up and introduced herself and when she did a Makah tribal member stood up and said, "Where in the world is *Philadelphia?*" The reporter replied, "It's a long, long way from here." Ralph Marschalleck spoke on behalf of the German film crew. He appeared slightly overwhelmed, as if he was in the midst of realizing that he was not going to be the only person attempting to film the hunt.

All the reporters took notes on what people were saying and sometimes what they were themselves thinking, and there seemed to be a feeling of gratitude on the part of the press corps for the tribe hosting the dinner, a feeling that they were—for the time being, anyway—welcome in Neah Bay. There was a moment of brief but intense panic when Ben Johnson, the tribal chairman, stood up and told the crowd that the Media Dinner was being held to distract the media from the hunt, which was being conducted at that very moment. Some of the reporters didn't immediately get the joke.

Members of the tribe began to stand and speak. One man said: "We're not any different from any other community in the world except that now everybody's watching us. Sometimes, I think it's unfair, for our grandfathers never had to deal with this."

Helma Ward, Arnie Hunter's mother, stood up and talked about traditions. "Somebody says, 'Don't you care about the whale? What's up with you?' But we have an understanding with the whale and I'd like you to know that." After that, Helma gave a few dollars to the drivers of the satellite trucks—*potlach!*

Imbedded in the ceremonial portion of the dinner was a tiny moment of news, a move in the political machinations of the hunt that was barely perceptible. Micah announced to reporters that he wanted to go to college and that he was leaving the crew. He might return at another time, he said. He spoke in his typical solemn, thoughtful manner. "I have decided to equalize my mind with those who have been working against us," he said. In the coming days, people would debate whether he left because he wanted to or because the hunt was no longer being run by his father, but that night the issue was addressed publicly, if obliquely.

"In this hall all differences are forgotten," George Bowechop said, getting up slowly from his folding chair. "We can agree to disagree."

John McCarty nodded his head at these words. Later, Micah danced and John McCarty danced and then they danced together.

Somehow the tables began to turn, and the dinner became a chance for the Makah to investigate the press. In the midst of the evening there was a question and answer session led by the tribe, a reverse interview where tribal members addressed questions to the press crew as they sat at attention in folding chairs:

Q: How many of you folks have been to Neah Bay before?
A: A small number of people raised their hands.
Q: How many of you have been to Japan or Norway or Iceland to cover their whaling?
A: A very small number of people raised their hands.
Q: I want to know if any of you have a cameraman half as good as the NBC *Today* show cameraman?
A: (*Offered by a cameraman who worked not for a national news organization but for a station based in the Pacific Northwest*): I'd be as good as him if I got paid as much as he does.
Q: How long will you be our guests here in Neah Bay?
A: Indefinitely, a representative of a news organization said.
A: Until the whale hunt, another one shouted.
A: (*Shouted by someone affiliated with a Seattle TV station*): You tell us.

32 / The Resident Issue

A procedural problem arose regarding a particular type of whale sometimes referred to as resident whales. Resident whales are called resident whales because they do not appear to migrate; they seem to feed and dive year-round in one area, in a particular bay or cove. Resident gray whales are not technically different from nonresident gray whales, as far as gray whale biologists know. The definition of a resident whale is a negative definition: a whale that is *not* migrating. They are the whales that people visit, that boaters get to know, in some sense, as opposed to the whales that swim out at sea in anonymity.

As an allowance, in part, to local interest in local whales, the Makah agreed that they would hunt only in the ocean, not in the strait. "It's a major concession on the part of the Makah. They are easier to catch close to shore," a spokesman for the fisheries service said. But now some protestors and whale biologists argued that all the whales on the other side of Cape Flattery, all the whales along the Pacific coast, were resident whales, that the migration had not yet begun. This seemed like semantics to the whaling commissioners. The tribe held meetings with the National Marine Fisheries Service and the Secretary of Commerce. Officials of these groups came to Neah Bay or conference-called. In one meeting, people were screaming and shouting. The Makah felt they couldn't wait much longer to hunt. They were worried about the weather getting rough, about winter coming.

The issue never seemed completely resolved to me—except that Makah officials said they would wait for the migration, which could begin at any time. So during the day, Dan Greene went out on his boat, sometimes with Wayne, sometimes with Donnie or Arnie Hunter. They scouted for whales coming down south from Alaska bound for Mexico.

Meanwhile, Sea Shepherd and some of the other groups protesting the hunt set out to name the resident whales, with the idea that whales that had names would be less likely to be hunted or would perhaps elicit more of an uproar if killed. Accordingly, the whale down at Snow Creek, where In the Path of Giants was based, became known as Buddy. Other names given to the gray whales were Angel Face, Monica, and Neah. Lisa Distefano, the expedition leader of Sea Shepherd's Gray Whale Protection Campaign, kept a journal on the Sea Shepherd Web site in which she wrote about the resident gray whales. "Whoever it may be," she wrote at one point, "I hope that the last days of Buddy or Angel Face or Monica or Neah, as they quietly move through the kelp forests, filled with an ancient intelligence, will contain some joy. Whether it's an extra tasty bite of something, or a sudden rush of wind, or an unexpected warm current. May they have some peace before they experience an agonizing, drawn-out, torturous death."

33 / The Prince of Monaco

Press conferences were held everywhere, all the time, in almost every conceivable station of Neah Bay life, causing the entire village to seem on occasion like a twenty-four-hour press conference, during which all the meticulously monotonous, everyday moments of life in Neah Bay were being covered *live!*

An example of a typical press conference during the wait for the hunt was conducted one day by Keith Johnson, the president of the whaling commission, outside the Makah Maiden. As soon as he began speaking to one reporter, others crowded around, so that soon he was surrounded by about a dozen people, and you couldn't see his short, compact frame behind the crowd. He was standing out in back of the restaurant where the parking lot turns into a gravel path that runs out on a little jetty. Behind him was Waadah Island, the strait, the protest boats, the white-and-red Coast Guard cutter. The gray sky drizzled.

The specifics he used to discuss the hunt just served to tantalize the reporters. He talked about the storage of the whale that might be caught, about how the whale that might be caught might be butchered, about the possible length of a whale that might possibly be caught, possibly very soon. "The thinking was that if there was a thirty-footer and a forty-footer then they'd go for the thirty-footer," he said. He added, "Everything is a factor—location, tides, time of day. Everything."

When Johnson talked about the resident issue, I had trouble following him—he was using a kind of self-help version of the Socratic method. "I keep quoting that Steven Covey book," he said. He was referring to *The 7 Habits of Highly Effective People.* "I don't know, maybe he'll call me up one day, but it says, 'Seek to understand before you seek to be understood.' So we *understand* the whale. We *understand* the whale rights people. We *understand* that they really love the whale." And then he asked the reporters if they understood the tribe. He said, "Do you know that we would be doing this if nobody was here?" He ended the press conference by saying, "I challenge you to go into that museum and look at those paddles. What do those paddles tell you?"

Now, at this point a lot of the reporters on hand had to get back to their motel rooms to file stories concerning the resident issue, but if I had any strength in my own circumstances as a reporter there in Neah Bay, if I had any counterpoint to the satellite feeds and computer arsenals of the other journalists on the scene, it was perhaps that I had all the time in the world to kill. So when Keith Johnson suggested people check out the paddles in the museum, I went over to the museum to check out the paddles—to see if they had anything to say. When I got there, Wayne and Donnie were out in front. They were standing in the rain and watching a child as the child slept in the car, a Volvo. Wayne and Donnie told me that the child was the child of the Prince of Monaco, who, with his wife, was in the museum getting a tour. I was a little skeptical, but according to Wayne and Donnie, the prince had met the tribal members and become friendly with them at the International Whaling Commission meeting.

Wayne and Donnie asked me if I could watch the prince's child, who was sleeping in the prince's car—they had promised an interview to a *Vancouver Sun* reporter who was waiting for them across town. I said I would. They went off and I stood in the rain watching the baby in the backseat of the car. After a couple of minutes, the baby began stirring. I panicked. I ran inside the museum to tell the Prince of Monaco. In the museum, I saw Marcy Parker, with whom I had spoken very few words up to that point. I looked at her and said, "The prince's kid is waking up." She said, "Huh?" and looked at me with a scowl. I repeated myself, and this time Marcy said, "Oh! Okay," and ran off to get the prince, who came out with his wife and carried the groggy child inside.

After the prince left, I went in and looked at the paddles—the paddles that had been dug up at Ozette in the big archaeological dig. I looked at them for a while and couldn't figure out what they meant in the scheme of things so I asked the interpretive specialist at the front desk, and he told me that the paddles came to a point so that water rolled off them quietly: it was another piece of technology that made the whaling canoe stealth, which, as the specialist saw it, indicated that paddlers might have approached a whale in the relatively calm water of the bay in addition to the ocean, meaning they might have hunted so-called resident whales.

Later, I went over to the tribal center to ask Keith Johnson about the paddles. I couldn't find him—though I did find out that the Prince of Monaco was not, in fact, the prince but a scientific adviser to the prince who ran an oceanographic institute in Monaco, and who looked like a prince to Wayne and Donnie. I ran into Marcy. She sat there on a chair in her office and looked at me skeptically. She had just finished talking to a protestor who claimed to belong to the tribe of the whale. "I said to her, 'What's your quantum?'" Marcy told me. "'You know, like what percentage whale tribe are you?' And she didn't know *what* I was talking about." Marcy's face broke into a big smile.

I asked Marcy if she thought the old whale hunters would have hunted resident whales.

"If there had been a whale and they didn't have to go out in the ocean they would have hunted that whale," she said matter-of-factly. She folded her arms. "You know," she said, "our ancestors weren't stupid!"

34 / On the Beach

On a night that went on and on, on a night that emphasized, in its clear black darkness, the interminable wait for the hunt, not to mention the soundstage quality of the peninsula at night, of this distant wilderness—a place where everyone seemed to be seeing a different version of what was or, more precisely, was not going on—on such a night, I walked over to the Makah Maiden from my shanty to treat myself to a piece of pie and a cup of coffee. Wayne and Donnie were there with some other guys from the whaling crew. (I ran into them everywhere I went.) They were all sitting around a big table and talking to a group of reporters from *The Seattle Times*. Wayne waved me over and told me that they were planning a trip the next day down to Ozette, near the site of the ancient whaling village, and that I should come along. When Wayne said that, *The Seattle Times* reporters looked up at me in a way that gave me the impression that they would not appreciate me distracting the crew, so I declined. But Wayne and Donnie insisted and then *The Seattle Times* reporters began insisting and I accepted the invitation since, as usual, I had nothing else scheduled.

I went back to the shanty and slept for a few hours and then woke up at around four in the morning and stood on the main street just off the bay with two reporters and a photographer who were waiting for the whaling crew. One of *The Seattle Times* reporters offered me some coffee, which she had told me was bought from a coffee company in Central America that paid the growers and pickers well, if I remember correctly, and I drank it gratefully as we watched shooting stars fling themselves across the huge sky and fade quickly away. Then, suddenly, the crew raced by in a fleet of old cars that I thought for certain would wake up the entire town but didn't. We all drove in a caravan for an hour to the trailhead at Ozette. When we parked, I saw that we were about to take a hike to the beach with the German film crew.

The Germans wanted to get more film footage for their documentary, which had been featured briefly in the local news when Dan Greene took them out on his red boat at night to get some photos of a whale that was feeding in the strait. Sea Shepherd and In the Path of Giants had swooped down and reported them to the Coast Guard, saying that they were illegally operating a boat at night without lights, although the Germans were using a spotlight to film. (The Coast Guard dismissed the incident.) On this early morning excursion to the beach, Ralph Marschalleck planned to film the crew alongside the ancient petroglyphs that were carved on the rocks along the shore. The petroglyphs were a local attraction, presumably carved by ancient relatives of the Makah. One of the rocks on which a petroglyph is carved is known as Wedding Rock; the carving is in the shape of a whale. Wayne and Donnie and the rest of the crew said they could show the Germans where the petroglyphs were. "This is our land," Wayne was saying. "We know this land like the back of our hands." At the trailhead, the Germans put on backpacks to carry tripods and other camera gear, and then we took off single file in the dark through the path in the woods.

The sky was still bright with stars and what was left of the moon, which had been full a few days before, but the path was slippery and nearly invisible in the cold fall morning. In the middle of the trip, we stopped in a prairie and saw a deer. I think it was Donnie who said, "Damn! That could have been dinner!" Then we pressed on over one more set of hills, which eventually dropped us down onto the beach, where the sun was just coming up. The black sky was lightening to blue on the horizon. Just offshore were the Flattery Rocks and Ozette Island, and the assembly of craggy, offshore volcanic formations looked like giant chess pieces or carved heads and faces, watching patiently in the dawn. The ocean was calm and the waves lapped gently at the gray, rocky sand. The tide was going out, and as the water receded, it teased little bits of bleached driftwood, the carcasses of huge uprooted trees.

After resting for a few minutes, our party set off south down the beach in search of Wedding Rock.

I walked with Dan Greene, who was part of the whaling crew's support team. He walked behind the German film team with his girlfriend, who had come along for the hike. A fisherman in his late thirties, tall and strong, Dan wore jeans and a hooded sweatshirt. He jammed his hands into his sweatshirt pockets. As we talked, we crackled through dried seaweed; we crunched through sand.

I mentioned that I had grown up on the East Coast and Dan told me that he had lived in New Jersey for a few years. He said his mother had moved the family there after his father had been in a logging accident on the Olympic Peninsula. His father was hit in the head. He survived, Dan said, but his mother was afraid he might be injured more severely the next time, so they moved to Bayville, on the Jersey shore. He recalled that when his mother died, his father told him and his sisters that they should pack one duffel bag and leave everything else, that they were moving back to Neah Bay. They moved the next day, his father abandoning everything and driving straight back toward Cape Flattery. "My father still sleeps on the couch," Dan said. Then he mentioned that he remembered loving the pizza in New Jersey as a child.

Dan has children and he told me that being a kid on the reservation can be a lot of fun with all the woods and the beaches. He said that once he was hiking in the hills with his son and night came and the guy who was supposed to pick them up didn't. It got late. Eventually, he gathered tree branches and they went to sleep in the woods. "I covered him with hickory boughs and he kicked them off. He was too warm," he said.

I pointed out the rocks offshore, and Dan told me that he had once accompanied an elder on a walk along the beach and that the elder had described the names of the rocks as they were known in the old days. This had been part of a cultural heritage survey that Dan was involved in. We talked about the Ozette archaeological dig, which he said was difficult to handle at first. "It was like digging up graves. But then it ended up being a pretty good thing. It gave us a lot. It gave us an amazing museum. It gave us something that the kids can see and really grab on to. It helped us with our fishing rights. That really opened up the sea to us. Now, the rest is coming back." He said that he was concerned about the kids learning only from the museum. "An old woman put it best to me. She said she was worried because the Makah are learning their history from books and they're no good because you have to *hear* the history. You have to *hear* the stories that were handed down."

At this point, Dan stopped to watch the Germans, who were setting up the camera and filming the sunrise, a perfect scene. In the distance we could see Ralph, his tall, lanky figure waving directions to his camerman and his soundman. Ralph was wearing his red bandanna, a black denim jacket, and green Army pants. He was standing behind the camera directing, one arm folded, one arm stroking his chin. Dan said he heard a marbled murrelet but I just heard the sound of the waves and the long stalks of kelp that tumbled onto the shore as the tide went farther and farther out.

"Do you want us to be quiet, Ralph?" Dan shouted across the beach, teasing Ralph.

"No, no," Ralph said. "It is okay. We are discussing the picture here." He pointed to where there were hundreds and hundreds of logs scattered along the beach like a giant fan. "This drifting wood . . ." Ralph paused in his conversation with Dan and asked a question of the cameraman in German then turned to Dan again. "This driftwood," Ralph said, clarifying.

Then Ralph called out to Andy. Ralph apparently wanted to film a Makah whale hunter in his ancient natural habitat.

"Okay, Andy," Ralph said. "Now, can you walk like this?" Ralph pointed in the direction he wanted Andy to walk.

Andy watched Ralph patiently. He was wearing a maroon windbreaker that said PUYALLUP POWER PADDLE 1998, baggy, hip-hop-style jeans, Nike running shoes, and a baseball cap that said NATIVE. His dark shoulder-length hair rustled in the breeze.

Dan called out to Ralph. "Hey, Ralph, do you want him to do his Clint Eastwood?"

Ralph smiled impatiently. "Something a bit similar," he said. Then Ralph directed the rest of the little crowd on the set: Donnie and Wayne and Paul Parker, another crew member, and *The Seattle Times* reporters. "Okay," Ralph said, "now everyone be quiet please for a while!" Ralph turned to Andy. "Could you come back just thirty feet?"

Andy moved the wrong way.

"Okay, come back," Ralph said.

Ralph pointed at Andy and said, "His long hair is . . ." He turned to the cameraman, who was crouched down in his red jeans, and said a word in German, *funkelord,* which the camerman translated as "sparkling." Ralph turned back to Dan and the others. "Sparkling," he said. "His hair is *sparkling!*"

The sun was farther up now and the tide was low. We walked out into the tidepools and sat down on rocks covered with barnacles and mussels and sea urchins, a kaleidoscope of crustaceans, starfish, and skittish squid. The sun was hot. Wayne took off his Raiders jacket and his *Today* show baseball cap, putting the cap down on the rocks. We sat in the warm sun and talked and watched the film crew walk farther out on the rocks with Andy. Now Andy had a rifle, and the film crew was filming him as he fired at a seal.

One of *The Seattle Times* reporters was dismayed that the Germans were setting up shots for their documentary. The reporter was grumbling that the documentary was, as a result, not realistic, an incorrect portrait of the Makah.[5] The reporter was also concerned about the legality of a gun being fired in a national park and the legality of a dead seal.

At Ralph's command, Andy fired. He missed the seal and we all turned to see it bob its head back underwater. Ralph directed a second take. Andy missed again. In a few minutes, the Germans packed up the heavy equipment and we all walked back to the beach. The tide was coming in, so Wayne and Donnie and the reporters and Paul Parker decided to get in closer to shore.

Ralph and I chose to walk farther south down the beach to look for the petroglyphs that no one had seen yet; Wayne and the rest of the crew weren't certain anymore about where they were. We approached the last large rock, hoping we would see it on the side that hadn't been visible. As we walked around it, I crossed my fingers for good luck. I asked Ralph if Germans cross their fingers for good luck.

---

[5] When Melville wrote *Typee* and *Omoo*, people didn't believe that these accounts of his adventures in Polynesia could possibly be true, even though they mostly were. *The New York Evangelist* called Melville a liar. Even his publisher doubted him, telling Melville that his books would sell even better if he could prove they were true. His British publisher requested "documentary evidence." One day, the sailor who had deserted the *Acushnet* with Melville, Richard Tobias Greene, wrote a letter to a newspaper testifying on Melville's behalf. Melville quickly went to see Greene, a house and sign painter in Buffalo, and returned to New York City with a daguerreotype of Greene and a lock of his hair: proof. His publisher still seemed to doubt him, and, subsequently, Melville was forced to cut a lot of the antimissionary passages in his books. When Melville wrote his third work, *Mardi*, which was intended not as a true-to-life narrative but as a romance, his publisher told him that people preferred his true-to-life narratives, that he was "the man who lived among cannibals," not a fiction writer, which Melville did not want to hear. With all this in mind he sat down to write *Redburn*, his account of his first time at sea, as a young man. Laurie Robertson-Lorant, author of *Melville: A Biography*, writes: "As he wrote about his first voyage, calling his autobiographical narrator/protagonist Wellingborough Redburn, he realized it would be painfully easy to follow the formula established by such writers of nautical adventure and picaresque novels as Captain Marryat and Charles F. Briggs—so much so, in fact, that his own youthful experiences began to seem fictive and clichéd to him. He began to toy with the idea that life imitated art, not the other way around...."

"No, we go like this," he said. He made a fist with his thumb tucked inside and showed me. "With the thumb in."

We turned the corner and looked at another field of just-now-under-water shells.

"No luck," Ralph said.

On our way back Ralph explained that the scenes of Andy shooting at the seal didn't work. "We took some pictures but the shot, it came up too quickly, too suddenly. It was no good," he lamented.

We regrouped and hiked north toward the old Ozette village site. On the hike, Wayne told me that the whaling commission had been working with the Germans for several years. The Germans had filmed them when they went to Monaco for the International Whaling Commission meeting. In fact, Ralph had recommended the hotel that Wayne had stayed in just outside of town, in France. Wayne suddenly borrowed Ralph's cell phone. I asked who he was calling. "Don't worry," Donnie said, "just some woman he met in France." The tide was nearly in now, and when someone pointed out how far the water had come up, Wayne realized that he had left his *Today* show cap "out on the rocks," which was now surrounded by the Pacific Ocean.

As we trudged along the beach, Donnie said, "After we hunt the whale we can pretty much go anywhere we want in the world, like on tours and stuff."

"That's right," Wayne said.

When we stopped for lunch, Ralph offered everyone dried salmon and hard-boiled eggs and German chocolate bars. Crows watched us eat. We walked a little farther and someone noticed Wedding Rock and the petroglyph of the whale but Ralph decided not to film them.

Wayne was impressed with the petroglyph. "I've only ever seen 'em in postcards," he said.

Ralph said, "They are in the *National Geographic*."

The petroglyph was of a sad-eyed whale, and alongside it were faces, like faces of the moon, one with what looked like tears: I was struck by how the carvings simultaneously looked like something incredibly ancient and like something I might see Micah McCarty carving at his house back in town while his tape deck was playing reggae.

We hiked on for another mile or so. We passed a dead seal on the beach and the stench followed us for a while, like a bad memory, before we finally came to Ozette, the site of the ancient village. There was a memorial where the famous dig had been, a longhouse with carvings and shells and bones left as ornaments. Inside it was a little chapel made with fallen logs and cedar planks, filled with shells and sea animal bones. At the back of the wall a plaque said:

FROM OZETTE ENDINGS
HAVE COME
BEGINNINGS.
AT OZETTE COMES NEW UNDERSTANDINGS . . .
FROM THIS SITE WE HAVE GAINED
APPRECIATION OF THE WISDOM OF OUR FOREFATHERS.
FROM THIS WE GAINED NEW STRENGTH . . .

I stood inside the memorial for a while. Outside, Wayne, Donnie, Paul, and Andy were lying on the beach, breathing hard, exhausted, relaxing in the afternoon sun. Dan, who was still fresh and sitting with his girlfriend in the grass on a hill, called out to Ralph, who was standing with his hand on his hip, gazing out at the ocean as if he were critiquing a set design.

"Hey, Ralph," Dan shouted. "Do you want to film them doing the nettles ritual, where they beat themselves with nettles? Or do you want to film them doing the sand flea ritual where they lie in the sand and let the fleas cover them? A guy showed me how."

Ralph smiled and tried to laugh. He acted as if something were on his mind.

On the beach, looking out, you could see how Ozette had once been the perfect village site. You could see how the crescent shape of the bay was guarded by huge volcanic rocks and islands, like lions on the steps of a mansion. You could see how the great concave curve of the land acted like a net to the creatures of the sea, all the creatures that filled the rocks at low tide, that passed by this bay at the tip of the Olympic Peninsula, here where the continent jutted out boldly into the sea: seals and sea lions and otters and whales. You could see the sun making the water shine and sparkle like a field of rippled ice.

Donnie pointed out into the bay toward the large rocks that resembled two profiles and were called Father and Son. He said they had nearly caught a whale there a few weeks before.

"We could have had him," he said. And then he lay back and rested again.

I asked Ralph how the day had gone for him film-wise. "You know, I didn't like the sunshine," he said. "At Ozette, I prefer the fog with this magical sunlight in between the sea and the fog. Do you know this sunlight?"

I said I did.

"I do not prefer the sunshine," he said. "I prefer the fog."

I left early and hiked back with the photographer from *The Seattle Times*. We had a nice long walk through the woods that had been dark and a little ominous in the morning but now were deckled with thousands of peaceful shades of green. We stopped at the Lost Resort, a little store a half mile from the trailhead, and had pizza and beer (Lake Ozette was not a dry town). The owner showed us a map of all the petroglyphs, dozens of them, and he said that there was a road that went almost to the beach, a road that would have saved us all a lot of time. That evening, when we got back to Neah Bay, we discovered that some of the reporters who were in town had taken the absence of the crew and the German film team and *The Seattle Times* reporters as an indication that the hunt was on. Panic had ensued, and several of the reporters set about renting a boat to take them down to Ozette.

Before Wayne and Donnie got back to town, they also stopped in at the Lost Resort for sodas and saw the petroglyph map and heard about the road. They were excited about both discoveries, especially the road, which was news to them.

"We could use that road," Wayne said.

35 / Evil

In the vacuum of inaction, criticism of the hunt began to grow, and an example of criticism in action occurred on an otherwise good-natured day in the midst of the wait for the hunt, when a couple of dozen cars driven by protestors blocked a road on the reservation. They had wanted to drive into Neah Bay, but the tribal police stopped them just out of town, in front of the cemetery, the fenced-off clearing in the woods decorated with flowers and clumps of fresh dirt with totem poles. The press rushed out to cover the event: newspaper reporters and photographers and TV camera crews lined up to film the cars, the little crowd. Some of the whaling crew members showed up too. Eric Johnson, the captain of the crew, had been keeping a low profile around town during the previous days, but he drove out and stood watching as the protestors stopped their cars and climbed out with their signs and their concerns. Wayne and Donnie were there too.

Initially, both sides stood on either side of the road but then the two sides mingled along the yellow line that ran equatorially through the standoff. At one point, the protestors walked into the cemetery and were shouting from the grave-covered hill. The whaling crew members present noted this. Marcy Parker was writing down license plate numbers, whispering to the police chief.

Very soon, a woman shouted at the crew. "Real men don't kill animals! Only a coward kills whales! You are a coward and a sissy!" Another woman shouted that the Makah shouldn't have special rights just because they were Indians. Another woman said her soul was connected to the soul of the gray whale.

And then a woman pointed at Wayne, the holder of the gun in the newspapers, the giver of interviews on TV, the guy who the press had reported to have been in jail, the guy who—as the protestors were now pointing out over and over—had slugged a man, had missed a court-mandated anger management class, was a criminal, was unworthy, a slaughterer of whales. Wayne was being singled out.

"You're *evil!*" the woman said. "Evil as hell!" She said it over and over. "Macho man!" she shouted. "You should be proud! *Real* proud!" The veins in her neck bulged; she seemed maniacal. "Big man, you can kill!" she screamed. "You're evil!" she said again. She later told everyone who would listen to her that she had not felt so strongly about something since she protested the Vietnam War. "You're *evil!* You have a black heart," she said to Wayne.

At first Wayne looked embarrassed. He put his hands in his pockets, lit a cigarette. Then he looked angry and then frustrated and then not exactly certain he knew what he was going to say or do. The protestors continued to shout. Wayne mumbled nervously to Donnie, who appeared relaxed, almost unperturbed. The woman continued to taunt Wayne.

"You don't know what you're *doing,*" she said, leaning toward Wayne, pointing at him, shouting, fuming. "You've never done it before. You don't even have a clue."

Now the protestors in the cemetery up the little hill were shouting down taunts as well. Wayne was slumped over smoking, and for a second he looked at his feet. Then, all of a sudden, he held his chin up, his chin wobbling a little as he did, looking as if it might fall back, lose its nerve. "Save the beef," Wayne finally said. "Go stand in front of McDonald's." Donnie rubbed his stomach.

Eventually, the protestors were back in their cars; the crew applauded when the car of one of the protestors, a heavyset fisherman from Port Angeles, finally started up after engine trouble. The protestors drove off, shouting that there was nothing traditional about the Makah hunt, that it meant nothing to the Makah.

Afterward, I walked over to Wayne. He appeared a little shook up. He still didn't seem to know exactly what to say. He mentioned that the crew wasn't happy about where the protestors were protesting.

"They shouldn't be doing this here," Wayne said, shrugging his shoulders toward the cemetery. Donnie was nodding. Wayne looked at Donnie and then Wayne began nodding again. "If it were a couple of years ago, we might have acted different," Wayne said, "but for now we're just gonna play it cool."

36 / Slaves

The configuration of the whaling crew was changing behind the closed trailer doors, around wood stoves, and in the council chambers room where the whaling commission met at night. I didn't know what was happening exactly but I knew that it had to do with personalities and politics and with history. Personalities and politics change but history is indelible in Neah Bay. It is in the rocks, which were named for people, for their resemblance to animals, for events that had taken place in their sight years and years before: Seal Rock, Sail Rock, the rock called Father and Son. History is in the rivers, where particular bends were identified with great fishing successes or sunken cars. It is in the sacred songs, which the whaling crew were arguing over when they met one another in the evenings, when they were asking: which song should we sing when we get the whale?

And history was in the social scheme, even if the scheme had changed, even if, when the representational system of government was instituted, the powers of the chiefs fell, and the powers of the commoners rose. Families who believed they were descendants of chiefs remembered. And no matter what, people still talked about slaves.

Slave: the word that stung, that was the highest insult, that was fought over and denied, the ultimate slur. Along the Northwest coast, in the villages that were ruled by a tradition that was built on the accumulation of wealth and prestige, in the land of the potlach, the slave was the person without, the person with absolutely no worth. At the time of first contact with whites, there were a lot of slaves along the coast, a lot of great, wealthy kings. A scholar has noted: "The data available . . . suggests that slavery on the northwest coast among the natives was of nearly as much economic importance to them as was slavery to the plantation regions of the United States before the Civil War." Slaves were prohibited by the Indian agents installed in Neah Bay by the American government. The Indian agents also took away the power of the chiefs when they moved people out of the distant villages and into Neah Bay, when they imposed a representational government on the Makah. The traditional balance of power was inverted. A chief who had once wielded great power in his village now had one vote on the reservation, just like each of the descendants of his many slaves.

While the whale hunt was on hold, while the political alliances that had made a whale hunt possible strained in the wait, that word—*slave*—was being whispered around Neah Bay. People disputed birthright and lineage and family trees, the right to hunt a whale, the right to speak for a family, for a village, for a tribe. *Slave*: it was being whispered like a dirty word. Slaves and chiefs, whalers and commoners: everyone seemed to have a different idea of who was which. I could visit with people around the reservation and hear all kinds of reasons for the whale hunt's delay. One man told me that the problem involved a chief who had had many wives many years before. There were families politicking against families, arguing lineages and ancestral rights, or just arguing. Whale commissioners resigned or threatened to. It was a matter of tribal politics and family politics and jealousies and other things all at once.

I was confused, and the more I heard, the more I realized that I was not likely to understand, but I could see that John McCarty, for one, was furious with how the hunt was proceeding, seething with the transgressions he saw or imagined. I would watch him from time to time talking to reporters. He was in support of whale hunting but against this particular whale hunt, and, as such, he had become a one-man Greek chorus.

One day I was walking along the road and he picked me up and we drove back to his house. He gave me a cup of coffee and an apple and we discussed the hunt while he filled the dishwasher. He was saying that the hunt was not traditional. He was ticked off, to say the least.

"I'm thinking of having a press conference," he said.

One of the television reporters later managed to talk John out of a press conference. But there was no stopping John from being upset.

"I know where these guys come from, and they know I know," he said.

Micah was back in town—it looked as though he wouldn't be going to college, for the time being anyway—but this morning, as John spoke, his daughter, Maggie, dropped by. At the time, she was working in the business development office out at the tribal center, where she was trying to train people in Neah Bay to be tour guides. She wanted to talk to him about arranging a court date in Olympia. He gave her advice on her lawyer.

Then, John got to talking about the hunt again and got upset about methods and people and politics and power, and put his fist down on the table. *"Slaves!"* he said. Maggie was sitting on the arm of her father's chair and she put her arm around him and hugged him and cooed. "Oh," she said, "Chief of Waatch."

37 / The Negatives

At last, with the hunt under attack on the reservation and all around it, something happened—something bad, something that ended up being reduced and condensed into a front-page picture, into a thirty-second video of what we, the assembled media, seemed to have wanted all along in one form or another: violence.

On a cold and drizzly Sunday morning, the flotilla of protest boats moved slowly into the marina, a few yards from the shore of the town. Sea Shepherd steered the *Sirenian* up near the boat launch, across the street from the espresso stand. Steph Dutton boldly kayaked around. Heidi

Tiura was in *Sea Dog*. There were Zodiacs zooming about the harbor and a Jet Ski—all there to demonstrate, to taunt. The protest boats played whale sounds, people shouted at the tribe through loudspeakers, calling them whale killers. One banner said: STOP THE GRAY WHALE SLAUGHTER. In no time, crowds assembled on the waterfront. Kids began shouting things back, and then adults did too. The *Sirenian* moved closer. Soon there were dozens of cars parked on the bluff overlooking the water. People honked and got out of their cars and shouted. Teenage boys ran out on the docks with rocks and firecrackers.

In a few minutes the confrontation escalated. The boys hit the protestors boats with their rocks, shattering a window on the *Sirenian* wheelhouse. The boys used slingshots, threw firecrackers. The protestors videotaped the teenagers' attacks.

At first, the tribal police watched the rocks being thrown and people laughed. There was a kind of malicious glee. But then mothers in the crowd complained. Eventually, tribal officials consulted the police and the police stopped the boys.

A group of tribal members stepped down to the edge of the boat ramp and brought out drums and began singing songs. Micah was at the boat ramp with Wayne and lots of other people. Eric Johnson got a few crew members together and paddled the canoe around.

In the midst of this mayhem, Alberta Thompson, the tribal elder who opposed the hunt, went out on the dock at the end of the boat ramp and called out to Lisa Distefano, the expedition leader of Sea Shepherd's Gray Whale Protection Campaign, who was in a Zodiac moving about the harbor. Thompson invited Distefano to dinner at her home in Neah Bay.

Distefano immediately accepted the invitation and came to the shore in her Zodiac, making a jump for the dock. She was pushed into the water by a tribal member out on the dock and after she waded ashore she was detained by the police, whisked away. She held her head high, in a pose of defiance.

In the huddle of people standing and singing and shouting on the boat ramp, Alberta Thompson cried. A few feet away, another elder who supported the hunt also cried and looked to the sky and wept through a prayer.

Someone then grabbed the line on Distefano's Zodiac and it was dragged up on shore. As the crowd became a mob, Donnie, Wayne,

Micah, and a few others climbed aboard the commandeered Zodiac. They held a Makah flag aloft. People cheered. Another protestor waded into shore from a small boat, and he was shoved to the ground as he was arrested by the tribal police, who said he had slipped. When he got up blood ran from the cut on his head.

Camera shutters clicked. The shambles was magnetized onto video-tape. Hosts of reporters gathered around the carcass of the Zodiac, its engine dead from having been dragged ashore. Photographers and TV camera people bumped into one another, crammed into the small melee, getting into each other's shots, focusing on the blood. Appalled by the scene as individuals, their coverage as a group nevertheless gained a momentary vitality in documenting the violence, a burst of life that broke through the days and days of hunt-free monotony. I have to admit that I too felt the call of the mob: a rush of feverish excitement in view of the clash of opposing sides.

Afterward, when it came time for the inevitable press conferences, for the flurry of accusations and the highlighting of wrongs, Watson held his on the *Sirenian*. He said he was, in his words, "here doing a peaceful protest and we were attacked by rocks and slingshots."

I saw Harriette Cheeka, the ambulance driver and poet.[5] She was worried that someone would get hurt when there weren't enough ambulance attendants on call. She shook her head and said, "When anger is in control, everyone loses."

The Makah called a press conference on the violence too. It was at the tribal center. Ben Johnson was somber. He seemed to know that somewhere in this squall of violence the tribe had been beaten, that Sea Shepherd and the other protestors had gotten what they wanted out of the tribe—a rise. "Well, it was a sad situation that happened," Johnson said. "It was uncalled for. Sea Shepherd, to me, violated our rights. And our treaty rights run very deep. I'm very appalled that Sea Shepherd was push-

---

[5] In *The Enchanted Flood: Or the Romantic Iconography of the Sea* (1950), W. H. Auden, the poet, said, "To understand the romantic conception of the relation between objective and subjective experience, *Moby Dick* is perhaps the best work to study. . . ." In addition, Auden noted the following about the owners of the *Pequod*, the whaling ship in *Moby-Dick*: "The proprietors of the *Pequod* are Quakers, i.e., they profess the purest doctrine of non-violence, yet see no incongruity in this [that they kill whales for a living]. . . . So always in every life, there is a vast difference between what a man professes and how he acts."

ing our buttons, making our people react." He seemed to become more angry as he spoke. "This is low-down," he said. "I'm disgusted. He knows how Indians feel. He knows how serious we are." And then he made a kind of plea to the reporters. "I just hope the wrong things don't get on TV. You know, you could make things look awful bad out there, and there are some things I wouldn't want to see. You know the negatives."

The negatives were played up that evening and the next day—the tribe looked like a bunch of vigilantes. But just after the tribal press conference ended, Eric Johnson, the crew captain, and his brother, J.L. walked in and cornered their mother, Marcy Parker, who had been on the phone with the tribal attorney during the press conference. Eric's jacket said, FIVE VILLAGES, ONE NATION. His brother wore a Yankees hat bill-backward. J.L. had filmed the protest too and they came to show the tape to their mother.

They rewound the tape. As they did, Marcy looked at Eric. "Is that my jacket?" she said.

He nodded distractedly and then said, "Look, they threatened us."

"They did?" Marcy said.

"It's on the tape," he said excitedly.

The videotape showed a protestor videotaping the canoe. "They said, 'This is for our wanted poster,' or something like that," Eric said.

Marcy folded her arms.

In a second, the man on the tape said, "For the wanted poster, boys."

The tape went on. It showed the paddlers paddling quietly and steadily, with chaos all around them. The paddlers paddled.

"See that?" Eric said to his mother. "No talking in the canoe. Quiet. No hate."

Marcy nodded.

"No hate," Eric said again. "If you've got hate, you can't be in the canoe."

Marcy nodded more vigorously.

And yet, beyond the council chamber, the damage was done. It was all getting ugly.

A few days later, Sea Shepherd called another press conference, and passed out articles that showed the tribal police chief in Neah Bay had stolen a gun while working as a police officer on an Indian reservation in Nevada. "What we're doing now is showing the real Makah," Distefano said.

38 / Cast Away

Trapped, I was trapped. The weather turned even worse and the rain pounded on the roof of the shanty and when the sky cleared for a day or two at a time and the crew didn't hunt, I wondered, just as everyone else wondered, if I would be waiting in Neah Bay forever. I sat around for a week and then another and then I drove seven hours home for just one night—just long enough to dump the expensive rental car at the airport after it had taken a rock in the windshield on the drive home ($400 extra)—and I raced back to the shanty. By day, I was amid scores of comradely reporters and I had a nice enough time talking to them, and I enjoyed seeing the people of the village, the people whose backyard I was camping in, but at some point I began to feel like an imposition, like jetsam, like unnecessary ballast—like a castaway, lost at sea and floating directionless in the sometimes kind of awesome midst of an unending controversy. In the evening, away from my land-based, non-whale-hunt-obsessed family and friends, I sat alone in the shanty, and I picked up my copy of *Moby-Dick,* which was tattered now and Scotch-taped, and amid plywood walls, I wallowed in the awful loneliness that is in the middle of the book: it made me want to give it up, just go home, hug my wife and children, and sleep in a warm bed. I did not do this, though, mostly because every time I was about to toss it in and drive away, a whale hunter approached me and said to stick around, said it would be soon. Once a news photographer grabbed me and said, "It's gonna be tomorrow, I *know* it." And so I stayed and roamed the town by day and watched the protest boats from my camp stove as they patrolled the area and then returned to the shanty, where I kept notes:

Yesterday, a woman who is a couples' counselor drove into town. From Seattle. Set up her tent near my shanty, spoke to the protestors, spoke to the Makah, and then packed her tent back into her car and drove home. Irreconcilable differences.

Halloween: went to a logging bar in Clallam Bay and watched people dance and couldn't decide if the guy dressed as a logger was in costume or not.

The Makah press conferences are like experimental one-act plays, scattered with non sequitur dialogue. "Where's CNN?" Keith Johnson asked yesterday. "Here," someone from CNN said. "Oh, haven't seen you guys before," Johnson said back. "Is the History Channel here? MTV?"

One of the TV cameramen is reading *American Cinematography*.

A newswoman told me that, even if I didn't want to admit it, I was there for fame and fortune, like all men, at the expense of my children. I took said comment to heart. Sat alone in the shanty and felt very sad and even angry until I went to a pay phone and called my wife. She said, "You can't leave *now*! What if you miss the hunt?"

Cellular phones are monitored by everyone. The other day, a reporter was sent back to the newsroom in Seattle after making disparaging comments about tribal members on her cell phone.

Craig McCaw, a Seattle cellular communications magnate, helicoptered a representative into Neah Bay to ask the Makah not to hunt. (McCaw had previously helped send Keiko, a killer whale formerly based at the Oregon Coast Aquarium, to Iceland. A few years before, Keiko had starred in the movie *Free Willy* and was subsequently discovered languishing in a Mexico City aquarium.) McCaw reportedly offered the Makah money not to hunt, and the Makah reportedly declined.

A young female protestor claimed to have once had intimate relations with a dolphin. At first I doubted it. Then I was told by an expert on cetaceans that dolphins have reportedly sought to engage in sexual contact with humans. The expert also told me that some scientists consider recreational sex a barometer of intelligence in mammals, which is one reason why the intelligence of whales and dolphins is considered to be high.

A Seattle reporter said to Darrell Markishtum, one of the crew members, "How was your powwow?" Darrell replied, "We don't have powwows. Powwows are Plains Indians. We have potlaches." The reporter said, "Okay, well, then *potlach*..I'm not very good with Native American terminology. Did you have a potlach?" Darrell said, "Well, no, but I think they had a meeting."

A newspaper reporter bought me dinner when I had completely run out of cash.

Guy operating the fishing boat that was to take reporters out to see the hunt in the event of it actually happening left town. He said he had looked in the eye of one of the whales and felt that the whale had been trying to communicate with him.

The producers of *Lethal Weapon* faxed reporters to say that they were against the hunt.

At the crowded Makah Maiden, a reporter who had been waiting for her food for a long time suddenly stood up and said, "This isn't funny anymore," and stormed out.

One night at the Makah Maiden, a photographer had to run out before he could eat his dinner and when he came back hours later, the people working there had saved it and reheated it for him.

Standing in the lobby of the Cape Motel one day, word came in over the radio that the hunt had happened, that a whale was being towed in on the Sooes River. Raced across town. Passed a woman and her children who had driven down to the beach after hearing from a friend in Seattle that a whale had been caught. Passed Wayne and Donnie, who had heard that a whale had been caught and were wondering if maybe Sea Shepherd was up to some trick, and then at the mouth of the Sooes River, I met a newspaper photographer who said, "*I'll* tell you what this means. This means we don't have any idea what's going on."

In the market, early one morning, when it was still dark, a woman said to me, "Did you hear that sound? It sounded like a whale." I ran out to the parking lot and stood there a long time and didn't hear anything.

The Seattle Times published a story comparing the Makah hunt with *Moby-Dick*. It read in part, "In the end of *Moby-Dick,* Herman Melville's epic tale of obsession on the high seas, the peg-legged Captain Ahab finally gets his white whale, and in the process, the whale gets him. I know this because I watched the movie. I couldn't get through the book. It was too ponderous for my late-20th-century sensibility. The story unfolding in Neah Bay has had the same effect. My attention has begun to drift. . . ." At another point the reporter wrote: "We were the biggest clowns of all— the people with the notepads and microphones and cameras. We came with leviathan expectations. We wanted a Steven Spielberg blockbuster and were disappointed when we got, instead, a reading of *Moby-Dick*. My edition of the book is 700 pages long. Apparently, Melville, too, thought there was more to whaling than killing a whale." Reading this, as *Moby-Dick* stared at me in the shanty, confirmed the gnawing feeling I had that maybe *Moby-Dick* and the Makah whale were somehow related, sharing some kind of semiparallel universe.[5]

---

[5] As he was beginning to think about *Moby-Dick*, Melville reviewed *The Red Rover,* a book by James Fenimore Cooper, for *The Literary World.* Melville biographer Laurie Robertson-Lorant writes: "Melville was fascinated by the 'Red Rover,' an enigmatic character through whom Cooper explores mysteries of identity that Melville, too, was pondering. Oddly, his review

After weeks and weeks of waiting around, I woke up one morning and went over to the restaurant to get some coffee and I heard a TV report in the restaurant that said, "The hunt is likely to be soon." I just laughed and laughed until I felt a little loopy after a while, a little insane, like a drowning victim, asphyxiated in the unrelenting pressure that surrounded an unpressurable event. I felt a little like King Lear's fool, except not so literate, not so smart, and mostly foolish. As the days went on, however, and the hunt continued to not happen, this ended up being a better vantage point from which to view events. After that the days passed more quickly, and I began to think that it didn't matter when the hunt would happen, that it didn't matter at all. I tried to tell this to a few reporters and a couple of people on the crew and they looked at me as if I were insane.

39 / Stories

With a new if tenuous perspective on things, with a kind of melancholy patience that seeped into my being with each passing day, I spent the remainder of the wait for the hunt that fall seeking out stories that were as seemingly unrelated to the whale hunt as possible, that were the stories of the Makah.[5] I forgot about the hunt and listened to some of the stories that the grandmothers told in the warm living rooms or in the senior center or in kitchens in the wake of a simple meal—grandmothers being the secret glue on the reservation, the homes of grandmothers being the child's

---

focused so much more on the way the volume was designed than on the text that it was published as 'A Thought on Book-Binding,' a Melvillean joke. By writing about the book's binding, which is a costume or disguise, and a surface identity, Melville implied the ultimate unknowability of the text, and the mystery of the text beyond the text, both of the book and of the universe."

5 Like any story, like any telling of an event, *Moby-Dick* can be interpreted in as many ways as there are interpreters. Here is the interpretation of Robertson-Lorant: "*Moby-Dick* draws from a deep reservoir of Native American folklore and myth. It is a vision quest, a narrative sweat lodge or purification ritual, and a Ghost Dance mourning the closing of ancient spiritual frontiers. It is Melville's lament for the extermination of the Indians by white settlers and the importation of Africans as slaves, both of which sowed seeds of sin and death in the New World Garden. It is an apocalyptic vision of industrialization and imperialism, an elegy for the medicine man supplanted by the gunslinger."

momentary refuge, the secret coves where the matters of the tribal health clinic's counseling sessions for drug abuse and alcoholism were maybe momentarily immune, forgotten, conquered.

I heard the story of the clamshell woman, who came from the woods and took away misbehaving children, dragged them off the beach, threw them in a cedar basket, put pitch in their eyes. I heard the story of the elk, the biggest animal, the haughty animal who shoved the small animals aside, who thought he was so big, so great, until the wren flew up his nose and made him sneeze so that he was weak when she flew out, and he learned his lesson and was nice to all the animals after that. I heard the story of the raven who tricked the crow. I heard the story of the buck who one day was curious, always looking, always watching everyone else, who was burning the splinters off the bottom of his canoe (to make it faster) with a torch, when the beautiful little canary birds came along and distracted him and he burned his canoe in entirety and upset his wife, a deer. I heard the song in which the woman watches a sail in her husband's canoe fill with wind and carry off her heart. I heard the story of Thunderbird, who brought the whale.

And, always, I heard the stories of Kwatee. Kwatee, who conquered the monster at the cape, who cut off his hair and disguised himself. Kwatee, who paddled to the cape in a small canoe and was swallowed by the sea monster and then cut away at the heart of the giant, undestroyable creature using his mussel shell. Kwatee, who could feel that the monster was dying and was then thrown up onto the beach just before the monster died, at which point the raven invited everyone to come to a big party on the beach. Kwatee, who was crafty, cunning, astute, who taught the people of the cape lessons, who changed himself into different animals, who was always changing, making people see things, making people understand. Kwatee, the trickster.

And then, after hearing the stories, walking through the rain. Walking and wondering and winding up at the market to see Wayne come in with Arnie after they had been out on Dan Greene's boat, from which they had pointed their whale hunting weapons to the water as if they had fired and raced off dragging a float, a mock marine mammal. The protestors chased them but insisted later that they weren't fooled at all, that they knew there wasn't a whale. But Wayne and Arnie sat in front of the market that night, cold and wet, recounting the event, laughing so hard they almost rolled over, almost turned inside out. *Kwatee!*

40 / Truce

The break in the standoff came at the end of November, just before Thanksgiving. Representatives of the Makah tribe met with representatives of Sea Shepherd at the Coast Guard base. It was their first face-to-face meeting.

The representatives of the tribe—Marcy Parker, Keith Johnson, and Ben Johnson—drove down to the base. Before the meeting, they took questions from the reporters.

"Do you expect the meeting to be productive?" a reporter asked.

Marcy Parker shook her head.

"Certainly, we're going to have a fine lunch," Keith Johnson said.

"It's gonna be interesting to see what the guy's gonna say," Ben Johnson said. "Look what the guy started. . . . It started about protesting whaling and now it's anti-Indian. . . . It's a complete turnaround. He's turning white people against the Indian."

Captain Paul Watson came in his dress uniform. Lisa Distefano was there too. As soon as they arrived, all parties sat down in the Coast Guard cafeteria for lunch with the Coast Guard commander. After an hour or so they came out.

Captain Watson announced that Sea Shepherd would leave Neah Bay. "I think that Sea Shepherd's responsibilities can very soon be taken over by Mother Nature," he said.

Lisa Distefano announced, "I think it's an important first step."

"We are not backing off here," Captain Watson said.

Lisa talked about death threats she had received on board the *Edward Abbey*. She brought up the tribal police chief controversy and made further allegations of tribal corruption. She claimed that she was concerned for the safety of the children in Neah Bay.

The attorney for Sea Shepherd stood beside them during the press conference and then got in a car with a bumper sticker that said, WAITING FOR GODOT, which, given the state I was in, meant a lot to me.⁵

---

⁵ Something or nothing, nothing or something: Melville pondered this Beckettian question. On occasion, he would worry that all the symbols he was pouring into "Whale," all the Shakespeare and Dante and Byron and Milton, would, in the end, be only, in his words, "sound and fury, signifying nothing." His heart suffered in other ways too. When Melville was sitting at his

Back at the tribal center, reporters asked Ben Johnson what Watson and Distefano had said when Johnson told them he felt they were being anti-Indian. "I think they were a little red-faced on that," Ben said.

"Do you respect them?" a reporter asked.

"Oh yes," Johnson said. "That's a long time to be standing there on a ship."

Keith Johnson informed the reporters that he had been disappointed with the lunch.

41 / The Problem

After Sea Shepherd left, the tribe didn't hunt a whale. I went home. Later, I discovered that the big problem for the tribe was not so much logistical as climatic, or environmental; for reasons that might have to do with global temperatures or Arctic food supplies or something else altogether, the migration was unusually late. Even the gray whale biologists didn't have a good reason as to why this might be. But, in short, the problem with the whale hunt turned out to be that there weren't a lot of whales.

42 / A Promotion

After winter had set in, after the protestors had left, after the hunt had vanished from the newspapers and the nightly television news, after the German film crew had flown home, I drove back up to Neah Bay. The trees were draped with ice. Clouds covered the wet forests like a thick, comfortable blanket, and when the tops of the Olympic Mountains peeked through they were white with snow. When I got to Neah Bay, I threw my

---

desk in Massachusetts composing *Moby-Dick*, in view of Mount Graylock, and his family was away visiting relatives, he would miss them so much that he would tremble.

stuff in my old shanty—it was frozen and covered with thick green moss and water was beginning to seep through the ceiling. I went over to the market and then mailed a letter at the post office and walked down the road along the bay a little ways. In a few minutes I saw John McCarty in his pickup truck. He told me to get in.

We drove across town to the senior center, where John made me coffee. He was working, for the moment, in the job that Alberta Thompson had had before she became friendly with the protestors; he was managing the lunch program at the senior center. He gave me the lowdown on the hunt: the players had changed somewhat. Marcy Parker was no longer on the council, but the person who replaced her was pro–whale hunt. The council was still for the whale hunt. Ben Johnson was still tribal chairman, and he was pro–whale hunt. Marcy's son, Eric Johnson, remained on the crew but he was no longer captain. (Eric later told me that he didn't want to deal with all the hunt politics anymore.) He said that Wayne Johnson was in charge of the crew and, moreover, was for all practical purposes in charge of the hunt itself.

"Wayne Johnson's in charge," he said. Then he said, "They're not ready." He was referring to the crew.

I met Wayne the next morning at the Makah Maiden for coffee. The management had recently installed a new stove—the place was luxuriously warm.

Wayne looked different to me; something about him had changed but I couldn't say what. He was dressed in a cap and a blue windbreaker and he was carrying a small briefcase that Denise Dailey, the executive director of the whaling commission, had given him: she had been telling him that he had to be more organized now that he was in charge of the crew and the details of the hunt. He looked like the cruise director on an inadequately financed adventure tour. When I walked in, I was a few minutes late. I apologized.

"You're fired," Wayne said. He smiled.

I was about to hear all about how Wayne was planning his version of the whale hunt, but he brought me up-to-date on other stuff first. He had stayed in for New Year's Eve the week before. He had bought a car just after Thanksgiving, after the press had gone, partly with some money he had been owed by the tribal government—for whaling duties and for Beautification Committee work. He had driven his new used car across the

peninsula, and when he was getting onto the highway near the Tacoma
Dome, a woman coming out of a bingo game and not looking sideswiped
him with her car and all but totaled his new car. He waited on the highway
to have it towed to Tacoma, where it sat in a car yard and eventually froze
and, as a result, needed a new engine block, which Wayne did not have the
money for at the time. Donnie had gone into Port Angeles the night
before the accident to see a band and relax, and Wayne used his cell phone
and just happened to get Donnie while he was in bed and watching cable
TV at his motel the next morning. So Donnie drove out and picked up
Wayne and brought him home without his brand-new used car. "The guy
said he'd only charge me a couple of bucks a day to store it, but now, I can't
afford to get it out of the yard," Wayne explained.

Wayne told me that he had finally started going to the anger management classes that the court had sentenced him to after he had hit the
machinist outside of Port Angeles. The classes weren't as bad as he had
thought they would be. The guy running them was an ex-Marine, a tough
guy, as Wayne described him. The last time Wayne had showed up at the
courthouse, he had run into a bunch of reporters who wanted to film him
dealing with his assault charges, but he managed to stave them off. "I told
them, 'Please don't do a story,'" he said. "I told them I'd give them some
more story later." He said he still wasn't comfortable with the press. "I read
some story a newspaper did on me," he said. "It was full of lies. I felt so
stupid."

I asked him about the situation in the tribe, the new council members
and the changes on the crew. He held his hands out and seemed to almost
plead with me. "We're stronger now," he said. "We're stronger."

We went out into the rainy cold and got into the van that Wayne was
driving. It was a military surplus van from Fort Lewis. The words DRIVES
GOOD were scribbled across the cracked windshield in wax pencil, and the
inside was covered with shag carpet. We picked up Donnie. Wayne lit a
cigarette and Donnie drank a can of Pepsi. I sat in the back on a milk crate
and finished a cup of coffee, and as I did I noticed a sign on the dashboard
that read, ABSOLUTELY NO SMOKING, EATING, DRINKING. A bus passed by
us heading in the other direction, and an advertisement on its side said:
ARE YOU THINKING OF COMMITTING SUICIDE TODAY?

Wayne was upbeat about the van. He said, "It's the Indian van! It never
breaks down."

We were headed out to meet Arnie Hunter at the tribal fisheries office.

Wayne was going to try and get some money for the crew, for all the time they'd put into practicing so far.

He told me that there were a lot of differences among the crew but that they were all trying to stay together. Wayne said that sometimes Darrell got upset with him if he threw a rock at a heron or something, so he was trying to be careful about that. He rolled his eyes and shook his head, looking at the sky and making a gesture with his wiry arms outstretched, palms up, as if to say, Can you believe this? "Some of these guys get upset if I smoke," he said, adding, "I'm thinking I might appoint a spiritual adviser to the crew."

We drove around in the rain for a while. We passed the marina, where crab boats were getting ready to head out into the icy water for Dungeness crabs off the Washington coast. Planks of yellow cedar were in the back of the van—paddles to be carved. Wayne was talking about finding more funding to take a trip over to Vancouver Island to see some other Nuuchah-nulth tribes, to get more yellow cedar, which historically is difficult to find in Neah Bay. It was pouring now. The windshield wipers seemed exhausted. Donnie pointed out a stream running down a hill: a stream he remembered drinking from when he was a kid and there was a problem with the water supply, like the time there was a dead cow in the reservoir. "The water in that stream is always good," Donnie said as we drove by. "You could drink out of it now."

Wayne said that after the whale hunt he and Donnie might finally be able to get their adult Indian names—an event that necessitates a big party and a gathering of a lot of relatives and, of course, some money to pay for the festivities, which would mark their ceremonial entry as adults into the Makah tribe. They were talking about having one together, to save costs. "We wanted to have them for the whaling, but as it is right now, we don't," Wayne added.

We met Arnie at the tribal center, as he was getting out of his pickup truck. Inside, Wayne went off to talk to Denise Dailey. I could see them down the hall. Denise was dressed in jeans and a flannel shirt. Wayne was now wearing his whaler's cap, the thick wool cap circled with little gray whales that looked like the whale on the petroglyphs at Cape Alava. Wayne seemed to be imploring Denise to do something. She was staring at him, squared off in her stance, her arms folded. When he came back, Wayne and Arnie and Donnie sat in the conference room, trying to figure how to make out a memo to the council to ask for $800 for each person on the crew, on orders from Denise.

"It's got to be official," Wayne said, as he wrote on a page of loose-leaf paper with a red ballpoint pen. He wrote out the hours of crew practice sessions for the past few months. "I've got to justify the hours," Wayne said. He spoke as he wrote; he'd put his whaler's cap on a chair. "One hundred and twenty hours," he said.

"Put *at least* in there," Arnie said.

"Yeah, *at least*," Donnie said.

Wayne read his memo out loud, the first he'd ever written.

Arnie was relaxed. Donnie flipped through a catalog filled with expensive fishing gear, pointing out cool-looking equipment. Wayne looked anxious.

"How does that sound?" Wayne asked.

"Good," Arnie said.

Wayne took the memo across the way to the tribal council chambers and into a meeting with Ben Johnson, George Bowechop, and Denise, who looked upset. She was in charge of keeping the whaling commission's paperwork straight. She looked at Wayne's handiwork and shook her head. "I need more justification here," she said.

I left the room, but later when Wayne came out of the meeting I asked why Denise looked so perturbed. "She's upset because she doesn't think the crew should be paid to train," he said. "But I told them, 'How can I run the crew when some of these guys are getting their lights turned off? They're gonna have to leave and get real jobs if we don't do something for them. I mean, it's just an appreciation of the council.'"

Wayne had gotten each of the crew $500, but George Bowechop said that before the money could be released Wayne had to get signatures from all the commissioners.

Before we left the council chambers, one of the secretaries came in with Wayne's paycheck, which wasn't much. Wayne said, "Thanks, you're back on the team," and everyone laughed.

The secretary laughed too and then she said to no one in particular, "When I saw you with the briefcase, I said, 'Is that Wayne Johnson? That couldn't be Wayne Johnson.' But it was."

We got back in the van and went out to get the signatures. Wayne was anxious to cash his check. He was going to lend Donnie $50. Donnie needed the money to drive to Bremerton, on the other side of the peninsula, near Seattle, to bring his daughter to a dentist. (There is no dentist in Neah Bay.) It's a three and a half hour drive; she had cavities that needed immediate attention—you could see them when she smiled her big smile. As he drove, Wayne shuffled through paperwork. He said, "What's a per diem?"

We stopped at his house for a minute so he could pick up some more paperwork. The house was on a dirt road back by the high school. Wayne's mom was there, playing with one of her grandnieces. She was friendly and exceptionally hospitable, and I asked her about the picture of Wayne on the wall. It was of him and the gray whale he had accidentally caught years before: he wore fishermen's rain gear and a big smile and looked younger; the whale, covered with barnacles, was lying on the beach. "That was his first whale hunt," his mom said. "After that, the law was after him already."

We went outside. Wayne shrugged in the direction of his mom's house. "As soon as I get a couple of paychecks I'm going to be getting my own place," he said. Then he realized he'd lost his hat.

On the dashboard he smoothed out a diagram of a gray whale that had come from a historical document, an ethnographer's report from around 1910. The diagram showed how each portion of the whale was going to be cut up and to which crew member it belonged. He propped it up against a soda can.

"Look at this," he said. "Look at all the stuff we gotta do with the biologists when we get the whale. We gotta assist in measurement of ovaries and earplugs, measure the"—he sorted through a stack of papers—"measure the whatever, but I mean, look at all this! And I've gotta get my butchering team up. I never knew how much work there was to be done but then I was always out in the boat." He continued, "There's all kinds of things we have to do. There's spiritual training and there's butchering. The saddle of the whale, it has to be cut out and it hangs for three days in the house of the captain with the eyeballs."

Wayne and Donnie drove through town getting signatures. Donnie waited for Wayne in the van as Wayne went into the houses. Wayne would walk into a house with his briefcase and talk for a while and then come out and get back in the car, close the door, and say, "*Yes!*" We went to John McCarty's house. When Wayne went in, John wasn't there. But when Wayne came out he wasn't thrilled: he'd heard what John had been saying.

Donnie said, "Until I started on the commission, I didn't care about politics. But in the last two years I've learned a lot."

Toward the end of the afternoon we were at the beach. We got out of the car, stood on the little cliff, and looked into the winter ocean: it seemed to be boiling over with foam beneath the gray winter sky. Wayne knew the cliff as Sadie's Cliff, named in honor of his mom, who had accidentally rolled off the cliff in a car one time. We looked northwest, where you could just see the rocks near Cape Flattery, toward where the land ended and the Pacific began. Wayne recalled being in Alaska and hearing about how the Alaskan whalers watched the clouds to look for openings in the ice. Wayne said that just around the corner there was a little cove called Skagway, where the water was never rough, an out-of-sight place of calm water.

"It's always calm in there," he said. "That's where our fleet used to tie up in the storms before they built the marina."

Donnie threw a rock out onto the beach. The waves grabbed angrily for it.

"We could get a whale in there," Wayne said.

Back in town, at the market, a little boy got out of his mother's car and spotted Wayne, the whaling captain, the new man in charge of the hunt. The little boy pointed at Wayne and shouted a phrase he'd apparently heard often, "Damn it, Wayne!" he said, smiling until his mother dragged him away. "Damn it, Wayne."

43 / Follow the Whale

A trip! A trip! I'd spent the fall in a wooden shack covered with moss and the shack was still there and it was raining all the time in the rain forest now and sometimes at night I would half wake up and think I was out to sea, and so now I wanted to take a trip, an exploration, a journey into far-off lands in search of the gray whale. I already knew enough about the gray whale to know that such a search was not impossible. I myself was unable to see them off the shore of Cape Flattery no matter how often I looked, unless I was taken out and shown one by a whale biologist or by Arnie Hunter. But it is a verifiable fact that gray whales migrate up and down the West Coast of North America, the way the buffalo once roamed the Great

Plains. People see them all the time. Put another way, a search for the gray whale did not mean endless meanderings over the seven oceans of the world, a crazed journey from ocean to ocean that might take months or years; it was not an absurdly hopeless-seeming task. The search for the gray whale was a no-brainer.[5]

I had the idea that the hunt wasn't going to happen for a while—at least until the spring gray whale migration began—and I wasn't going to worry so much about it: I had learned my lesson. I had been thinking a lot about gray whales. I read about them in the shanty, and I kept hearing about them from the protestors, who had all described being moved in their presence, who had said that I ought to learn more about gray whales, that I had to understand them. I called up a marine biologist in Oregon and asked him about a trip to see the gray whales in the lagoons where they mate and give birth, and he described an incredible-sounding tour that he himself offered to the gray whale–interested public—boats went out for about a week or so with the whales—but that cost several thousand dollars. I was looking for a less expensive version. As a second option, he told me to drive down the Baja Peninsula in Mexico to a town called Guerrero Negro, stop in at the last bar on the right, and ask to see the gray whales. The name of the bar, he said, was Malarrimo.

Those directions sounded good to me, so I set out driving the gray whale migration route from the tip of the Olympic Peninsula almost to the tip of Baja, Mexico. It was to be a long and only slightly circuitous trip, in which I planned to take in the sights, get in some whale watching, possibly meet some of the protestors in their natural habitat. I would generally explore the land-based version of the gray whale's long migration route. I started out in my own car, but a few hours into the expedition it broke down, in Hoquiam, Washington. While my car was at a service station I found an old copy of *Moby-Dick*, one that had a different ending

---

[5] One whaling ship Melville served on had such difficulty finding whales that they ended up hunting turtles instead. From reading about Melville, I also had the feeling that he could change plans on the spur of the moment, in his adventures and in his writing. For example, *Moby-Dick* appears to have started out like a very matter-of-fact book about a whaling adventure, possibly featuring just Ishmael and Queequeg, but then it changed. He wrote his publisher in the summer of 1850 to say that the manuscript would arrive that fall. A year went by without any sign of it. Melville took a completely other tack. Finally, it was handed in, in the fall of 1851. In a book called *Melville's Reviewers*, Hugh W. Hetherington writes: "The long interval, it is now known, was the result of an extensive revision Melville began in August 1850, better called a total transformation."

from the ending Melville wrote. After getting towed back home, I rented a car, and set out again.

My first stop after Neah Bay was a town called Moclips on the Washington coast. Wayne had told me that a gray whale had washed up dead on the shore there. Wayne had been to see it the day before, along with Al Ingling, the veterinarian who was doing ballistics test for the tribe, and some biologists from the National Marine Fisheries Service. They had hoped to shoot the whale to determine if the whale hunting gun was humane, but when they got there the whale had already begun to decay. (It had been a cold and wet and miserable day; the sky couldn't decide between hail and snow. "I didn't even bother to get out of the car," Wayne said.) I pulled into Moclips and walked onto the beach through a cut in the sandstone cliffs. I saw a tiny group of people standing around what I assumed to be the whale. It was silhouetted and now almost silver: against the gray clouds and the wet creamy sand, it reminded me of a ballet slipper. I walked to it and paced out its long body but stepped back after I walked downwind from it—I was shocked by its putrid stink. When the kids in the group suddenly smelled it too, they all screamed and ran away.

I drove south toward the Oregon coast, where the cliffs grew higher and more dramatic and I looked over the edge at the cauldrons of surf. Already, on too many occasions, I was stopping to look out at the sea, mistaking rocks and sea stacks for the tail end of the whale migration. Then, about halfway down the coast of Oregon, just outside of the town of Waldport, I saw the black plumes of smoke that I had heard about on the radio but was not prepared for just the same.

A wood chip barge had gone aground near Coos Bay and leaked seventy-two gallons of oil. To mitigate the disaster, the oil on the ship was being burned off with napalm, dropped from warplanes. I reevaluated my itinerary; I was running late on account of my car breaking down in Washington. I cut inland and got on the interstate going south and, a short while later, I was soon driving just north of San Francisco. A few weeks later, I went back to the scene of the barge grounding, when the wreck was being towed piecemeal out to the ocean. Since I had been through, hundreds of rare and threatened and not-so-rare birds had been found dead, covered with small fractions of the oil that had leaked from the tanker. More birds would have been killed if most of the Oregon coast's birds hadn't been away at the time, on their own migrations south. The barge was still there, waiting to be towed away to sea to be torpedoed: it was a giant, neighborhood-sized mistake, sitting like a fallen-down drunk on lovely shorefront property.

On this morning at the beginning of my trip south, however, on my own winter migration to Mexico, all my thoughts were on how different the ocean looked off the coast just north of San Francisco Bay. It was calmer, greener, almost tropical. It wasn't raining and it wasn't winter anymore.

44 / Save the Whales

As I enter the San Francisco Bay area, let me take a break from my logbook entries of this gray whale migration excursion-in-progress to briefly consider the history of the public interest in saving whales, and let me begin by noting that before people sought to save whales, they enjoyed just looking at them. Of course, beached whales have most likely been ogled since the indeterminable time when the first whale beached near a human settlement, but one of the first intentionally exhibited whales was a skeleton that traveled all around Europe from 1827 to 1834. It was the skeleton of a ninety-five-foot-long blue whale that had washed ashore in Ostend, Holland, and it was called the Ostend Whale. In the 1860s, in New York City, P. T. Barnum exhibited beluga whales in a tank in the basement of his museum. "It was a very great sensation and it added thousands of dollars to my treasury," Barnum wrote. An embalmed finback whale toured Europe and the United States in 1954. Leif Søgaard had harpooned the seventy-ton whale off the coast of a Norwegian island called Haroy, which gave the whale its name. To preserve it, the whale was injected with eight thousand quarts of formaldehyde. It was exhibited on a boxcar, and ended up at Coney Island, where it soon began to smell. A WHALE IN BAD ODOR, the headlines in *The Times* read at the time. CONEY MERCHANTS COMPLAIN OF VISITOR FROM EUROPE. "Neighboring hot dog and soft drink concerns had complained, not that it was drawing business away from them, but that its odor was driving customers out of the area," the story read. The account went on to report that the whale's owner promised to telephone "experts" in Oslo to, in the reporter's words, "see what could be done to make the whale more socially acceptable." Within a few days, the whale's owner was issued a summons. Shortly thereafter, the whale mysteriously caught on fire. *The Times* report stated: "Mrs. Haroy, the seventy-five-foot whale that had been offending the nostrils of Coney Islanders lately, came to a fiery end yesterday."

Live whales have likewise been displayed in public for centuries, but the modern live whale exhibit dates to approximately the same period as the invention of the modern tourist aquarium, which, it can be argued, began with the opening of Marine Studios in St. Augustine, Florida, in 1938. Marine Studios featured a quasi-scientific exhibition of dolphins. It was so successful that Marineland opened in Palos Verdes, California, in 1954, and soon larger ocean-theme parks called Sea Worlds began to open in California and Florida and Ohio and then other states around the United States. These parks also featured dolphins, which were invariably described by the scientists who worked at the parks as being human-like. The oceanariums eventually displayed beluga whales, which were likewise deemed intelligent and friendly, and, a short while later, killer whales, which, Richard Ellis notes in *Men and Whales*, "are the most powerful predators on earth." The first killer whale was exhibited in Seattle in 1964. It was named Namu for the town near Bella Bella, British Columbia, where it was captured. Other oceanariums showed killer whales and named them Namu too. The idea was that the public would not realize that individual whales died from time to time. Cetaceans were subsequently popularized in movies and books and on TV. In 1963, the movie *Flipper* featured a little boy and a dolphin who helped save people in the face of bad guys and bad animals. (*Flipper* went on to become a TV series.) In 1973, the movie *The Day of the Dolphin* starred dolphins that could talk and that, in the face of nuclear Armageddon, helped save the entire world.

As people were getting to know cetaceans on vacation and at the movies, magazines and newspapers simultaneously began reporting on the demise of the species. For example, in 1967, *Scientific American* published an article entitled "The Last of the Great Whales." In 1968, *The Undersea World of Jacques Cousteau*, a television show, reported that whales were being slaughtered throughout the world. Cousteau showed photographs of whales underwater, some of the world's first. (Cousteau had to tie up a sperm whale to film it.) The recognition of the damage that commercial whale hunting was inflicting coincided with the discovery that the whales made a kind of music. In 1952, Frank Wattlington was monitoring underwater listening devices called hydrophones in Bermuda. Originally, hydrophones had been placed around the Atlantic during World War II to find airplanes that crashed into the sea. When an airplane hit the water, a pressure-sensitive dynamite charge exploded in the fuselage—thus, the plane's position could be triangulated and the pilot rescued. After the war, scientists such as Wattlington continued to study underwater acoustics. One night, Wattlington was startled by strange, moaning sounds coming through his hydrophone. He happened to ask an old whaler who lived in Bermuda about the sounds. The whaler said the moaning sounded like the sounds of whales that whalers heard coming through boats on the ocean. Wattlington and other scientists eventually determined the sounds to be the sounds of humpback whales.

Whale songs were a big hit with the public. In 1967, Roger Payne and his wife, Katy Payne, two whale researchers, determined the humpback's sounds to be types of songs in that they included phrases that were repeated over and over. Roger Payne even released a record entitled "Songs of the Humpback." In his book *Among Whales*, Payne argued that human music and whale music were "strikingly similar in many basic ways." "The length of a whale song falls between the length of a modern ballad and a movement of a symphony." Subsequently, Judy Collins released "Farewell to Tarwathie," a New Zealand whaling song that featured humpback whales on backup. Paul Winter, a saxophonist, recorded with whales.

A person who was instrumental in the Save the Whales movement was Joan McIntyre, a writer who Richard Ellis, in *Men and Whales*, refers to as "the 'high priestess' of the love the whale movement." Her book *Mind in the Waters: A Book to Celebrate the Consciousness of Whales and Dolphins* is a collection of scientific and not-so-scientific writings about cetaceans. To me, *Mind in the Waters* is most remarkable for its descriptions of relationships between humans and cetaceans. An example of this is an essay by Malcolm Brenner, author of "In Contact: An Interspecies Romance." In the essay, Brenner describes attempting to teach a word to Ruby, a female dolphin he had developed a personal relationship with, and subsequently realizing that Ruby had taught a word to him: *keee-orr-oop*. McIntyre's book ends with a plea for the reader to join the fight to stop whaling in the world, to, in the words of the movement that was about to be born, "save the whales." "Every twelve minutes a whale is killed—the living tissues blown into agony by explosive harpoons," McIntyre wrote. As the "founding mother" of Project Jonah, an organization based in Bolinas, just north of San Francisco, McIntyre helped enact the international whale hunting moratorium. She quit before the moratorium was enacted, however. She had given herself five years to end commercial whaling, and when her five years were up, in 1975, she moved to Hawaii. "My profession, so to speak, had been the politics of whale saving," she wrote at the time, "and that profession had wearied me and turned me into a bitter person filled with doubt and anger."

45 / On Late-Twentieth-Century Pictures of Whales

Yes, the Old Masters painted the biblical whale, the wide-jawed creature that swallowed up Jonah, the great vengeful-seeming fish that staved ships and inspired fear in the hearts of land-bound men, the Leviathan. But, as I resume the description of my long, gray whale–inspired journey, it seems to me important to point out that the whale art one sees everywhere on the West Coast of the United States is a different kind of whale art altogether, that modern-day whale art, it might be argued, seems an outgrowth of the more compassionate view of cetaceans that came about in America and elsewhere as a result of the battle to save the whales. In lieu of the terrible whale, the angry, sea foam–mouthed whale that hangs on the walls of old European museums, we have the calm-inspiring gray whale murals that are on the walls of car dealerships and the sides of parking structures in West Coast towns and cities. We have peace-inducing blue whale paintings that adorn the T-shirts and coffee mugs of the populace. We have artists renderings of killer whales that crash up from the amniotic water that decorate the posters sold in nature-oriented retail stores. We have humpbacks that are shadowed by dolphins which, in turn, rise from the water to peer out on a land of waterfalls and blue skies and streams that are clean and pure and perfect, like airbrushed Platonic forms.

In Neah Bay, during the wait for the hunt, I had learned that the whale artist who had painted the small Sea Shepherd submarine to resemble an orca was named George Sumner. I also learned that he refers to himself as an "environmental artist." When I was in his vicinity, in the hills just

north of San Francisco and still days away from the gray whale lagoons in
Mexico, I stopped at a pay phone and called him. Sumner's wife, Donna
Lei, answered the phone. "Come on over!" she said.

I drove to a modest home in a modest suburb in Marin County and
Donna Lei answered the door. She was wearing a headset telephone—she
runs the business side of her husband's whale art enterprise. She called for
George, a fifty-seven-year-old man of medium height and medium build,
who came to the door wearing jeans and a button-down shirt, a neatly
trimmed beard, a fisherman's cap, and a big relaxed smile. He walked me
through a living room filled with giant ethereal aquatic paintings, past a
sketch of San Francisco drawn by Tony Bennett and dedicated to Sumner,
and finally into the family room, which was filled with giant paintings of
his own. Then, George opened up a bottle of red wine, and he told me the
story of his career as a whale artist.

He was born in the Tenderloin, a tough, working-class district of San
Francisco. He parked cars at the Blackhawk, a jazz club where he used to
hear Billy Epstein. He grew up wanting to be a cartoonist and did science
fiction illustrations: lots of spaceships and robots. "I'm a hippie street
artist from the sixties," George said, proudly raising his glass. As a street
artist, he supported himself by gardening. He designed the floral arrange-
ments at Golden Gate Park for many years, and it was while he was working at Golden Gate Park that he did his first whale. Greenpeace was then a
young environmental group and it was throwing a benefit concert at the
park featuring Crosby, Stills & Nash. George painted a whale mural for the
stage. "The painting was nine feet across," he remembered. "It was a
mother and a baby gray whale and I hate to say it but, in all honesty, it probably looked more like a frog. But then with the strobe lights and all the people smoking pot it probably looked okay. And that was the first painting in
what turned out to be a long career." He was smiling but his face quickly
turned serious. "And I have said," he went on, "and I will say it again now,
that I will not stop painting whales until they stop the senseless slaughter."
He smiled again. "Actually, with painting, I never even thought of turning
it into a profit situation. It was primarily my podium to speak out about an
incredible disgusting slaughter that the world should hang their head
lower on."

When painting became a profit situation, he was painting mostly
abstract landscapes, not whales. "We traveled from Canada to Mexico," he
said, recalling traveling with his fellow artists. "We'd paint in shopping cen-

ters. At that time, the indoor malls, they'd just started, and you could paint for five days. We all had school buses and vans and we used to have long hair and beards but that was part of the show. We stayed at the finest hotels. What a wonderful lifestyle—where you had people feeling sorry for you and you were making lots of money." He poured more wine and then he added, "Just so you know, when I start painting I'll do twenty hours straight. I paint wet on wet. It can't dry." In the seventies, the United States was still whaling, and many San Franciscans were against it; Sumner remembers what he called "the Mendocino Whale Wars." It was then that he switched to full-time marine-mammal painting, which was a risk. "I started painting marine life and the galleries thought I was out of my mind," he said.

His early methods weren't at all scientific—as much by choice as necessity. "At that time there wasn't a decent photograph of a whale in the world," he explained. "If you look at the photographs then, the whale looked just like a greenish glob in the water. So up until 1983, everything I painted was out of my imagination, just out of my belief system. I mean, now we know a lot of it is true, but then I asked myself, Why wouldn't whales hold themselves together like lovers with their fins wrapped around each other?" In time, Sumner was seeing whales firsthand, diving and on boats. "I can show you pictures here where I've my hand on the calf *and* the mother at the same time in a Zodiac, and it's just a real emotional experience when you feel what kind of a being these are." His own inspections eventually led him to find links between whales in the water and outer space. "If you are lucky enough to find yourself eyeball to eyeball with any of these creatures, you'll see a whale has total neutral buoyancy. It will not move a quarter of an inch. That's like total deep space." This observation, in part, eventually led him to paint whales for NASA. "I was the first guy to put a humpback in space," he told me, proudly.

We walked around the room and talked about his individual paintings, which were in varying shades of blue and featured whales and all kinds of cetaceans cruising through ethereal blueness. Some of them sell for as much as $150,000. Over the years his clients have included Jimmy Buffet, Neil Diamond, Andreas Vollenweider, Muhammad Ali, Clint Eastwood, Patty Hearst, and Jean-Michel Cousteau. He showed me lots of his paintings. Most of them were of whales, but there were several paintings that had world peace as their theme. He played a videotape for me of his handing one of the latter-themed paintings to Mikhail Gorbachev, the leader of the Soviet

Union at the time. During the video George and Gorbachev hugged. Viewing the tape of his meeting with Gorbachev made George become suddenly emotional. He turned to me. "I've never told anybody this," he said, "but I was in the Navy. I felt like all young people—you know, guys. I liked to feel macho. Anyway, I was in the Navy and I used to fuel U-2 spy planes, you know, with fuel. And I don't know, since then, I've always felt the need to make my peace because I was part of the ultimate war machine. I mean, I didn't beat my chest about it but when I hugged Gorbachev, I thought, You know, maybe this is what life is all about."

I was enjoying listening to George talk about his work and he seemed to be having a good time telling me about it. He was getting more and more expansive and enjoying the wine, which was good. In hopes of learning something about the history of contemporary West Coast whale art, I asked him about other whale artists and he named a few who were friends. But then when I asked him about a muralist whose work I had noticed up and down the coast, George was quiet for a minute and changed the subject.

At that point, Donna Lei, who had been walking in and out of our conversation, took me upstairs and showed me the small bedroom that she uses to run the Sumner family operations. "I'm trying to do the balance," she said. "It's a balance of making enough to survive, which is a tough thing for an artist to do." She spoke hopefully about a deal with Sharper Image, a catalog company and upscale gadget retail store chain, and she talked about her school education program, for which George painted a blue whale on a bus. But then she began talking about other whale artists, and it suddenly became clear to me that there had been some bad blood between George and another whale artist whom George had once welcomed into his studio. George had even shared his techniques with this artist, such as using cloth diapers instead of brushes. The artist had then gone off and upset George, apparently by using George's techniques without fully crediting him. Donna Lei made it clear to me that George was too hurt to discuss it. She took her headset phone off as she emphasized this. She had to go out and pick up their daughter from softball practice. (Their son studied marine biology at UCLA.) Before Donna Lei left the room, she made certain I understood one thing. "There's a lot of these guys who are painting the walls, doing whale murals and other stuff," she said. "But do you know why they are doing it? It's commercial. And do you know why George does it? Because he vowed to do it until the whales stopped being killed. I can't say that George created a movement but I really hope that these other guys doing it . . ." She made a sigh of exasperation. "Well, it's known."

George called for me from down in the living room and we drove up into the hills behind his home, to his studio. I followed his minivan. At the first stoplight, George suddenly got out of his van and ran back to my car to tell me to tune my radio to the local soft jazz station. We drove past old farms and ranches and through woods and along a stream and up a semi-treacherous muddy road. We arrived at his studio on the top of the hill, and I looked out at the panoramic view of the Pacific. Inside the studio were huge canvases with whales on them and whale books and whale posters. The studio was made with wood from old buildings in San Francisco. He showed me the nautical-themed bathroom, the hot tub, the surrounding woods and sculptures, and the big deck that the helicopter of one of his patrons once landed on. It was a nice place.

I hung out at his studio until it started getting dark and I had to get back on the road to Baja. He gave me directions to San Francisco and a drawing of a humpback whale that was blowing bubbles in the shape of hearts. He took me outside and said good-bye and he hugged me. When I got in the car I read the inscription on the drawing. It said, "Remember to believe in the magic (!!) of the impossible. George and Donna Lei (signed).

46 / Good Versus Evil

I spent the next day in San Francisco, in the Haight-Ashbury neighborhood, where I ate a big breakfast, and went to the City Lights bookstore to read some Beat poetry, and then got back on the road down the coast of California. I drove down Route 1 as it meanders along the side of hills turning more and more brown, which I took as a hint of the desert to come. I passed through Golden Gate Park and then looked out on the Pacific at a little beach marked on my map as Gray Whale Cove. I drove through Half Moon Bay, where surfers in wet suits dotted the ocean swells like seals. In Davenport, at the Whale City Bakery, Bar & Grill, I picked up a cup of coffee and a gray whale migration bumper sticker and climbed on top of my car to look for whales but I saw only a small group of German tourists. The woman who sold me the coffee said, "*I* haven't seen any whales but my coworkers have." Every turn was so scenic that I took too many photographs; I was like a migrating whale stopping in every cove.

When I got to Monterey, I decided to look up Steph Dutton and Heidi Tiura of In the Path of Giants. I was a little nervous about seeing Heidi, given that she'd been so mad at me the last time I saw her in Neah Bay. Nevertheless, she welcomed me and gave me a glass of water and we sat down in the back of her house overlooking the hills behind Monterey Bay.

Steph wasn't there; Heidi explained to me that he had been studying for a boat captain's license. I asked her if they were planning on returning to Neah Bay in the spring to continue their attempt to stop the Makah whale hunt. She said she was; they had retooled their injured boat, *Sea Dog*. "To fight the Makah we needed to have a boat that was the biggest, the baddest, the best boat out there. Our boat can go anywhere," she said.

"It's a huge commitment," she went on to say. "You know, I don't want to sound like a whiner or anything but we really got blindsided on this." She said that the fight against the whale hunt had taken up a good deal of the resources that were intended for their gray whale migration study, adding that since the previous fall, groups all around the country had been asking her and Steph to come and give their presentation, to speak about gray whales and the hunt. She summed up the argument between the protestors and the Makah this way: "They are definitely in a fight of good versus evil."

As I was getting up to leave, Heidi recommended I go out and look for whales and maybe go whale watching, which was what she still hoped the Makah might want to do instead of hunting whales, so I drove into Monterey and looked around town for a whale watching tour.

In downtown Monterey, I saw the old Monterey whaling station, the place from which Portuguese fishermen would go out in small boats and fire guns at whales and drag them into Monterey Bay. The whaling station is a museum now; I read that the beach in Monterey in 1861 was white with the sun-bleached bones of dead whales. I visited an old theater that was constructed in part with whalebones, where there was a small memorial to the actor Henry Brandon, who was born Henry Kleinbach in Berlin in 1921, and who, the literature said, "portrayed Indian Chiefs 26 times." I read about the Italian fishermen who had fished for the canneries on Cannery Row and I watched a group of men playing boccie and speaking Italian for a while. Finally, I walked over to the pier and strolled through the smells of fried foods and cotton candy and saw a guy hawking whale watching trips. I bought a ticket.

A man standing next to me on the pier bought one too, and he asked, "Do you guarantee we'll see a whale?"

"Guaranteed to see a whale," the ticket seller said, looking out for more whale watchers.

On the boat were kids and their parents and a group of teenagers and a couple from Spain. Just as we pulled out, a woman said to her husband, "If I had known you get seasick, we wouldn't have gone."

"We never know what to expect on each trip," the captain said over the public-address system. He added, "We have many different varieties"—he sighed—"I mean, fifty-six varieties of seabirds."

Of course, I was hoping to see a gray whale. But I was in the minority. The captain announced that we would probably see gray whales but that there was a chance we would see killer whales, and at this news the little crowd let out a cheer.

The winds were strong and the water was slightly rough and before long a father saw his child fall down on the deck. When he was pulled up, the child's lip was bleeding.

"What happened?" the mother asked.

"He's all right," the father said. The boy was screaming.

"He looks like he's bleeding," the mother said.

"He just hit his mouth, that's all," the father said.

Off the back of the boat, a man threw potato chips at the seagulls following us. The woman with him said, "That looks like the movie *The Birds*." She took a flash picture.

The kid with the bleeding mouth began to throw up.

I walked up to the front of the boat and spoke to the Spanish couple. The man said he was from La Mancha. He began to describe La Mancha to me but then the boat suddenly changed course because it had spotted a pod of killer whales, which in a minute were racing beside the boat. We *ooh*ed and *aah*ed at the killer whales. They crested the water alongside of us. They were huge, and their black-and-white crispness reminded me of a cedar carving. They followed us for nearly fifteen minutes, or else we followed them. I snapped a picture. As the boat turned back, the captain was apologizing for the lack of gray whale sightings and mentioned offhand-edly that a young gray whale had been killed the week before by a pod of killer whales.

On the way back to Monterey Bay, I went to the cabin and spoke with the captain. He said that he had been a fisherman all his life until the fish began disappearing and he began whale watching. He enjoyed it because it allowed him to develop his skills as an orator/naturalist. "At first, you know, I didn't know much," he said. "I'd talk about the whales and then, you know, maybe bullshit a little, but then I started to read and I really learned a lot."

His first mate, a young guy in his early twenties, piped up. "You should hear him talk about the grays," he said. With his hand moving like the mouth of a puppet, he mimicked someone talking at length. "He knows every little thing about the grays," the mate said.

"Well . . ." the skipper said, slightly embarrassed.

"And it's funny," the first mate continued. "I've only been going out for a year and I already know a lot about them."

"Well," the captain said. "I've read a lot but there's a lot I would learn. I'm no marine biologist. There's a lot I would learn."

As we pulled into the pier we passed a seal that would have been a threat to the fisherman five years ago, when seals and fishermen competed for salmon, but was now a harmless talking point on the ex-fisherman's eco-tour. I mentioned that I was on my way to Baja to see the gray whales as part of a study of the Makah whale hunt. The captain said that he had heard of the Makah's plan to hunt a whale from Heidi and Steph. The captain was against the hunt, though he was loath to explain his reasons. I pressed him. "Well, if they hunt the whales then there won't be any left for their kids to hunt," he said. "That's my feeling, anyway."

47 / Los Angeles

At last, I saw gray whales. I saw them from Highway 1 as I drove south through Big Sur. I saw them as the road wound along the side of the long hill covered with cypress that strained back from the ocean wind, a rough green hem on the cape of jade-blue water: the infinite, great-drive view of a car commercial. When I stopped on one of the high overlooks on the edge of a tall cliff and looked down into a cove necklaced by rocks that turned out to also be seals, I saw a little group of gray whales. They were less gray than silvery, a small herd of ghostly apparitions that slowly torpedoed down and then back up in the iridescent water. Occasionally they spouted Big Sur coastal water, which, at cliff height, was visible only with binoculars.

I was ecstatic. Four days' drive from Neah Bay—my first whales! Sighting them confirmed everything: I was on the right trail; I wasn't too late. They were still headed due south toward Mexico, even if they were, like me, running behind schedule. I got back in my car and got out again and looked at the whales some more, and, by the time I was back on the road, I was finally imagining myself in Mexico. I drove past the Hearst mansion at San Simeon, as the mountains turned into mesas; into San Luis Obispo, where I noticed the women walking around in bikinis and then wondered if it was raining in Neah Bay. I wondered what might be spiritual about a hunt as I stopped in an old mission, a little stone church. I could see the Channel Islands, off past the oil refineries, and I knew whales were out there but I had stopped looking for them. I wanted to get to L.A., to the apartment of my cousin John, to eat and sleep and see if he would drive with me on the rest of the trip to Baja.

John is an actor, and he agreed to go to Mexico, but not before he finished up a job: a scene on a television drama where he was to be killed—pushed off the side of an aircraft carrier that he was stealing money from, to be precise. (John is tall and has a big, crooked smile and often plays tough guys and bad guys and really bad guys or just guys with an attitude when he is in movies or on TV—although, in my own personal experience, he is one of the nicest guys you would ever want to meet.) John diligently consulted his director and we concocted our plans, which involved my hanging out in L.A., waiting for John to be killed.

The next day, while I waited, I watched the TV traffic reports, which showed a color-keyed map that pulsed with simulated traffic-flow intensities. I read headlines in the Los Angeles Times. One said: CANCER RISK FROM AIR POLLUTION STILL HIGH. Another: INVASION OF FIRE ANTS POSE NEW THREAT TO AREA WILDLIFE. Yet another: SOUTHERN CALIFORNIA ALREADY IS LABELED A "HOT SPOT" OF EXTINCTION WORLDWIDE. I went to a coffee shop and heard someone say, "Really? You like to write the treatment *before* you write the screenplay?"[5] And then I went back to John's apartment and read about Mexico and gray whales and then wandered off into John's Irish history books. I read a passage from a speech given by Terence MacSwiney, the lord mayor of Cork in March 1920: "This contest of ours is not on our side a rivalry of vengeance but one of endurance—it is not they who can inflict most but they who can suffer most who will conquer." This caused me to think about American Indians and then the Makah and then Neah Bay, so that I borrowed John's phone to call up Wayne, who, his mother said, wasn't around. His mother said that he and the crew were out. "Target practice," she said. They were testing a new whaling gun, given that the .50-caliber was having some trouble shooting through water. She asked me where I was and I told her I was in California and she said that once she had been out fishing along the coast of Neah Bay and that after a while the boat drifted and they wound up off the coast of California. "It was something," she said.

Around then, John came back and we went out to pick up a script at his agent's office and then to eat at this great Lebanese restaurant where the owners knew John and smiled at him when he came in, patted him on the back.

48 / A Vision

It was my second day in L.A., and my cousin still had not been killed—there were apparently some difficulties with his scene—so I drove over to Venice, to the headquarters of Sea Shepherd, where I arranged to meet

[5] John Huston also directed a movie version of *Moby-Dick*. Huston wrote the screenplay too, with Ray Bradbury. Gregory Peck played Ahab; Orson Welles played Father Mapple, and Richard Basehart played Ishmael. I didn't see the movie—I was too involved with the book. But, according to Richard Ellis in *Men and Whales*, Huston's *Moby-Dick* followed Melville's story closely. The film company couldn't get ahold of a whaling ship for filming purposes; they had to make do with a schooner that was not seaworthy. They used models of great white whales, one of which disappeared in a storm in the Irish Sea. Afterward, Huston wrote: "*Moby-Dick* was the most difficult picture I ever made. I lost so many battles during it that I even began to suspect that my assistant director was plotting against me. Then I realized it was only God."

Captain Paul Watson on land. In the traffic on La Brea I felt less like a migrating whale than one little nervous fish in a huge school of fish being chased by sharks. Sea Shepherd headquarters were in a small office complex located next to the Chabad of the Marina and across the street from a Thai restaurant. Inside, a small staff of young people was busy on several ocean conservation campaigns that had to do, variously, with an oil spill off the coast of Germany, the gray seal conservation off the coast of Denmark, and an investigation into the overharvesting of ocean krill. Captain Watson took me on a tour through the offices, where people were making calls on behalf of sea life around the world. He showed me posters and literature from past battles to save seals in Canada and photos of Sea Shepherd personnel with celebrities such as Pierce Brosnan and William Shatner, and then he took me to his office, where we sat down with coffee. He was wearing a black Sea Shepherd T-shirt, black sneakers, and jeans. Books decorated the walls—titles such as *The Seven Military Classics of Ancient China, A General History of the Pyrates, The History of Christianity,* and *Narrative of the Most Extraordinary and Distressing Shipwreck of the Whale-Ship* Essex, *of Nantucket.* He had a bag of seal hair—Watson had shown that seal hair could be marketed, that the seal was more valuable alive than dead. He had a large collection of different editions of *Moby-Dick.*

Despite his often harsh rhetoric, he was quiet and personable in the quiet of Sea Shepherd headquarters. I felt comfortable in his office, and, at my urging, he recalled his childhood with his Danish-German mother, who died when he was twelve, and with his French-Canadian father, whom he had trouble getting along with when he was young but who then later served as a cook on some early antiwhaling ship tours. I later learned that Paul Watson was named after his grandfather's brother, Paul Watson, who was killed in World War II while serving as a torpedo boat commander in the Canadian Navy. Watson grew up close to his mother's father, a native of Denmark who was, according to Watson, exiled from Denmark for "political reasons." An art professor at the University of Toronto, the elder Watson enjoyed painting animals at the zoo. Prior to that, the elder Watson had been a prizefighter, a lumberjack in Oregon, and a Rough Rider with Teddy Roosevelt during the Spanish-American War. Watson idolized his grandfather.

When he was five, Watson moved to New Brunswick and lived in a fishing village on the sea. One of his earliest memories is of a summer spent with a beaver that lived near a pond where Watson played. "That really was my best friend when I was nine years old," he told me. The next year when Watson returned to the pond he found out that the beaver had been trapped and killed. Watson began destroying beaver traps.

He ran away from home as a teenager and rode freight trains to British Columbia, where he eventually found work on a boat delivering paper, potash, and sulfur to places like Iran and Malaysia. As a mariner, he once nearly died when he went into a bar in Mozambique and woke up in the jungle the next day without any cash and with two Zulus suggesting he owed them money. In 1969, he became involved in a Canadian organization called Don't Make a Wave, which protested a planned American nuclear detonation at Amchitka in the Aleutian Islands chain: the group feared the explosion might cause a tidal wave along the Northwest coast. From that group came Greenpeace. Watson was one of the founders— though he eventually left. "Greenpeace always says that I was asked to leave because I was so violent," he said, "but that is total revisionist history."

I asked him about the tomahawk on his bookshelf, and he explained that it came from the Battle of Little Bighorn. It was a memento he had picked up, when he was at Wounded Knee on the Oglala Sioux reservation in 1973, at the time when two hundred members of the American Indian Movement seized a trading post and a church. He had been working as a landscaper in Stanley Park in Vancouver when he heard the news that AIM members had taken over the buildings to protest the degradation of Native American rights on the reservation and elsewhere. He and David Garrick, a cofounder of Greenpeace, decided to drive down to South Dakota to offer their help. Watson had never been to South Dakota and he knew little about Native Americans at the time. "I knew that the Oglala Sioux had saved the buffalo," Watson wrote in his memoir, *Sea Shepherd*. "[F]or David Garrick and me, that was enough."

At Wounded Knee, Watson was immediately arrested but eventually got past the FBI agents surrounding the reservation by pretending he was a reporter with *The Vancouver Sun*. Once inside, he was appointed a medic by the AIM members. The only equipment he was supplied with was sanitary napkins. He stayed for seventy-one days of the siege, during which the store and church were surrounded by federal troops, U.S. marshals, and FBI agents. When it was over, Garrick and Watson were given Indian names: Two Deer Lone Eagle and Grey Wolf Clear Water, respectively. "Indians are a spiritual people in general," Watson wrote later, "and it is difficult to be around them without feeling something of that creeping under your skin and into your bones. But the practical side of me resisted total surrender, even as I experienced events that I could not explain except in mystical terms. Further, shared danger always draws people closer, and the risks we had taken at Wounded Knee knitted me into the Oglala Sioux as fully as the solemn ceremony conducted by Wallace Black Elk, acting for himself[,] and Leonard Crow Dog as tribal leaders as well as on behalf of all Oglala Sioux.

"Even without my membership in the tribe now," Watson went on confidently, "even without my tribal name, I felt like an Oglala Sioux, and I always would, from that time forward."[5]

It was while in a sweat lodge at Wounded Knee that Watson realized his life's work was in working to conserve the environment. "I saw a huge buffalo, the great animal that is to the Great Plains of North America what the elephant is to Africa and the whale is to the world's oceans," he wrote. "The buffalo seemed to talk to me as I lay sweating and gasping for air inside the incredibly hot lodge. It seemed to say that I should look to the whales, that I should not dissipate my energies on the full range of animal life, but that I should concentrate on the mammals of the sea, especially whales." In looking back on the events at Wounded Knee, Watson also recognized a new greatness for contemporary Indians. "The American Indians learned that they still produce great leaders," he wrote then.

After Watson told me about his own personal experience at Wounded Knee, we talked about the Makah whale hunt.

Watson said that he was planning on returning to Neah Bay in the spring, if the Makah tried again to hunt a whale. "We are very happy about

---

[5] Though he was never adopted by a tribe, and although he never publicly claimed to be an Indian, Melville probably had some contact of his own with Native Americans on the trip he took west after he returned from his youthful whaling adventures. He visited his uncle on the frontier in Galena, Illinois. While there, he traveled to the headwaters of the Mississippi. He came home via Mississippi riverboat. His experiences on that trip were the basis of the last novel published in his lifetime, *The Confidence-Man,* a long and difficult-to-encapsulate novel full of ambiguities and elaborate conceits at the center of which a confidence man plays a practical joke while aboard a riverboat called *Fidèle. The Confidence-Man* includes a chapter entitled "The Metaphysics of Indian-Hating." Some of Melville's contemporary relatives definitely came in contact with Native Americans. In fact, while Melville was writing *The Confidence-Man,* his cousin, Guert Gansevoort, an often-drunk naval officer, was commanding the U.S. *Decatur* in Puget Sound. Gansevoort's mission was to defend Seattle from Coast Salish tribes who had lived there. He eventually won a commendation for helping to rid the Northwest of its original natives. Melville seemed to think that Indian policy being conducted in his own time was a kind of con in itself, a giant confidence game in which the U.S. government was the genocidal perpetrator, U.S. citizens the dupes.

what was accomplished there," he said. "No whale was hunted." Sea Shepherd, he felt, had exposed the connection between the Makah and world whaling interests, even if the press didn't necessarily believe Watson. He argued that his group was not against the rights of Native Americans but just out to protect the international whale hunting moratorium. "This is not an animal rights organization. This is a conservation group and this hunt jeopardizes the moratorium," he said. "This has nothing to do with Makah culture." He admitted a public relations disadvantage. "From the media point of view, this isn't very good. You've got a big black boat and they're going to come out in a canoe." He talked about a "reverse racism," which he explained on the Sea Shepherd Web site: "A sympathetic national media . . . has been saturated with the reverse racism inherent in the 'noble native' take on the hunt. They have effectively created an atmosphere in which concern for the welfare of whales is now perceived as a de facto attack on native rights and the cultural heritage of an oppressed minority."

He said that he doesn't believe the Makah treaty is valid in that, as he reads it, it gives the Makah the right to hunt whales in common with U.S. citizens, and U.S. citizens no longer whale. He talked about Indians having "rights above the rights of other Americans." He said that he couldn't understand why the federal government was so insistent on backing up the Makah and that he suspects the United States doesn't want to get sued by the tribe. "I told the [tribal council], 'You want to make some money on this, you sue their ass,'" he said. He said that he still believed the Japanese and Norwegians were ultimately involved and that the Makah planned to send whale meat up the British Columbia coast and perhaps to Japan by holding potlaches during which whale meat would be distributed.

He predicted that the hunt was not going to be spiritual in any way; he said it was all about money. "Native Americans are as inclined to greed as anyone else," he said. "It all comes down to individuals. At Wounded Knee, they told me that to be a Native American is in your heart."

We were interrupted and he asked a Sea Shepherd member to hold his telephone calls. "We know everything that's going on up at that reservation because we've got elders just telling us everything," he said.

He continued with his assessment of the progress of the hunt. He reiterated that, in his opinion, the hunt was in no way sacred. "What you have here is a bunch of boys from the hood. Wayne Johnson. He's just a thug." Watson was shaking his head as he repeated himself. "This whole thing with Wayne Johnson taking over, it means that the thugs won."

After that, I looked at the foreign translations of his memoir. There was a French edition—*Les Confessions d'un Eco-Guerrier*—and a German one—*Mein Kreuzzug gegen das sinnlose Schlachten der Wale*. In the main Sea Shepherd office, we stood for a while over a videotape machine and watched a collection of news coverage and videos taken by Sea Shepherd volunteers. On the tape a Makah tribal member said, "I guess the big reason I've been for this hunt is that it's a birthright. It's been predestined for me, before Christ ever walked this earth." When Watson heard this, he immediately shook his head, looked at me, and said, "There's *no* evidence for that."

In a few minutes we were headed across the street to eat lunch at the Thai restaurant. Before we left Sea Shepherd headquarters, Watson gave me a gift—several copies of *Sea Shepherd Log,* the group's magazine. I thanked him. When we got to the Thai restaurant, we talked a little about the movie that was being planned about Watson's life. He was very excited about it. He said that he hoped Martin Sheen would play Cleveland Amory, the animal rights activist who first supported Watson. "Right now, it looks like Woody Harrelson will be playing me," he said. At some point a Sea Shepherd supporter seated on the other side of the room recognized Watson and came over to our table. Watson greeted the supporter warmly. Then Watson picked up one of the copies of *Sea Shepherd Log* that he had just given to me as a gift and took it back from me and gave it to the supporter.

49 / On the Road to Baja

John, my cousin, came home to his apartment to say that he had finally been killed and that we could leave for Baja, and after he packed and picked up the cedar shavings from the cat litter box that his cat had dumped over just as we were walking out the door, we were on our way to a healthy sandwich place where a lot of actors worked, and then on to the highway in traffic, and then, an hour or so later, in downtown San Diego, looking for a place for me to cash traveler's checks. At sunset, we crossed the border at Tijuana and descended into a deep valley of smog and smoke. In

Ensenada, we turned off the highway and watched as waves broke dramatically onto the little road into town: seawater scattered in our headlights. We stopped at a roadside food stand and John ate a taco and I drank a Coke and then we got lost for about half an hour trying to get back on the road to Baja. When we did, we saw that the road to Baja was a two-lane road through hills that rolled out all around us in the bright moonlight. I was driving but then John took the wheel and we talked and listened to music until we were stopped at a military blockade and approached by several soldiers with rifles. A man, who had a machine gun pointed in our general direction, watched us from the top of a truck off to the side of the road.

The situation made me nervous but John was cool; he continued to smoke his cigar and dangled his leather-jacketed arm from the car. John doesn't speak Spanish, but he said, *"Buenas noches,"* anyway. The soldier responded with a question in Spanish, to which John responded, "Uh . . . what?" and smiled. Next, John turned to me and said, "What's the word for *whales?*" and I bumbled through my whale watching guides and Spanish dictionaries and shouted out, *"Ballenas!"* which John repeated to the officer, after taking a drag on his cigar. At that, the soldier motioned for us to get out of the car and open the trunk. I opened the trunk and began taking everything out as fast as I could, and, when the soldiers told me to stop, that it was not necessary for me to take everything out of the trunk as fast as I could, I packed it back up and looked over at John, who was still smoking his cigar and now casually laughing and chatting in broken English with the armed soldiers, who were laughing and chatting and being casual too.

We got back in the car and drove for a few more hours in the darkness and came to El Rosario, a seaside town, where we checked into a hotel. We asked the desk clerk what brought guests to the hotel.

"We have very few activities," he replied, "although we have a lot of people who are coming to watch the birds. I don't know if you guys are interested but we have a lot of people who come here with bird books and look for birds that are gone or endangered, and they check off the ones that they see. Which is kind of funny to me 'cause I didn't even know we had those birds. But our best season is the whale season. That is our best season. We have people who come and they want to go see the whales. They come and they want to be with the whales. They come back over and over again and they want to pet them and touch them and be with these giant creatures."

We asked the desk clerk how many hours it was to Guerrero Negro, and he said it was about seven hours. So we went to sleep in a big room that looked out on what sounded like the sea. In the morning, as I walked to breakfast, a hotel guest who was also from the United States stopped me. He was wearing a jacket with the logo of an Arizona ballooning club, and it seemed as if he had something important to ask me.

"Are you hunting?" he said urgently.

"No," I said. "Why?"

"Well, there are a lot of men down here and, you know, they hunt brant."

"What's brant?" I asked.

"It's like duck."

"Oh," I said. I pointed to his jacket. "Are you ballooning?"

"No," he said, and then he just laughed.

After breakfast, we drove for hours. We drove up into the desert hills that are at the center of the Baja Peninsula. We passed ranches with windmills that did not turn. We passed through an area that a British company had hoped to transform into "the bread basket of Mexico" in the late 1800s but apparently didn't. We passed through dry desert valleys and through fields of tall cactus that looked like pre-clear-cut forests—we passed through hundreds of miles of desert wilderness. Sometimes we saw vast rock garden-like vistas of rubbled mountains. And all of the time, over the hot hood of the rental car, over the yellow-striped black highway with its hallucinatory shimmer, over the cactus and the sand and the rocks, was a sky that was so blue it was almost the idea of sky.

Somewhere around Valle Jesú María we stopped at a small plywood shack and bought tacos. Two women cooked them up and while they did I read the lumber company's stamp on the inside of the unfinished plywood that was the shanty-like ceiling and roof—it said Dawson Creek, British Columbia. The tacos were so incredibly delicious that we ordered more. John tried to find out if the two women were related, if they were mother and daughter, and then he tried to tell them that he and I were cousins, but in the end we realized that we couldn't communicate at all. They gave us fresh sugar cookies that were huge and also delicious and wouldn't let us pay for them. The younger woman pointed to John and said, "*Mucho alto*," which, later on, we guessed meant she thought he was tall. We left liking them and with a vague feeling that maybe they had liked us but we couldn't be certain. We were coming out of the mountains now, out of the interior of Baja, and we could see the silvery Pacific, the last few miles of ocean on the gray whale's long trip (and also my own). At last, we arrived in Guerrero Negro, which was a little fishing village with one big salt factory on the edge of town and it immediately seemed to me like the Mexican version of Neah Bay.

We found Malarrimo, the bar with the whale watching tours that the gray whale biologist had told me about. The tour operator told us we were too late for that day's trip. We took a room in the adjoining motel and went out and found another taco stand—John was crazy for the tacos. I went to the bar and read an article pasted on the wall that explained how things from all over the Pacific Ocean seemed to wash up on the beach just outside the lagoon, on the beach called Malarrimo; it said Malarrimo means "bad approach." An old *Los Angeles Times* article described the beach as "the junkyard of the Pacific." "A beachcomber," said one of the beachcombers interviewed, "could exist for months on Malarrimo, and clothe, feed and house himself in reasonable comfort with all the necessities he would find readily at hand." Among the objects that the article mentioned beachcombers finding there were: a wrecked airplane, a torpedo, a life jacket from the S.S. *President Madison,* boxes of ammunition, steamer deck chairs, a bushelful of sandals from Asia, cans of meat and fruit and dried coffee and K rations, unopened containers of emergency drinking water, and huge redwood logs from the Pacific Northwest.

I went into a gift shop and chose from a selection of gray whale postcards. The gift shop also carried locally made crafts—small sculptures of whales, whale-themed crockery and sweaters. While I was there a group of retired people touring Baja in recreational vehicles came into the gift shop too. A retired woman took down a locally crafted sweater and in the process broke a locally crafted plate. Her husband came into the shop and scolded the local woman running the store. "You shouldn't have put that sweater there," he said. The wife shook her head and *tsk-tsk*-ed the local woman and then left without paying. The local woman said nothing—she didn't speak English—but looked at me and sighed. It was all I could do not to say something to the retired couple. Instead, I went and had a beer with John in the bar, where we met a guy who ended up joining us for dinner. He was from Georgia and he had just sold his corporate-lawn-care business and was going to live for a while on the the edge of a lagoon on the Sea of Cortés with his dogs, who were waiting for him in his VW van. John said he thought that was a good idea.

50 / Scammon

The lagoon in town where we would whale watch the next day, Laguna Ojo de Liebre, is also know as Scammon's Lagoon, and while we were hanging out at the hotel, I told John more than he probably wanted to know about Charles Scammon, the nineteenth-century whaler who first whaled in the lagoon. I mention Scammon again here because I am of the opinion that no attempted exploration of a modern-day gray whale hunt would be complete without looking into some of the details of Scammon's life and work, even though some of them don't seem, at first glance, to have anything to do with the whale hunt of the Makah.

Charles Scammon was born in Pittston, Maine, in 1825, during the height of East Coast whaling. He loved the sea and when he grew up he sailed westward, since at that time East Coast whaling was in decline. He arrived in San Francisco with dreams of captaining a clipper ship but he ended up captaining a whaler instead. Glamour-wise, West Coast commercial whaling was a watered-down version of the glory days of East Coast whaling, and San Francisco was a poor-man's Nantucket; when Scammon sailed to San Francisco Bay, in 1850, people were mostly there for gold, not for whales. The waterfront of the young city was littered with boats that sat at interminable anchor because their captains couldn't find enough men to sail back East. Some of the boats were made into general stores, with planks to the shore for customers; others rotted away while everyone went mining. Scammon's father, Eliakim Scammon, was skeptical about his son's aspirations in San Francisco and thought Charles should return to Maine. Apparently, their relationship was rocky. "[T]here seems to be a mighty rushing to California," Eliakim wrote to Charles. "I do not know but it would have been better for Maine if California had not been heard of."

Despite his father's wishes, Scammon took a job on an eighty-foot-long brig, the *Mary Helen,* which had a crew of sealers and whalers who had probably planned originally to get rich mining gold. Scammon had been hoping for more prestigious work but he desperately wanted to get to sea. The *Mary Helen*'s crew hunted elephant seals with clubs and lances and muskets along the shore and on the little islands from San Francisco to Mexico, and the crew went after the occasional whale. Though he was a reluctant whaler, Scammon proved good at it, and in 1852, he took command of the *Rio Grande,* a full-fledged whaler. On this boat, his wife and son sailed with him until his son was suddenly sent back to Maine—difficult father-and-son relationships were a Scammon family trait. In a few years, Scammon specialized in gray whales, which, from a whale hunter's perspective, were not as profitable as other whales but were easier to catch, in that their path was more predictable and they were relatively simple to find in the bays along the California coast. For these same reasons, other West Coast whalers soon began going after gray whales, and subsequently Scammon found himself in the midst of a gray whale shortage. "A landsman cannot imagine the disheartening situation of a whale ship that has sighted not even the shadow of a whale in it's sojourn," he wrote. "During these discouraging times, men are likely to reject order and discipline. From the moment the captain steps upon the quarterdeck until the voyage terminates, he leads a life of constant care and anxiety, for the expedition is fraught with uncertainty as to its results." There came a point in Scammon's career when gray whale uncertainty was no longer an issue because, in 1855, sailing the *Boston,* he hit the gray whale hunting jackpot. He discovered the shallow lagoon near Guerrero Negro.

He discovered the lagoon either on a tip from a sea captain or by his own ingenuity—it is not certain which. He entered the lagoon carefully; the entrance was dangerously shallow. The expedition was a gamble—there might not have been any whales and there was a chance he would strand his ship—he discovered quickly that he was on to something. "The waters were alive with whales, porpoises and fish of many varieties," he wrote in his log. He realized later that he was at the end point of the gray whale's long migration, one of several lagoons where female gray whales give birth. Inside the lagoon, he sent men to the shore in the smaller whaling boats to collect firewood. The particular crewman left to watch the boats decided to take a bath while waiting. He pulled out the plug in one boat to let in some water and accidentally let in too much. The boat capsized. He swam to shore as the other boats all began to float away, completely jeopardizing the entire expedition. Some Hawaiians on Scammon's crew used planks to make what Scammon described as "surf-boards," which they used to paddle quickly after the boats, to no avail. The crew's carpenter, "an excellent swimmer," by Scammon's account, ripped off his clothes, dove in after the boats, and drowned. It looked as if the entire whaling expedition was over until the tide brought back the boats that evening.

The next day the crew managed to catch one gray whale. The following day, when they went out again, a gray whale attacked them—it staved the whaling boat. Men with broken arms and legs waited in the water for a rescue boat, which a gray whale also wrecked. Scammon's wife, Susan, was on board the *Boston* and took care of the injured crew for a few days; Scammon called the *Boston* "a floating ambulance." A few days later, after the whalers had recovered, the crew went out whaling again. They approached a gray whale to harpoon it, but when they did, everyone jumped overboard. Scammon described the panic in his journals: "On one occasion, a bulky deserter from the U.S. Army, who had boasted of his daring exploits in the Florida War, made a headlong plunge, as he supposed, into the water; but he landed on the flukes of the whale, fortunately receiving no injury, as the animal settled gently under water, thereby ridding itself of the human parasite."

The whales impressed Scammon. "The testimony of many whaling-masters furnishes abundant proof that these whales are possessed of unusual sagacity," he wrote. His crew did not. "It was useless to attempt whaling with men who were so completely panic-stricken," he said. Eventually, Scammon sent the whalers back out on the water with a new invention: a Greener's harpoon gun, a swivel-mounted gun that fired a harpoon. Scammon ordered the whaling boats to position themselves alongside a small channel in the lagoon, which the gray whales navigated with difficulty. The crew was to shoot the grays as they passed. The old whalers on the crew laughed at this idea, but it worked. They brought in several whales a day for months. "From that time on, whaling was prosecuted without serious interruption," Scammon said. The tryworks, where the blubber was rendered, burned continually, stopping only to cool down from time to time. The *Boston* sat for weeks in the tropical lagoon, hauling up gray whale carcasses and spouting thick black smoke. The crew emptied out barrels filled with food to carry the extra oil. As the ship set out toward the open sea, the weight of the oil nearly stranded the *Boston* on the bar. Mexicans already knew the lagoon as Laguna Ojo de Liebre, or Jackrabbit Spring Lagoon. Scammon renamed the lagoon Boston, though it would later be renamed for him.

For a while, Scammon attempted to keep the lagoon's whereabouts secret. Scammon's brother-in-law, Jared Poole, seems to have driven him crazy in this regard. Poole was also sailing with his wife, Susan Scammon's sister, and when Scammon was on a whaling trip to his secret lagoon,

Poole taunted Scammon by sailing up alongside of him. "Poole!" Scammon shouted at him. "Stay away from my ship, damn you!" The following winter other whalers visited Laguna Ojo de Liebre, and finally the lagoon was traffic-jammed with whaling boats—even if some whalers thought shooting gray whales in their birthing lagoons was a strange way to whale.

"I shipped to this ship to go a-whalin'," Scammon recorded one whaler saying to his captain. "I'd no idea of being required to go into a duck-pond to whale after spotted hyenas. Why, Cap'n, these here critters in this bay ain't whales!"

"Well, if they ain't whales what are they?" asked the captain, an old whaler from New Bedford, in a husky voice.

"Well," replied the mate, "I don't know rightly what they be; but I have a strong notion they are a cross 'tween a sea-serpent and an alligator."

After about four years, the Laguna Ojo de Liebre and other nearby lagoons were all but emptied of gray whales. As a result, gray whales were nearly extinct. "The mammoth bones of the California Gray Whale lie bleaching on the shores of those silvery waters, and are scattered along the broken coasts, from Siberia to the Gulf of California; and ere it long may be questioned whether this mammal will not be numbered among the extinct species of the Pacific," Scammon wrote, sounding as if he perhaps lamented what he had wrought. Natives in villages in Alaska and Siberia who hunted gray whales for food starved when the grays killed by commercial whalers in the Baja lagoon did not return. By 1880, gray whaling was no longer profitable, the gray whale population was so small. The population rebounded somewhat and commercial whalers returned in 1914. Norwegians, Soviets, Japanese, and Americans whaled off the Baja lagoon into the 1940s, years after an international agreement was signed to protect grays. Today, the lagoon is used by whale watchers and by salt mining companies.

Scammon found other lagoons to whale in—Laguna San Ignacio, for example, which was just south—but then he moved on. He referred to himself as a "civilized whaler," but he also fancied himself a sea captain and a naturalist. He went on to captain a revenue cutter out of San Francisco. He got caught up in an Alaskan telegraph scheme that didn't work out and—thanks to some long letters that he wrote while he was drunk during his stay in Alaska—sullied his reputation forever. He patrolled the San Juan Islands and the coast of Washington, during which time he became familiar with the Makah hunt. In time, Scammon the whaler became Scammon the writer, and he described gray whales and whaling in general in articles in *The Overland Monthly*, a magazine edited by Bret Harte that featured articles by Joaquin Miller, John Muir, and Mark Twain ("Roughing It" first appeared there). Eventually, Scammon published a book called *The Marine Mammals of the North-western Coast of North America*, which for many years was the definitive book on the subject. For a brief time, Scammon was a small literary sensation, the marine adventure writer of his day. The book was a commercial failure, however: Scammon bought them from the printer for the cost of the paper and gave them to friends. In his personal life, he pressured his son, Charley, to become a sailor but Charley didn't. In *Scammon: Beyond the Lagoon*, Lyndall Baker Landauer writes of Charley: "He never had a profession, never amounted to anything. He was a gold-seeker, a gambler, a ne'er-do-well." Charley died living in a shack in Alaska, where he claimed to be having the time of his life but was eating boiled caribou tongue and potatoes night after night. Scammon's own father seems to have mellowed on his son's career. When Scammon sent copies of *The Overland Monthly* to Maine, Eliakim wrote back, "We did not know we had a literary Don in the family." Charles Scammon, the great gray whale hunter, died in 1911, twenty-four hours after his wife. They are buried in Oakland in an unmarked grave. "In the final analysis," Landauer writes, "Scammon the writer can be said to have done a great deal with a modest talent."

There is another summary of Scammon's life in *Beyond the Lagoon* that jumped out at me when I read it:

Scammon's actions made him noteworthy and immortalized his name. That is a privilege or a curse granted to only a few. . . . The lagoon in Mexico is forever Scammon's, though it is still Laguna Ojo de Liebre on Mexican maps. The whales still flock to it, and today so do the whale-watchers. Its use and importance has varied over the years, but it will forever be Scammon who found the way in and who opened it to everything from the slaughter of the gray whale, to salt mines, to a prime area for the study of these animals by scientists. This is not the sum of his life, only a small part of it. He explored and mapped the northern seas and islands. His name is still on maps, in Scammon Bay in Alaska as well as the Lagoon. The premier gray whale parasite is called *Cyamus scammoni*. He had many interests and tried to learn as much as he could about each. He was a man who lived in his own age, held 19th century ideas and acted according to 19th century morality. No one can do more. Many have accomplished less.

I read this section over and over. Sometimes I found it a little uplifting. Sometimes it made me sad and a little depressed.

51 / Salt

It was cloudy and windy in Guerrero Negro on the day we set out to see the whales, but a little bus left the bar and headed for the docks at Scammon's Lagoon anyway. We rode with small groups of people, including a woman in a wheelchair, whom we recognized from our hotel the day before. There was also a family from California who came in two large sport utility vehicles: their name was Dove. "We came down before," one of the Dove party said. "It was pretty incredible." On the bus, Julio, a Guerrero Negro resident in his twenties, told us a little about Guerrero Negro and the whales. He told us about the salt production company, which is the big employer in town, and the largest salt production facility in the world—it produces thirty-five million pounds of salt a day. He said that the salt mines were expanding and with it the town. "People are saying that in six or five years it's not going to be a town anymore," Julio explained. "It's going to be a small city." We all listened patiently. He talked more about the salt mines. "It's hard to get a job there. You have to have a brother or a sister or you have to kill someone over there." Everyone on the bus turned his or her head to look at him. "No, no, I'm just kidding," he said.

We passed through the edge of town and headed out toward the lagoon, through the salt flats. The salt along the road was slightly dirty from the salt company truck tires, so that it looked like the streets of a big Northern city just after a snowstorm. I had read about the controversy involving the salt mining company: whale biologists and environmentalists were concerned that the barges from the plant might disrupt the whales as they came in and out of the lagoons. Some feared that the liquid used to process the salt might jeopardize the gray whale habitat in the lagoon and in the other lagoons in Baja. Julio played down the ill effects of the salt company. "The salt company, it gets a lot of benefits for a lot of people," Julio said. He deflected some of the attacks. "Some religions of the Japanese kill whales," he said, "and then eat it, I think, so that's what is bad for the whales. But the salt company has been here for fifty years and every year there are more whales." (The following year the Mexican government decided against an expansion of the salt production facility, in part to protect the gray whale habitat.)

From the road we could see a barge filled with seven thousand tons of salt. The tour guide said it took eight to nine months for the salt to evaporate. He listed more facts: 79 percent of the salt goes to Japan, with much of the remainder going to Canada; 49 percent of the operation is owned by Mitsubishi, 51 percent by the Mexican government. He told us that there were 1,850 gray whales counted in the lagoon last year and this year there were approximately 1,500. He said that the whale had been late and slow to come down from Alaska and that no one really knew why.

As we got closer to the lagoon, he prepared us for the whale watching itself. "There are a lot of rules," Julio explained, "because in 1970 there were some tourists in the lagoon and they got drunk and they were with the whales and they were playing rough so that the whale even bled. The one guy had gotten on the whale like a horse and the whale got mad and turned over the boat. And then for eight years the government said no one—no one for eight years. Now, there are lots of rules."

One of the Doves asked a question: "How often do you get to touch the whales?"

"Two days ago, everybody touched the whale but it is always different," he said. "A girl touched a whale a couple of days ago but she got mad. Do you know why? She got mad because she had no film. She said, 'No one is going to believe me!'" Julio became very serious, and then he went on, "You are going to see sea lions, maybe dolphins, and if you are very lucky, whales."

There was a noticeable silence; people looked out at the lagoon that was now in sight and seemed worried at these words. Julio smiled. "No," he said. "I'm just kidding you. You *will* see whales."

Everyone laughed.

52 / Touched

We put on life preservers and long yellow raincoats, both of which were too small for my cousin John. We got into two small blue skiffs. The Doves were in one boat, the *Susanna*. John and I got in the other, the *Leviathan*. The motors quickly took the *Susanna* out into the lagoon; we waited as the woman in the wheelchair was assisted into the *Leviathan*. John and I were in the middle of the boat when we set out. The man behind us was reading the instructions for his digital camera, while his brother advised him. The woman who had been in the wheelchair was in front of us and holding on tight. The man piloting our boat was a fisherman who no longer fished for a living; he spoke no English.

We cast off and soon passed a buoy covered with seals and then headed out into the lagoon. The sky was light gray like the water. We were surrounded by low rolling hills of white salt. It was a landscape of ocean and desert where distances all faded together in the grayness. We saw pelicans, and I thought of Scammon: *"The waters were alive with whales, porpoises and fish of many varieties."* We continued out into the huge lagoon. People acted halfheartedly impressed with the seals and porpoises but you could tell that everyone just really wanted to see a whale. After about forty minutes, the sun was starting to break through the layers of low clouds, but still we saw no whales. I was preparing myself for the idea that I might have come all this way, the fifteen hundred miles from Neah Bay, and not see a whale when someone shouted, "There's one!" I saw nothing at first, but then I could make out a little gray lump sticking up out of the water in the far distance: it seemed less like a living, breathing cetacean than a distant, mechanized parade float. In a minute, the blunt gray heads were all over the horizon. In another minute, I could make out the tails of gray whales and then I saw an entire creature, closer to us now, maybe a hundred yards away, rise from the ocean, turn, and then fall thunderously down. At last, whales all around us were doing the same thing: it was as if they were putting on a show.

Everyone on the boat was ecstatic. The digital camera of the guy in front of me was beeping frantically. The guy was saying, *"Oh yes! Yes! Oh yes!"* One of the women behind us was creaking forward her film advance knob on picture after picture. And the whales were closer. John turned to me and said, "This is incredible." I agreed. I tried to take a picture of a whale as it breached and I missed.

Before I knew what was happening there was a gray whale within a few feet of our little boat. The captain slowed the boat down and began pointing and nodding. Someone translated his words, saying, "This one is friendly." The fisherman seemed to recognize the whale. The whale came closer and everyone was standing, which made it difficult for the disabled woman to see. For a second, the whale disappeared and then reappeared again, underneath the boat, as if to emphasize how big it was in comparison to our skiff. I saw its vast, island-sized back, gray and nearly black but covered with barnacles, shiny and wet. The stink from its blowhole was excruciatingly dank. Generally speaking, the experience was like watching a tractor trailer truck come up underneath you, a huge, nonnegotiable formation of living rock that all of a sudden turns to reveal its grapefruit-sized eyeball.

When this happened, everyone immediately leaned over to one side of the boat in a frenzied attempt to touch the whale, like fans running for a foul ball. I could feel the boat tilting so that I felt certain for a moment that we would all drown in the warm salty water or be baleened to death. I looked back to see precisely how close we were to a watery end and as I did I noticed the disabled woman sliding slowly to the floor. Her face looked worried as the boat tilted, as a crush of hands reached past her, reached over and around her—as the whale simultaneously rose from the water to look at us or to be looked at or maybe to be touched or possibly for no reason at all. I turned to John, who saw the woman falling too, and then I tried to climb back, saying, "Look out!" Attempting to crawl back, I alerted the man behind me, who then saw the woman sliding down to the floor of the boat. By this time, the whale was submerging again, returning to the depths of the lagoon, so other people noticed the woman's distress, and now were helping her up, asking her if she was okay, which, after looking a little shaken for a minute, she was.

Out of all the passengers on the *Leviathan* there was only one person who had touched the whale. She was a woman in her early fifties in a light blue windbreaker. She seemed nonplussed, almost put out when everyone looked back at her expecting her to describe what it had been like to touch a gray whale in Scammon's Lagoon, what it was like to have experienced a palpable connection with a whale that would likely pass out of the lagoon and travel the West Coast, past Los Angeles, past Cape Flattery, past Vancouver Island to Alaska and swim in the Bering Sea one day. The woman who had touched the whale did not seem to want to discuss it. Her arms were folded; she practically grimaced. "Like a hard-boiled egg, without the shell" was all she said.

In the bus on the way back into town, everyone agreed that the day had been a success, for the Doves had seen whales too. Julio, the tour guide, was pleased. "Some people, they say, 'If I don't touch the whale, I want my money back.' And I say, 'But it is called whale *watching*, not whale *touching*.'" He passed around a book for everyone to sign. Among the pages were many comments by people who had taken the trip before us: "Experience of a lifetime . . . My dream of seeing the whale has come true. . . . Our fifth trip & each one better than the last! . . . Super cool! . . . *Wundervolle!* . . ." But a few more pages back there was evidence that something had recently gone wrong with a whale watching excursion. It was in the entry of an Italian tourist who had signed the guest book. "It was the fact that [when] I went to see the wells [sic] there was an Insident. . . . We were almost killed by a momma well protecting her baby." Another Italian seconded it. "Almost killed by a momma," he or she wrote on the bus ride back, "a momma whale protecting her baby whale . . ."

I was reading these comments until we returned to the bar, where we had a drink and dinner and went to bed. We woke up and drove all the way to L.A. in one very long drive. We stopped for tacos at the place we'd stopped at on the way down, and the two women remembered John and welcomed him kindly. We landed at John's apartment early in the morning and I had to sleep in John's bed (a queen) since his neighbor, Seresh, had crashed on John's couch for I don't know what reason.⁵ But there on

---

⁵ In *Moby-Dick,* Ishmael and Queequeg end up sharing a bed due to the Spouter Inn being overbooked. Because of the description of this bed-sharing scene and other such innuendo-filled chapters, a lot of Melville scholars have devoted significant amounts of attention to whether or not Melville was gay. There were many reasons for this: *Pierre,* the novel he wrote right after *Moby-Dick,* is so psychosexual that it's difficult to follow: there are a lot of closets he could very well be subtextually coming out of. Also, some scholars asserted that Melville once made a pass at Hawthorne. Melville lived very near Hawthorne for a time, and the two were friends. (Mostly, Hawthorne was Melville's friend, since Hawthorne was reserved in comparison to Melville, who was not.) For a short while, they saw each other frequently, thoroughly enjoying each other's company by all accounts. In *Melville,* a kind of psychological biography, Edwin Haviland Miller describes Melville dressing up as a Spanish cavalier, getting on a horse and riding to the home of Hawthorne, who was reading the newspaper in a little grove of trees. Miller writes that Melville greeted Hawthorne in Spanish and at this point apparently made a

the bus, moments after our up-close gray whale encounter, at the end of my long West Coast journey, I looked through the window at the lagoon, and then over at John, who was engrossed in conversation with the woman who had fallen in the boat. She told him that she was traveling around the world—she'd been to London and Hong Kong and a lot of other places—and that her favorite city so far was New York City, even though it was a difficult city to navigate in a wheelchair. She said she found the people there friendly. On the drive back, as we passed through the desert, John told me more about the woman who had so impressed him. It was obvious to me that she had really touched him.

53 / Back in Neah Bay

After the trip to Baja, I went back up to Neah Bay. I arrived in the evening. At the restaurant, I heard that the power had gone out while I was away. Everyone went over to Washburn's Market, which is where everyone usually goes during a power outage, even though there wasn't any power there either. The gas station runs on electricity; everyone was forced to drive out of town to get gas. The power company had to get at lines back in the hills, back where mules are used to bring in repair gear. People in town who didn't have gas-powered generators lost everything in their freezers, such as elk and deer meat. A lot of people went out hunting after that to restock their freezers.

I called up Wayne and his mom said he was at the base, in the gym. I drove over to the gym by the tribal center. A bunch of people from town were using a weight-lifting machine and playing basketball; a little kid

---

pass at the author of *The Scarlet Letter*. Other biographers say that there is no hard evidence that Melville made such a pass, even if Hawthorne did move away from the Berkshires kind of suddenly (supposedly, Hawthorne never liked the Berkshires). The other reason it is argued that Melville was gay, or perhaps bisexual, was that he was at sea for a long time. In fact, *Moby-Dick* is full of puns on homosexuality—in the chapter entitled "A Bosom Friend," in which Ishmael sleeps in the same bed as Queequeg, for example. Robertson-Lorant argues in her biography that the debate over Melville's sexuality can sometimes take away from the image that Melville was trying to create with most of these references, which is an image of mutual understanding and democracy and brotherly love.

threw a ball at the hoop but couldn't reach it. I was told Wayne was in a back room. I walked over and saw the crew, sitting in a circle, in the bright whiteness of the racquetball room, listening to Wayne as he spoke—his wiry arms gesticulating, imploring, his hands inevitably finding their way back to his Raiders jacket pockets. He was kneeling on one knee.

I left them alone and went out in front of the gym and waited around until everybody came out. Darrell showed me his new pickup truck, which was actually an old pickup truck filled with a new engine that he had pulled out of an old car in the junkyard. The next morning, I met up with Wayne and Donnie. Wayne said that they had some new guys on the crew. "We've got a total of twenty-four people who are on the crew now," Wayne said. "Some more guys want to be on but I have closed the door." Wayne said they were talking to a newspaper photographer from Seattle about making a calendar with pictures of the whale hunt crew members to make money for the crew. (That didn't work out.) I wanted to show Wayne and Donnie some photos I'd taken in Baja of the whales jumping all around us, of the whale coming up to our little boat. So I spread out the pictures on the table.

Donnie said, "You were close?"

I told him that I could have touched them and that people really wanted to touch them and one person did. Wayne looked at me for a long time and I got the feeling that he was wondering about my experience with the whales.

Later, Wayne said, "Me and Donnie, we were thinking, when this thing's all over we might go to Mexico. Take a vacation."

54 / On the Job

Wayne was in the van. The van was malfunctioning. The driver's-side door wasn't working and something was wrong with the starter. He either had to stop it on a hill when he parked it or else he had to let the engine run. Wayne drove past a big cart filled with cut wood that sat out in front of the post office next to a sign: MEMORIAL WOOD RAFFLE—$1.00 EACH. The money was to go to the family of a diver who had drowned while picking sea urchins from the floor of the strait. Some people thought that a seal had tangled his air line, that he had maybe panicked, but no one really knew. Wayne passed the cart on his way out to the country, out to the tribal center. He picked up Donnie. He went by John McCarty. John saw Wayne and Wayne saw John. Nobody waved. Down the road a little farther, Wayne stopped the car and shouted to a teenager walking aimlessly down the street. "Want to come out training with us?" he asked. The kid looked down at his feet. "Keep you from spending your money on alcohol," Wayne said. The kid laughed. Wayne put the van back in gear. "See you 'round," Wayne said.

At the tribal center, in the council chambers, a video about the Makah was playing: it showed cliffs and water and people talking about whales and ancestry. Ben Johnson seemed to be watching it, but he wasn't really. "Oh, I've seen it so many damn times I don't know what it's about," Ben said. Keith Johnson was there too, just back from a speaking engagement, where he had talked about what the whale hunt meant to the tribe. As Wayne and Donnie were walking out of the council chamber, Ben stopped them. Ben was in his chair at the head of the long table, leaning back, playing with his pen. "So when you gonna get us a whale?" he asked.

Donnie and Wayne stopped dead in their tracks. They stood side by side. "There're no whales out there yet," Wayne offered.

"One right off Baada Point yesterday," Ben said and grinned. "Get us one by the fifteenth," he said.

Wayne and Donnie smiled and left. Donnie's outward confidence rarely seemed to waver but Wayne sometimes looked less confident when he got in the van, and that's how he looked now. When he looked past the windshield wipers, out into the rain that had been pouring down for weeks, Wayne said, "Everybody's kind of down, kind of blue." But he had been finding some middle ground with Denise. He sounded sympathetic, even, when he talked about how she had been ambushed at a conference at which the whaling commission was invited to speak. "Denise went to a conference in Oregon," he said. "She sat down and she got stuck talking to a vegetarian," he said. He shook his head. "We got to have somebody checking these places out."

Donnie got into his own pickup truck. Wayne headed for coffee with some of the crew. They drove over to J.J.'s Pizza and Bakery.

With the van's starter on the blink, Wayne parked up on the hill in front of the bakery. The hill was steep so that the van looked like it might tip over at the top but it didn't. After Wayne parked, a bunch of crew members pulled up in a small pack of pickup trucks and old sedans. They parked every which way so that within a minute the little parking area looked like a five-car pileup. Darrell went in first and ordered a latte. Donnie arrived in his own truck and grabbed a soda. Then Theron Parker arrived. He had a cast on his leg. He had injured his Achilles tendon.

Theron Parker: tall, strong, partly bearded, with eyes that could look at you and say *What do you want?* in a way that indicated he didn't require a reply. Theron was the harpooner who looked like a harpooner, the man so obviously capable of launching a long barbed pole into whale flesh. The cast made his harpooning status questionable for the moment, however. Theron didn't show up in the papers or on TV at all when they were covering the whale hunt; he didn't seem to like most of the reporters, much less the idea of doing interviews. And his physical presence was such that the reporters didn't want to push him on the subject, didn't want to rub him the wrong way. Whenever I ran into him, I'd say something and he'd just stare me down. It seemed to me he was trying to scare me, and it was working.

This menacing quality endeared him to some people in town, such as members of his family. "If we had more guys like Theron on the crew we'd have that whale by now," a relative of Theron's told me. This quality also made him difficult for other people to deal with—especially Wayne. Theron and Wayne had not been getting along lately and it was imperative for the hunt that they did. It was a matter of captain-crew unity. Earlier that day, in conversation with Donnie while in the van, Wayne had been optimistic about his relationship with Theron.

"He's talking to me again," Wayne said.

"He don't got no choice," Donnie said.

"There's a huge power struggle going on in town," Donnie told me. He was philosophical. "You see," he said, stuffing a wad of tobacco into his mouth, stomping the floor of the van to shake the wet cold out of his layers of sweatshirts and sweatpants. "It's easier to work with somebody in your family," he said. "It's like with me and him"—Donnie pointed to Wayne—"we know each other. We know how we do things. We have the same religion and everything. With somebody else, they might do things differently, you know?"

"That's right," Wayne said.

Wayne also saw it as a personal chemistry issue. "He's the kind of guy who will take a bear head and hang it on the front of his house," Wayne said.

"You should see his masks," Donnie said. Theron was a carver.

"Man, they're dark," Donnie said.

When Wayne and Donnie arrived at J.J.'s Pizza, the whaling crew members were standing in a circle with their coffee drinks. Wayne walked in and soon he and Theron were facing each other. As they talked, Wayne seemed to be hoping to take advantage of Theron's expertise with wood. The crew needed some new paddles and they were out of lumber.

"We need to make some paddles," Wayne said. "Can you get us some more yew?"

There was a short but dramatic pause. Then Theron spoke. "I know where some yew wood is," Theron said. "I could get it except for this." He pointed to the cast on his leg. "You could use maple," he said.

"Maple?" Wayne replied.

"Yeah," Theron said. He looked at Wayne. "It's gonna be just as hard as yew and you can cut it down to this." He held up a paddle.

Everyone talked for a while. It looked as if Wayne was trying to be nice to Theron and as if Theron was trying to be nice to Wayne, as if there was a moment of total crew unity. I was standing there drinking coffee too, and at one point, I spoke to Theron and he responded. I think the fact that he had even talked to me went to my head, so that a minute later I told Theron that if he needed help getting to the yew wood, I could maybe assist, that it was no problem, since I wouldn't mind poking around in the woods. Of course, as soon as I said that I wished I hadn't. Theron folded his arms and looked me in the eye. I thought he was going to growl.

"Did you ever read that book *Never Trust a White Guy?*" he said.

55 / Wayne to Court

I gave Wayne a lift to Forks in my car one morning. Over the fall, when the press had been in town and the whale hunt didn't end up happening, Wayne had missed his court-appointed anger management classes. ("I couldn't leave town *then*," Wayne said.) As a result, he had been wanted on a parole violation, a fact which the whale hunt protestors frequently publicized. Since the fall, he had gone to court and checked in and, now, to stay on track, he had to go to Forks to see a court officer. He didn't have any way to get there so I offered him a ride in my car. I saw him in the morning and we agreed to meet again at around noon, but then noon came and I didn't know where he was so I called his house and got his mom. "He has to come home and change before he goes to Forks," she said. I checked at fisheries, where I found him. He was looking for someone to pick up lumber in Port Angeles for paddles. He had settled on cherry—maple turned out to be too expensive. He said he was ready to leave. I mentioned to him that his mom had said that he was going to go home and change his clothes first. He looked at me and shook his head. "Pffff," he said.

While I waited for Wayne to finish talking to Denise in the whaling commission's office, I read the just-published first-ever issue of *Makah Fisheries News*. There was a photo of Darrell and Donnie and Donnie's brother Randall taking the Dive Safety Course. There was a photo of the fisheries Habitat Division, and a report on the efforts to monitor water quality, in light of the intensive logging that was going on, on the borders of the reservation. "Because of our remote location, no other agencies are looking at the health of our rivers. This land is our home, and we depend on these rivers. . . . Water quality standards will allow us to talk to the E.P.A. in their language, and show them how our federally-recognized treaty rights are being ignored." A story by Dave Sones talked about the work being done to improve the habitat in streams for the salmon; it talked about the fishing fleet dwindling, about the fall in salmon and black cod fishing. "My greatest concern is: How do we maintain our livelihoods?" Sones wrote. "We did not build our fleet overnight. It took the knowledge of our senior fishermen to teach crucial elements of our maritime skills to younger generations. It is my belief that our fishermen are the current warriors of the tribe. They risk their lives out on the open ocean to exercise our treaty rights each year. They provide food for the community and share earnings throughout their extended families."

Also while I was waiting, Donnie introduced me to his mom, who is a technician with the tribal fisheries.

"I used to go out fishing with my dad," she said. "I loved fishing with my dad. I went tuna fishing with him." She said that he had passed away in the seventies. "It seems like yesterday," she said. Donnie told me that his grandfather had been going to Vancouver Island to invite some relatives to his wedding. On the way back, there was a storm that came up suddenly. The boat hit a reef and he went down.

"The sea can go from calm to rough in a minute," Donnie's mom said.

Wayne came out of Denise's office, looking upbeat. We sat around and talked some more, and when we were on our way out, someone asked Wayne if he could take a call for the executive director of the whaling commission, because Denise had just left, gone home early. He said he would. He went down to the whaling commission's office, and put his briefcase and his cell phone on the desk. Donnie sat on the windowsill and watched him; Arnie Hunter sat in a chair with his feet up on the desk.

"Hello, this is Wayne Johnson," he said.

He looked down.

"Uh, yeah . . . Uh-huh."

He listened for a long time and then looked at Arnie and began shaking his head. Finally, he interrupted the caller.

"Do you think you could call back?" he said.

"Well, I'm not trying to be rude or anything," Wayne went on. "But I'm not the person who can answer those kinds of questions and, anyway, I could take your name and number and somebody could call you back. Can I do that?"

He found a pencil on the desk and scratched a number out. He hung up the phone.

"Jeez," Wayne said.

"What did she want?" Arnie asked. He was looking at his watch—he had to get to Port Angeles for his weekly bowling match.

"She's writing a novel," Wayne said.

"A novel?" Donnie said.

"Yeah, a novel and it's about a boy who—he's reading in the paper about Makah whaling and he finds out that he's a Makah and he moves to Neah Bay and gets on the crew."

"Huh," Arnie said.

"But that could never happen," Wayne said, leaning back in the chair. "We're all full. There's no more room on the crew."

*　　　*　　　*

♪ In 1843, after he deserted from the *Acushnet*, Melville worked in a Honolulu bowling alley setting up pins. The job was somewhat controversial given that American missionaries considered bowling indecent at the time. (King Kamehameha was converted from bowling to billiards by the missionaries.) Melville didn't stick around Honolulu for very long. He was listed in the shipping office as a deserter from the *Acushnet,* and he was afraid he would be noticed and end up in jail.

I threw my daughter's car seat in the trunk and we took off for Forks, an hour's drive through the pouring rain. We had been driving for a while when I noticed that Wayne was smoking and I freaked out and told him he couldn't smoke in my car because my wife would flip. He put out his cigarette and leered at me. "You're fired," he said.

Donnie sat in the front seat and read a column in the local paper that was written by an Olympic Peninsula resident of Irish descent who said that just because his ancestors ran around naked in the woods and beat people senseless with clubs didn't mean *he* had to do the same, which, the columnist implied, meant that the Makah didn't have to hunt a whale. Donnie critiqued the column. "This guy's an idiot," Donnie said. As we drove out of Neah Bay, I could see where the road had recently washed out. When I pointed this out to Wayne and Donnie, they told me about one of their relatives, one of the last sealers in Neah Bay. He was on the road in his car waiting for a landslide to be cleared when another hill gave out and washed his car down into the strait, killing him.

We got to Forks and went to the county offices. The receptionist told Wayne that he was a day early for his appointment. He showed the card in his wallet that said his appointment was for that day and the receptionist said there was nothing she could do. It was raining—still pouring. The three of us got back in the car and drove through the woods to Neah Bay, and we went to Donnie's house and sat in his living room and talked while his daughter watched *Titanic*. They talked about what they would do when the whale hunt was all over, when hunt preparations were completed.

Donnie said he'd maybe join the National Guard. "It's a good deal," he said. "You get benefits and you get to be a weekend warrior."

"I want to maybe move to Alaska," Wayne said. "Get away from this rat race."

56 / The Germans Weren't Around

As the winter progressed, the German film crew called every week to see if the tribe was ready to hunt. Ralph Marschalleck, the director, asked over and over if it was time for his crew to return to Neah Bay to film their final scene. I kept hearing that the Germans were calling, and I often thought about the author who Ralph had said had influenced them as boys, in Germany—Karl May. I went to a library and read about May and about his relationship with Native Americans, and I learned that Karl May is the most popular German writer ever. He was the German version of James Fenimore Cooper. His work inspired the invention of the spaghetti western. Hermann Hesse called him "brilliant." Albert Einstein loved him ("My whole adolescence stood under May's sign"). He was Hitler's favorite author. Of course, I was still interested in the progression of Makah whale hunt preparations but toward the end of the winter, with no actual whale hunting going on, with a lot of nights spent reading in the tent that I was using in lieu of the shanty (even a shanty starts to add up after a while), I felt it was good for me to ponder some of the foundations of the modern German perspective on Indians. And the more I pondered, the more interested I became in May's aesthetic ideals and reality. In other words, it was turning out to be a long winter.

Karl May was born in 1842, in the city of Hohenstein-Ernstthal, in Saxony. He was one of fifteen children. His father was a weaver, at a time when weavers were being put out of business by English textile mills. Weavers were working eighty hours a week and had no money left for food. In his memoirs, May recalls begging for potato peels at the local inn. He lost his eyesight as an infant. To help the family make ends meet, May's mother got herself certified as a midwife in 1845, and the next year her midwifery instructor operated on Karl May so that he was able to see. May was then sent to the local school, where he studied foreign languages and music. After school each day, he worked at the inn setting up bowling pins. The inn was also the local lending library, and May devoured all the romantic novels there. At home, his father forced him to memorize entire geography books. When he was thirteen, he ran away to Spain, which was, as he put it, *"das Land der edlen Räuber, der Retter aus Armut"*—"the land of noble robbers, the saviors from poverty." At least, he *said* he ran away to Spain. Just as he read romantic novels, so he romanticized his childhood as an adult; his biographers aren't entirely certain if he really did go to Spain or, for that matter, about much of anything in his childhood.

When he was fourteen Karl May was sent to a seminary, where he was trained to be an elementary school teacher. The seminary was strict, and he was repeatedly reprimanded for missing church services. In 1859, he was expelled from the school after being accused of stealing Christmas candles for his family. He was made an assistant teacher in 1861, but he lost that job after being accused of inappropriate overtures toward his landlord's wife. He lost his next job when he was accused of stealing a watch, a pipe, and a cigarette holder from his roommate. He spent six weeks in jail, where he worked in the prison library. "It was probably during his imprisonment that May first thought of becoming a writer," Karl Doerry wrote in an essay on the life and work of May. May claimed to have left prison with a stack of his own manuscripts, though most experts doubt this. May described the following years as a period during which he was torn between *hellen und dunklen Stimmen,* or "voices of darkness and light." When he listened to the dark voices he ended up in a work camp in Zwickau, at which point he apparently listened to the light voices and was released early for good behavior. It wasn't long, though, before he was in jail again, this time in Waldheim. His crimes usually involved impersonating doctors or teachers or government officials and then conning people out of their money. He didn't con people out of much, though. He seemed to be in it for the role-playing. He often said that he merely wanted to be known as a *Respektsperson,* or "person for whom you have respect."

When he was released from jail in 1874, May said he planned to go to the United States but instead worked as a book and magazine editor. In 1878, he published his first novel, *Im fernen Westen,* or *In the Far West,* which was set in the American West. In 1880, he married Emma Pollmer, who was from his hometown. He wrote for a Catholic family magazine and then he wrote a series of travel novels, in which similar protagonists pursue similar adventures either in the American West or the Orient, which were pretty much the same in Karl May's mind. Generally speaking, May's novels are didactic. A typical Karl May adventure will often begin in a lowland, with the climactic scene—the obvious moment of truth and enlightenment—happening, after much suffering, on a high point, like a mountaintop. The novels are full of local details that gave his readers the sense that they were reading an eyewitness account even if the author had never been to the places he wrote about. "Their main appeal derives from the reader's ability to experience vicariously a human, just, educated, and intelligent German hero triumphing over both primitive savagery and a corrupt modern world," Doerry wrote. One of his narrators was named Karl the German. Another was called Old Shatterhand. Old Shatterhand was so named because he could knock people out with one punch. Sometimes May would dress up as his character as he wrote.

His most famous novel is called *Winnetou, Der rote Gentleman*, or *Winnetou, the Red Gentleman*. It is the story of Old Shatterhand and his friend Winnetou, an Apache. (When Hitler was defeated on the Russian front he instructed all his generals to read the *Winnetou* novels.) May wrote it in 1893, and he used George Catlin's reporting on American Indians as background. It starts out with Old Shatterhand traveling to America and staying with a German family in a city for a while and then going out West, where as a "greenhorn" he immediately kills a grizzly with a knife. The America that Old Shatterhand sees is, as opposed to the stratified society of May's own Germany at the time, a place where natural ability takes precedence over birth and nobility. "This egalitarianism . . . must be considered an important contribution to the image of America in popular German imagination," Doerry wrote. As in all of May's westerns, the white men of the West are ruled by greed for land and gold and oil. Winnetou, on the other hand, is an Apache who has read all the great European works. He has given up what Old Shatterhand considers to be barbaric practices, such as scalping. Winnetou is a noble savage who has become even more noble by somehow having managed to attend finishing school in his spare time, and, with Old Shatterhand's help, the two combine the best of Native American nature with the best of European philosophical culture to create an *Über*-native.

In 1899, Karl finally visited some of the places where his novels took place; he traveled through the Middle East, Turkey, Greece, and Italy. The trip produced a crisis in his life and writing, as if seeing those places were too much after having imagined them for so long. Meanwhile, he was being attacked at home for calling himself a doctor when he wasn't and for some pornographic scenes in his early novels. From then on, he wrote allegorical novels—among them *Ardistan und Dschinnistan*, which is a novel about the narrator's trip from the lowlands and deserts of Ardistan toward the mountains of Dschinnistan. May claimed that *Ardistan und Dschinnistan* answered all the questions facing humanity, though critics questioned that. In 1903, May's wife divorced him and joined the people who were attacking him and his writing. He remarried the widow of a friend. In 1908, he took a trip with his second wife to the United States, where he had never been. He arrived in New York City and then visited Niagara Falls. He made a speech in Lawrence, Massachusetts, entitled "Three Questions for Mankind: Who Are We? Where Do We Come From? Where Are We Going?" He did not visit the West, the stomping ground of Old Shatterhand, the land where his doppelgänger wrestled with wild animals, had survived death-defying journeys, and dueled with what was for his fans almost palpable evil. In 1912, back in Germany, he died of a cold.

While the German film crew was still in Germany, I set aside *Moby-Dick* and picked up *Winnetou*. I read as Old Shatterhand came to America and killed the grizzly bear; as he encountered the corrupt white guys who were looking for gold; as he met Winnetou, who, like all the Indians, Old Shatterhand didn't understand at first but then was impressed by and then impressed—for Old Shatterhand was not the typical white man. I read as the bad guys killed Winnetou and then tried to get the gold, which was way up on a peak. I watched Old Shatterhand raise his rifle to shoot the bad guy and saw that at the last second he didn't have to shoot because a rock fell down on the bad guy, causing the gold and the bad guy to fall into an abyss. As it turned out, this was the way Old Shatterhand knew the story would end. He had seen it foretold in a dream.

57 / Responsibility

"I'm doing ninety-nine things at the same time here," Wayne was saying.

It was cold and raining. He was in the van heading over to the museum to check out the whaling canoe that was being carved, and he was running around checking on equipment and personnel issues—he was still trying to make certain that everyone on the crew had passed all their training tests. It was as if he were preparing for a religious service, an example of which he had never attended.

He pulled up to the longhouse: the incubating whaling canoe sat in a bed of red cedar shavings, the wood's sweet incense falling out the door of the longhouse into the cold, wet air. "It's coming along," Wayne said.

The carving was proceeding smoothly, given that it was a few months behind. Wayne figured it would be done any week now, though they didn't necessarily need this whaling canoe for the hunt; they could use their racing canoe, the one they'd been practicing in. The two guys carving it—Lance and Glen—were planning on steaming the canoe soon. Wayne was in charge of gathering the rocks that would be heated and dropped into the water inside the canoe, which would cause the canoe to expand in width, open up like a fan. Wayne had brought the metal milk crates he planned to use to move the rocks from the fires to the water inside the canoe. The carvers approved the milk crates. Wayne made the thumbs-up sign.

We picked up Donnie, and Donnie drove us down to the marina to look for some trolling poles, long wooden dowels that Wayne had seen being thrown out at the marina. Wayne thought the poles might make good harpoons. As Donnie drove, Wayne read from an ethnographer's report given to him by the museum staff, a historical account of the tribe and their whale hunting methods. There was a copy of an old drawing, a seating chart for a traditional whale hunt. Wayne kept this chart on the dashboard of the van as if it were a road map. "'The harpooner is in constant communication with the crew through hand signals,'" Wayne read.

He looked up.

"We're gonna throw a couple of harpoons," Wayne said.

"I'm gonna throw one from the chase boat," Donnie said. They had decided Donnie was worth more out of the canoe. He thought of something. He added, "And I'm gonna need a new bearskin. That one Micah has—it's too smelly."

"Yeah," Wayne said.

"Eric's gonna throw one," Donnie went on. "And then I'm gonna throw one. And I'm gonna have my diving gear on so I'll just throw it and then I'll dive in and tie its mouth shut." Donnie smiled. "I'll feel its body quiver when I swim by his tail."

Wayne laughed and shook his head, and pulled on his cigarette.

The van pulled into the marina parking lot. Donnie and Wayne looked for the poles in the trash to no avail. Next, we drove past some other popular garbage sites in town and then we drove to the dump. In Neah Bay, the dump is on a hill on the peaks that overlook the cape. We passed signs that said Makah Wildlife Refuge and then passed trash—first in bits and garbage bags and then in home furnishing–sized chunks. The trash appeared in larger and larger concentrations, until we were in the hilltop clearing that was the dump. There, the town garbage truck was unloading. A dozen stuffed animals were tied to the truck's grill—all of them abandoned and subsequently adopted by the garbagemen. In front of the truck, an unreeled cassette tape was streaming in the wind.

Donnie stopped the van. "We used to come up here and just shoot shit," Donnie said. He hung out of the van's window and shouted over the sound of the garbage truck emptying itself, over the hydraulics of the truck, over the sound of rain falling hard on trash of all species. "Hey!" he said. "We're looking for some trolling poles. They were thrown out at the marina."

"We were gonna use 'em for our harpoons," Wayne said from the passenger seat.

"Oh no," said a garbageman. "That woulda been perfect." He shook his head. "No," he said. "No, we didn't take them. They'd be perfect!"

"You don't have to plane them down," Donnie said. "Otherwise, it takes a long time to plane 'em down."

"Oh, fuck yeah," the garbage guy said. "That woulda been perfect!"

The other garbage guy came up now, away from the truck, which was now empty. He stumbled through the fresh trash, and nodded a greeting to Wayne and Donnie. "Hey," he said.

"Hey," Donnie said.

The first garbageman said again that he hadn't seen the poles. "No," he said, "we don't take 'em, too long."

The second garbageman looked at the first one quizzically.

"Okay, thanks," Donnie said.

"Thanks," Wayne said.

As they drove back down into town, Wayne pulled another list from his briefcase and went over the latest whaling crew certification qualifications, as revised by the whaling commission:

(1) Each member must be able to swim in the open ocean.
(2) Each member must pass a Drug and Alcohol test.
(3) Whaling crew must have expertise in shooting the rifle on land, in canoe, and practicing on a moving target.
(4) Whaling crew must have experience in use of harpoon on land, in canoe, and practicing on a moving target.
(5) Must be able to show that they have made attempts at approaching a Whale in a canoe.
(6) Must be able to tread water.
(7) Must be cross-trained in canoe.
(8) Chase/Support boat crew must be able to drive boat in open ocean, surface, etc.
(9) Chase/Support boat crew will be tested for Drugs and Alcohol.

The list ended with the following statement: "The responsibility of the Whaling Captain is to see that each crew member . . . is adequately prepared spiritually and physically to go on a hunt."

"These are a lot less strenuous than they used to be," Wayne said, pointing to the list. "They used to be a lot more strenuous and nobody could keep up, not even Donnie."

As we drove, the radio in the van shorted on and off, cutting off the radio psychologist who was advising a caller to break up with his girlfriend, and get on with his life. Water leaked through the roof on the carpet in back where the extra battery was. At one point, Donnie got out to talk to somebody and Wayne mentioned his son, whom I had never met—I didn't even know he had a son or that he had been married until that moment.

"You know, I really wanted him to come up here and be involved with this work that I'm involved in, but it's not time," Wayne said. His son was living in Oregon. He mentioned that he was worried about him. "I told him you're gonna end up being whoever you hang out with," Wayne said. "If you hang out with alcoholics, you're gonna be an alcoholic. If you hang out with crack heads, you're gonna be a crack head." He turned the radio off. Just as Donnie was getting back in Wayne said, "I don't want him to be up here now, not yet."⁵

Wayne drove over to the house of a crew member, Paul. Paul lives across from the high school. When the van pulled up, he came to the door.

"Going to go tread water?" Wayne asked him.

---

⁵ Melville had two sons. Malcolm was the oldest. He and Melville had a rocky relationship, partly because Melville, the increasingly unsuccessful writer, was difficult to live with. Malcolm ended up becoming a soldier, in hopes of emulating his ancestors' glorious military careers. (The Melvilles often talked about the glories of their ancestors.) Malcolm was a member of the New York State National Guard. When he was eighteen, he was staying out late and drinking, which upset Melville. Melville imposed a curfew. One night, Malcolm came home at 3 A.M., went to his room, and locked the door. He didn't come down for breakfast. Melville grumpily said to let him sleep and suffer the consequences. Finally, his mother went up to get him. Eventually, they broke down Malcolm's door. He was in his nightclothes lying in the fetal position, a pistol in his hand, a bullet hole in his head. Melville's second son, Stanwix, died when he was thirty-five. He had tuberculosis and had failed in his quest to make his fortune in California. Melville didn't write much about his feelings surrounding either of his sons' deaths. But, as Edwin Haviland Miller points out, there is a lot in *Moby-Dick* about loss. Starbuck has lost his brother and his father at sea. Ishmael is an orphan; Ahab refers to his own son as an orphan. The captain of the *Rachel*, another whaling ship featured in *Moby-Dick*, has lost his twelve-year-old son in a boat and he asks Ahab to help him search (Ahab doesn't; he's too busy going after the white whale). And the *Pequod* sets out on Christmas Day, on the anniversary of the birth of a boy who has no earthly father. "Paternal rejection lies behind the first sentence when Ishmael evokes the myth of Abraham and the son's loss," Miller writes.

"Gonna get my hair cut," Paul said. He stood in his doorway. Behind him was the cougar that his brother had shot and stuffed.

"We're gonna tread water at two-thirty today," Wayne said. "You can get your hair cut some other time."

"Do it tomorrow," Donnie said.

"Tomorrow, doing something else," Paul said.

"Well, now you'll have two things to do tomorrow," Wayne said. He got back in the van.

58 / Sensible

Up to now, I have maybe made it seem as if, while spending time on the Makah reservation, I only came in contact with people immediately involved with the whale hunt effort, but that was not at all the case. The case was that after I camped in the evenings—in the woods near Lake Ozette, or in the grassy area behind the Cape Motel—after I woke and crawled reluctantly out of my sleeping bag and then dressed and unzipped my tent to come face-to-face with another cold and wet Neah Bay winter day, I would make haste for the Makah Maiden, where I would drink cup after cup of coffee and usually see one of the people that I saw over and over in Neah Bay—someone like Helma Ward, Arnie Hunter's mom. It was a lot of fun to sit by the warm stove while it rained and hear her talk about Neah Bay.

She talked about the rivers and the cape and once she told me that she had heard of a great wave that a long time ago had come running up through the Waatch prairies and pressed on into Neah Bay, washing out the village. She said she had heard it from her elders and that she believed it to be true. She had also heard that the hills of the cape were riddled with holes, like Swiss cheese. This was the reason she had picked up her children from school when they were younger on the occasions that the school ran tsunami preparedness drills. The school took the children up into the hills, safe from any possible tidal wave. Helma feared the hills might crumble if a wall of water hit them, so during the drills, she drove Arnie and his siblings into Port Angeles.

"Do you remember?" she said to Arnie, who was sitting next to her.

"Yep," Arnie said in reply.

Sometimes she even told me stories about Arnie, her fifty-year-old son, still a little boy at breakfast. She remembered once putting a half-full bowl of berries in front of Arnie when he was a kid. "Aren't you going to pray?" she asked him. Arnie replied, "There's not enough."

One morning after coffee, I attended one of Helma's language classes at the museum. It was a slow day; only one student was able to make it. Helma wore a Makah sweatshirt and slacks and a sweater. On the wall behind her was a picture of her and Arnie dancing and a clipped comic strip, "They'll Do It Every Time." The student was Darrell Markishtum's sister, Jill. She began speaking Makah; at the beginning of the lesson, it was a struggle for her to become accustomed to the glottal stops that the language requires. Jill said that when she began her language class, months before, her throat suffered, so that once, after a class, she gave blood and the doctor told her she was sick and she said, "No, I've just been to language class."

Helma went over the worksheet. She said *babaqi·yuk^wi·k*, which is the question "What are you doing?" She had her student repeat it. They went over the vocabulary words: *ʔi·caq'aqY*, which is the Makah word for "sensible," and then they went over the Makah words for "middle-aged person" and "rosy cheeks." Then Helma told a story in Makah. Jill asked more about the Makah word for "sensible." She asked if an animal could be referred to as sensible. She gave an example of a horse that had waited for her when she had fallen and sprained her leg. The horse had walked her back to town slowly. Helma thought about the question for a while and then decided that you probably could apply the word *sensible* to an animal, and as an example she remembered the dog she had as a child, Prince. Once the family had very little food, she told Jill. This was very unusual because there was always fish, and in the old days if someone in Neah Bay was hungry the elders would simply send out some canoes. But at this time, for whatever reason, there was no food in their home, and Prince noticed this and, the next day, went to the market and found the load of food and supplies that were headed for the government lighthouse on Tatoosh and brought back a package of steaks.

When Helma said this, Jill's jaw dropped.

"And, well," Helma said, "we gave that dog a nice piece off that first steak that night."

59 / A Hand

Donnie kept saying that you had to be really tough to be on the whaling crew and I didn't doubt him, but he kept saying it over and over, and then he was having a fun time teasing me, saying that I could never make the cut, that I could never take the rigorous training regimen. Finally I said, "Fine, I'll take one of the tests," and I signed up to go swimming. The swimming test required that prospective crew members tread water in the open ocean for ten minutes, a cold and icy duty!

The day of the test was gray and cold and a wind was blowing over the strait from the north. It was so cold that I was wondering what I was doing jumping in the ocean during the winter. I got gym shorts out of my car. I put them on. I wore a T-shirt because I was freezing even though I wasn't even near the water yet. I thought maybe everyone was going to have to jump out of a canoe off Tatoosh Island or something but they were just jumping in the bay down by the boat launch, off the little wooden pier. I walked over there in my hiking boots and gym shorts and T-shirt in the freezing cold. Arnie was there to monitor the test and to time everybody. He was wearing a winter coat and a hooded sweatshirt and boots and a warm hat and thick gloves that were fluorescent orange and thickly insulated. He appeared as if he was ready for a blizzard. "Hey," he said, when I got down on the dock. He looked at me and smiled.

In a minute, a bunch of crew members pulled up—Darrell, Andy, Donnie, and some other guys. Andy jumped out of his van and his cell phone rang. It was sealed in a Zip-Loc storage bag to protect it from the rain, and he talked through the plastic. As he spoke he put on his wet suit. Darrell and Donnie and the others did the same. I said, "You're wearing wet suits?" And they told me that you'd be crazy not to. I didn't have one and I felt it was too late to turn back. Next, we all put on life preservers and stood around on the dock. The water was so cold it was a sheet of black glass. Arnie said, "Okay," and set his watch. Darrell jumped in first and he used a disposable underwater camera to take pictures of people as they proceeded to jump in.

I was the last to jump. I kind of wanted to just forget it but Donnie was now egging me on. I slipped off the dock as I jumped and fell in a bad sort of belly flop. When I came up, everyone was laughing and the water was

so cold it felt hot. I quickly climbed out and tried to jump in more grace-
fully, which I did (I felt). I treaded water for a minute or so, and I declare
to you that all the while I was wondering if I was in the process of dying of
hypothermia, if all the horrible controversy of the hunt would vanish
from my brain, if all the accumulating details of preparation would now,
in this ice-cold bay off the Pacific, fade from me with all my mental capaci-
ties, the way that anger, as whaling experts of old reported, faded in the
scent of the sperm whale's sperm, its so-called ambergris, the so-called
milk and sperm of human kindness.

After what felt like an hour but was probably only a minute, I no longer
had anything to prove. I dragged myself up onto the dock, looking like a
sea mammal that forgot to migrate.

This was when Arnie reached out and gave me a hand.

I dried off as quickly as I could and changed clothes up the hill and realized that no one in town was noticing that there were a bunch of guys
swimming in the bay in the winter. George Bowechop looked in on us and
then drove away. Denise Dailey drove down and looked unimpressed.
The big news in town on that afternoon was the new house that was
being put in across the street from the piers on behalf of a tribal elder: a
crowd gathered as a new double-wide trailer was towed in on a big truck.
I watched the crew get out of the water—a team made imperceptibly
more solid by a short midwinter swim. I was trembling by then and I can't
remember much of what happened but I think it was Donnie who was
showing everyone the little hole in the arm of his dry suit, where cold water
had leaked in a tiny little bit and caused him some slight discomfort. I tried
to tease him about it but my teeth were chattering so violently that I
didn't make any sense.

60 / Fish-in

On March 15, halibut season on the Northwest coast was ushered in with
a big storm—rains, winds, ocean swells that threatened to swallow up
small boats—but the fleet went out anyway because that was the day the
season was open and if they wanted to make money, any money at all,

then they had no choice. They also went because the tribe had always gone out for halibut. The Makah ate salmon in the old days, dried, or cooked on cedar stakes over coals of burning alder, but their staple was halibut. Halibut is the signature fish of the Makah, just as fishing halibut is a signature endeavor, what they consider, like whale hunting, a right.

Halibut is a large, diamond-shaped fish that lives on the ocean bottom. Halibut grows to between four and five feet long and up to five hundred pounds. The small ones are called chicken halibuts; the large ones are called whale halibuts. The Makah used to call halibut *shoo-yoult*, according to James Swan, but then they were told to call it *halibut*, which comes from the Middle English word *hali*, meaning holy, which refers to the fact that it was something that could be eaten in Europe during the Middle Ages on Holy Days. Halibut starts out life like the average fish, with eyes on each side of its head, and then as an adult it transforms itself, changes, morphs, so that both its eyes move to the same side as it lays flat on the ocean floor. Just off the cape, the ocean floor drops to an underwater valley. Halibut live on the valley's soft, rocky edge, feeding on the nutrients that well up from the deep, as do whales.

If you were sailing in a ship from Boston up along the Northwest coast in 1870, you would have seen that the roofs of the longhouses of the Makah, unlike the roofs of the longhouses of other tribes on your journey, were covered with halibut. "The appearance of one of the lodges on a fine day in summer when plenty of fish are drying is that of a laundry with clothes out bleaching," James Swan wrote. The halibut fisherman paddled out to the underwater banks known as Swiftsure, fifteen miles away. He dropped a line made of kelp, and a hook made from hemlock that was called a *chebood*. When the halibut was brought in, it was sliced thin, dried, and then dipped in whale oil and eaten. James Swan: "It requires a peculiar twist of the fingers and some practice to dip a piece of dry halibut into a bowl of oil and convey it to the mouth without letting the oil drip off, but the Indians, old and young, are very expert, and scarcely ever drop any between the mouth and the bowl."

Dave Sones, the director of the natural resources for the Makah Nation, told me that the Makah had fished with the old hemlock hook up until the forties, bringing in hundreds of thousands of pounds' worth of halibut every year. Then, commercial halibut fishing operations moved in and the tribe's take decreased annually. By the fifties the halibut fishery was depleted and the Makah stopped. The same sort of thing happened in their other fisheries, such as the salmon fishery. "We kind of got squeezed out," he said, "kind of like with the whaling."

Native American tribes in the Northwest began asserting their fishing rights in unison in the fifties and sixties. For a long time, Indians in the state of Washington were accused of overfishing the rivers, despite the fact that the total catch by the tribes was less than 1 percent of the total harvest. State officials ignored the effect of pulp mills, dams, and canneries in the depletion of fish runs; the tribes were made scapegoats. In fact, tribal fishing rights were often leased to canneries, without the tribe having any say. It was in the fifties, as non-native commercial fishing declined, that Indians were more and more likely to be arrested while fishing on the rivers running through their reservations, their ancient fishing sites. Their boats and nets were confiscated. Sports fishermen slashed tribal members' nets and sometimes even shot at Indians.

In the sixties, tribes decided to take political action against these laws. They believed their right to fish—their right to preserve or restore their traditional economy—was embedded in their treaties. A member of the Tulalip tribe, near Olympia, wrote: "They promised us we could fish . . . as 'long as the mountain stands, the grass grows green and the sun shines.' But now the State of Washington has declared the steelhead trout a 'white man's fish.' They must think the steelhead came over behind the *Mayflower*." According to some accounts it was the Makah who put out a call for action among Northwest tribes that resulted in what eventually became known as fish-in protests, during which tribal members were inevitably arrested, often in large numbers.

In the seventies, fish-ins on the rivers of the Northwest became well-publicized political events. Celebrities attended; Marlon Brando was arrested in a Northwest river, as was Jane Fonda. Tribes from all over the nation came to offer support: Navajos from New Mexico, Blackfeet from Montana, Iroquois from New York. The fishing rights of Native Americans in the Northwest meant a lot to Native Americans everywhere. Thousands of people were arrested. State fishing regulators physically beat the protestors, and many were hospitalized. State courts repeatedly came down against the tribes, but gradually federal courts began to rule in the tribes' favor. (Federal officials became especially concerned when the Yakima tribe got involved in protesting, as the Hanford Nuclear Reservation, a nuclear weapons manufacturing facility, was in the middle of the Yakima reservation.) In 1974, Judge George Boldt, a federal judge, ruled that Indians were entitled to half the fish returning to sites off their reservation that had been their "usual and accustomed places." White fishermen questioned Judge Boldt's sanity; they said that he had been given free fish by Indians or that he had an Indian mistress, neither of which was true. After the Boldt decision, some tribes had to station armed guards at their fishing sites.

In their own attempts to fish for halibut again, the Makah were at first allotted fifty thousand pounds a year by the federal government and only allowed to use hand lines and rod and reels. They caught their limit in the second year. They were then permitted to use commercial gear. Now, they go out once or twice a year during the winter and fish with long lines. They lay the lines out in the field across from the tribal center or sometimes on the school football field. There are about three thousand hooks on a long line set, each of which must be baited by hand with herring or squid or octopus before it is laid down on the ocean floor. An entire set can cost $10,000.

When the first halibut opening came that March in the year of the whale hunt, the wind in Neah Bay was out of the north and blowing at around thirty miles an hour and gusting up to sixty, as if it were perturbed. The little boats that set out from the marina were lifted up on waves that were two stories high. Some fishermen came in with a small catch, and they sold it at the fish dock for between $2.75 and $2.50 a pound. A couple of crews had to head back in as soon as they had thrown out their lines, leaving behind their gear. When the weather cleared and those crews returned and retrieved their lines, the halibut that was still on the hooks was good to eat but could not legally be sold because they were being brought in after the opening had officially closed. The fish were distributed free throughout the community.

On the night of the first halibut opening, in the middle of the storm, Dave Sones was worried about the fleet, so nervous that he went out to his own boat, which was up on blocks on his front lawn, just off the beach. He stood at the helm and turned on the radio and looked out the boat's windshield at the wind raking the gray Sooes Beach. With the wind whistling and swaying his boat, he could hear the older fishermen talking to the younger ones, keeping them calm. One boat was in distress. The captain had gotten his line caught in his prop and he was trying to get it untangled. He put on a Mustang suit, the orange-colored survival suits that are like whole-body flotation devices, and instructed his crew to tie a rope to his waist. He jumped into the ocean storm. He floated in the churning water and waited for the prop to be lifted from the water by a swell so that he could work: a window that opened for four or five frantic seconds at a time until the ocean heaved the boat down again. Sones was afraid the fisherman would get killed. This went on for close to an hour. Finally, the Coast Guard found the captain and towed his boat in.

61 / Painkiller

You could sense that the whale hunt was getting closer, that an actual hunt was looming, even though no one had any exact dates in mind. You could sense this, especially on the day, at the beginning of April, when I stopped by Wayne's house.

The clouds had lifted from over Neah Bay and the peaks like a dark lid from a little green bowl. Across the strait on Vancouver Island, you could see precisely where it was and where it wasn't raining at that particular moment—a natural weather map. At Wayne's house, one of two surplus Army trucks that Wayne had picked up at Fort Lewis was sitting out in front; he had driven it into town the day before after stopping at the dentist to have a tooth pulled and after stopping in Sequim to put in an order for ammunition for the new whaling gun—after much testing, after much firing of bullets through drums filled with water, Al Ingling had decided on an elephant gun instead of the .50-caliber rifle. The van was parked at Wayne's house too, although it was temporarily out of commission: it was currently tangled in the wire fence around the house, trapped. Wayne had forgotten that the car was in gear the last time he started it, and when he turned the key it had suddenly run off the top of the driveway and into the fence, nearly ripping it out. The car stopped only a few inches from the satellite dish that feeds TV into Wayne's house, which was a great relief. "If it'd got my satellite, I'd have cried," he said.

I dropped by as Wayne was slowly getting up off the couch in his living room. His mouth was still hurting from the tooth he'd had pulled. "This is all the dentist gave me," Wayne said, holding up a bottle of mild pain reliever. "Just pain reliever. I could have killed that dentist."

Wayne said he was concerned about taking the pain reliever. He said it might affect the drug and alcohol test that he had to take for the hunt. He and Denise were battling over the drug and alcohol test. She was not going to issue a whale hunt permit until everyone took his drug tests and passed it. So far not everyone had passed, and some crew members hadn't taken the test yet. "I'm confident *I* can pass," Wayne told me. He was so vehement that I wondered. "But I want to be totally clean." He broke open the pain reliever's childproof cap and threw some tablets in his mouth.[5]

Just then, a bunch of guys from the crew drove up and banged on his door.

Theron was there and even he was in a good mood, practically cheery. He shouted in to Wayne. He teased Wayne about the van, which sat there caught in the fence like a fly in a spider's web. Wayne walked outside.

"You been partying, Wayne?" Theron said. "You been out partying?"

Wayne told him about the starter.

"Yeah, sure, Wayne," Theron said, as the other guys started laughing.

"I got a witness," Wayne said. He was laughing too. "My neighbor saw the whole thing."

"Yeah, sure," Theron said again.

"No, really," Wayne said. "My partying days are over."

I sat there waiting for Wayne on his mom's couch, and, as I did, I couldn't help thinking that he said this as if he were saying it mostly to himself, as if he were convincing himself that after the whale hunt he wouldn't go back to hanging out in bars; everything would change.

Theron and the others took off for the docks. Andy stuck around, while Wayne stuffed gauze into the hole in his mouth. He needed to put

---

[5] Melville once made a reference to dental pain in a letter he wrote to Nathaniel Hawthorne during the time that he was composing *Moby-Dick*. In the letter, Melville said that he had not written any of "The Whale," as he referred to his work-in-progress, for three weeks. "I'm going to take him by his jaw, however, before long, and finish him up in some fashion," he wrote. He despaired about his reputation. "Think of it! to go down in posterity is bad enough, any way; but to go down as 'a man who lived among the cannibals!'" Melville burned most of his letters to Hawthorne, but in this one, which Edwin Haviland Miller describes as a "heart-exposing, life-weary" letter, Melville talks about how he had only recently bloomed as an artist. "My development has been all within a few years past," Melville said. "I am like one of those seeds taken out of the Egyptian Pyramids, which, after being three thousand years a seed and nothing but a seed, being planted in English soil, it developed itself, grew to greenness, and then fell to mould. . . . Three weeks have scarcely passed, at any time between then and now, that I have not unfolded within myself. But I feel that I am now come to the inmost leaf of the bulb, and that shortly the flower must fall to the mould." He closed the letter by commenting on Goethe's directive: "Live in the all." "What nonsense!" Melville wrote. He added that it was especially difficult to live in the all in the case of "a raging toothache."

down his cigarette to get the gauze all the way into the hole. The three of us got into the huge truck. When Wayne started it up, it sounded like a tank. Andy hung on the side of the truck as we drove out to the base on a back road through the marshy land near the junkyard. The skunk cabbage was in bloom: big yellow fronds of it in the bogs and slow creeks along the Waatch. It was a glorious day. After the turn we could see the silver ocean turning white at the shore, tumbling roughly onto the sand. On the side of the truck, the wind was blowing Andy's long black hair straight back; he was in Nike sandals, jeans, and a tank top. He looked as if he was already savoring summer.

Wayne had to shout over the thundering engine. "This is the best I've felt in days," he said.

At the base, Wayne showed Andy some more surplus military equipment that he and Donnie had picked up for the hunt. As far as Wayne was concerned, everything was almost in place. In the little shed behind the tribal center, he had amassed big orange floats and yellow lines and harpoons and flags to let the Coast Guard know when the canoe considered itself officially hunting. The heads on the harpoons were sharpened so that, as Wayne demonstrated, they cut paper. There were a couple of big stainless steel meat slicers, and flotation suits. The prize find was the new surplus Zodiac, a boat just like the boats all of the protestors had. It had a strong and fast Volvo engine in it, which Wayne would have liked to use, but would cost $18,000 to fix. He had taken the engine out and was looking for an outboard to put in its place. The Zodiac was on a trailer and Andy and Wayne and some people in the tribal motor pool who happened to be around lifted the trailer hitch onto the back of the two-ton truck, and we dropped the boat off across from the old military base in front of the whaling equipment shed.

Wayne let Andy drive the truck downtown. When he put it in gear, he cheered, and sped up slowly, and cheered again. Andy waved at everyone he passed, honking when he drove past his house. He bounced up and down on the big springs in the truck's seat. Wayne looked at Andy and shook his head and smiled and smoked, the gauze in his mouth making him look a little beat up. "Savage," Wayne said.

On the way into town, Wayne mentioned that some Shakers were coming to town to meet the crew. The Shakers were part of an old Indian religion, a type of Native American Christianity that originated in the Pacific Northwest.

"They've been having . . . what's the word?" Wayne said. "*Visions!* They've been having *visions* that we'll have a successful whale hunt. It ain't my belief, but I'll go listen to them, hear what they have to say."

"Me too," Andy shouted.

At the boat ramps, Wayne got out of the truck and signaled Andy as Andy began backing the truck down the ramp: the crew wanted to pull the *Hummingbird* out of the bay. They wanted to let it dry out for a while just before the hunt; it was a getting a little waterlogged. They were going to put the canoe on the trailer. Andy hesitated as he backed down the boat ramp so Wayne got into the truck and took the wheel. The canoe didn't fit in the trailer at first, but Wayne and Theron jury-rigged it so that it did.

The canoe sat at the boat launch, and two white fishermen approached it. "How'd you make that?" one of them asked Andy.

"Carved it out of a log," Andy said.

"Must have been a big log," one of the fishermen said.

"Yeah," Andy said.

"Well, good luck to you," the fisherman said, and he walked away.

Everyone was standing around the upside-down canoe, leaning across it, talking and laughing and joking, and it was one of those moments when it seemed as if the hunt were just about to happen, as if everything would work out for the whalers, as if it might be pulled off despite all the logistical difficulties, the problems with training and managing personnel.

Even Wayne and Theron were joking together, as Theron inspected the canoe, felt for holes in its bottom.

The crew's confidence was infectious, and when I caught it, I mustered up the courage to try and speak with Theron again. He had found a small hole in the bottom of the canoe, a little rough patch, and I asked him about the procedure for fixing it. He suddenly shot me a solemn look.

"Oh, that's a *very* spiritual process," he said, "a very, very spiritual process."

I thought maybe I had said the wrong thing again.

"First," he said, looking hard into my eyes, "you must go in a sweat lodge and you must pray and pray and pray." He raised his dark eyes to the blue sky. I noticed again how much bigger than me he was. "And then," he went on, "you must wait for spiritual direction. . . ."

I was holding still, trying to be respectful and cool when I realized he was smiling.

"No, I'm just kidding," he said. "You just sand it."

62 / Fuck-Ups

Some people on the whaling commission stood by Denise's decision not to issue a whaling permit until all the crew was certified. Others thought she was being too tough. One of the people who stood by her was John McCarty, whom I ran into in front of the market.

I had just been over to his son Micah's house. Micah had recently moved back to the reservation. He was no longer attending college. He was carving and looking for work. I had watched him carving a wolf mask. His new daughter was asleep in a little crib, and he had talked about how he had just returned from a whale conference in Hawaii, where many people were against the Makah hunt. He was spending more time working and trying to make money for his family but he was still speaking up for the whale hunt, even though he was no longer on the crew. "Every time I was introduced, there would be this long silence. It was weird," he said.

When I ran into John, he told me that he too had recently spoken at an event on behalf of the whalers. He spoke about the tribe's tradition of whaling, about their attempt to bring it back, and he said that after he did he was angry, on account of the current crew.

"Basically, they're fuck-ups," he was saying. "And I'm getting tired of lying for them. I go out and lie for them. I went out a couple of days ago and we talked to some schoolkids. But I'm getting tired of it. I'm getting ready to call *The Seattle Times* and tell them to write an article about it. You know, they wouldn't let me come to a commission meeting down here the other day."

He kept his hands in his jeans pockets and nodded toward the restaurant.

He went on, "That's where they said some of the guys were positive on their tests. They wouldn't let me in because they don't want to hear it. But it doesn't matter if I'm there because I hear it from the other guys anyway. Two of them are still positive! They didn't pass their test. And, you know, they said it was okay because their level hadn't gone up or anything. *Pfffft!*"

He was shaking his head, though still nodding hello to people as they walked out of the market. He stopped a woman, asked if she'd seen someone he was looking for around town.

"They're fuck-ups," he said again, as he smiled to another woman he waved to. "And you know what bothers me? They're representing our ancestors. Our ancestors were strong and pure and courageous. But these guys are fuck-ups."[b]

I asked him if he thought anyone on the crew would change, if preparing for the hunt might have any kind of an effect on anyone.

"Probably not," he said. "But it doesn't matter. I got me a new job. I'm a criminal defender."

He explained that he was working for the Makah judicial system and that he was defending a guy who had been charged with drunk driving and assaulting an officer. At that moment, he spotted a person he wanted to interview in the case. He said, "I gotta go," and he walked away.

63 / The Shakers Are Coming

A group of Shakers were coming into town to see the crew and to tell about their vision of the hunt, and because Wayne was in charge of the crew he was in charge of the Shakers—he had to figure out where to put them all when they arrived. He was not experienced in organizing this kind of thing, much less in dealing with any religious leaders. It was one more complication in a long list. The power had been out all night, and his toothache had kept him up. Theron was upset with him again, and he was back to battling with Denise. He wanted to whale in the next week or so but Denise wouldn't issue a permit. He left his house on that gray morning with a lot on his mind. As his mother walked out she told him to

---

[b] When *Moby-Dick* was finally published, not everyone immediately thought that Melville had done a good job writing about his whale hunt; some people thought that he had screwed it up, ruined a perfectly good sea adventure with overwriting. In England, where it was published first, it got a good review and a bad review. For some reason, American papers chose to publish the bad review. The bad review called it "an ill-compounded mixture of romance and matter-of-fact" and "so much trash. . . ." Melville's family began to think he should give up writing and get a government job—if only for the sake of his health. After *Pierre*, his next novel, failed, he had some luck writing magazine pieces. After *The Confidence-Man* failed he lost his confidence. He sold his farm, which took a while. At one point, a commission looking for a site upon which to build a new insane asylum for the state of Massachusetts was interested in Melville's farm but then declined to buy it, which made Melville more depressed. He got a government job. He began to write just for himself, mostly poetry.

tell Denise who was boss. Wayne rolled his eyes. "I don't really want to deal with this whole thing right now," he said. "But it's all on me."

He clipped his cell phone to his briefcase and said, "Okay, I'm ready for business."

We went for coffee at the diner. He looked out at the water, which was rough but no longer wintery. Sometimes, he looked to me as if he were in the midst of imagining the worst possible outcome—he could seem so morose. He was beginning to talk more often about safety during the whale hunt. "One swipe of that tail, it could kill three guys," he said. "And if somebody dies that's all on me too."

Wayne argued that the commission couldn't be so tough on the crew. "The commission tried to say that if you scored positive on the test then you were off the crew. But I said, 'No. That's not what this is about.' I said, 'You have to have your levels coming *down*.' With some of these guys, I ought to be able to say, 'It doesn't matter.' 'Cause they're gonna be so valuable. Like Donnie. He's gonna be too valuable. But it doesn't matter because Donnie is gonna pass his test this time. I know it."

We drove out to the log boom near the breakwater, out in the center of the bay. The wind was raging and it was beginning to pour again. Wayne found one of the operators, a man named Leonard Bowechop, who apparently was the Shakers' contact on the whaling commission. Wayne opened his briefcase and took out a pen and loose-leaf paper.

"Okay," Wayne said. "We just need a list of which Shakers are coming. And also, do you know what kind of Shakers they are?"

"Oh," Bowechop said. "Well, yeah, well, let's see. They'd be—what?— 1920 Shakers. No, 1900."[b]

"Oh, okay. Well, my mom will know which ones they are then. And now can you tell us which ones are coming?"

"Oh well, yes. Let's see, there's Jean Smith, that's the woman who first had the vision."

Wayne wrote down the names of eleven Shakers. The rain on the paper made the ink run. He took a ten-dollar donation for food for the Shakers from Bowechop and then he went to the tribal center. He picked up his paycheck, $150. "A tough day in the dress factory," he said. "Now, I gotta find room for eleven Shakers tonight and I don't know how I'm gonna do it."

[b] When Melville lived in the Berkshires and was writing *Moby-Dick* he used to love to go and visit the Shaker community nearby. He was charmed by their communal life.

Wayne went around looking for advice and volunteers. A woman in the maintenance building told him to make Buckskin Bread instead of Indian Bread for the guests because the Buckskin Bread was easier. He told the woman that he had some frozen halibut in his refrigerator. Someone suggested that he put the Shakers in an empty cabin where the fisheries department used to be. He liked the idea. People gave him a few more five- and ten-dollar bills to help defray the cost of hosting the Shakers. He stopped at Arnie's house and Arnie said a few Shakers could stay in the VFW hall. He saw Denise having lunch at the Makah Maiden and mentioned the cabin that he was thinking of putting the Shakers in. She barked at Wayne. "You can't make them stay in there," she said. "They'll feel like dogs."

He went to see Marcy Parker, who had lost her reelection bid to the tribal council. She was watching *Days of Our Lives*. Even though she was no longer a council member and no longer on the international delegation to the International Whaling Commission, when she made a few calls and got Wayne the house next door to her for the evening, she looked like a still-practicing professional politician. The house was the one the German film crew always stayed in and so was empty. Marcy hung up the phone. "It's all set," she said.

Wayne seemed amazed at his own progress on the Shaker housing issue, but he still needed to find someone to cook on Saturday night. He finally drove over to Ralph Butterfield's house.

Ralph Butterfield was the person whom Wayne had appointed to be in charge of butchering the whale when it came in, and he had taken over the job with gusto, drawing up lists and questions regarding the carving up of the whale. (An example: Will the butchering crew need food-handling permits?) On most mornings, Ralph ran on the beach, he did so with the long, pole-like butchering knives. "He's into it," Wayne said.

Ralph's house is at the top of a hill overlooking Neah Bay, and as we drove up to see him, Wayne seemed uneasy and I couldn't figure out why. I thought it might have to do with the Shakers—he was saying "I'm not really into this spiritual stuff" over and over—but that didn't seem to be all. I knew he was upset by what Denise had just told him. "She says I've burned too many bridges. She says I won't be able to get anyone to cook. But I didn't burn any bridges. *Jeez!*"

We were talking about something he'd learned in anger management class—about the importance of noticing a person's body language—up to the very moment Wayne knocked on the door. A woman answered, and when she did, Wayne's body seemed to fold up: he was looking down, almost at the ground. He didn't introduce me.

"Ralph here?" Wayne asked.

"He's at work," the woman said.

Wayne told her that he was in charge of housing and feeding the Shakers, whose arrival was imminent.

The woman shook her head, folded her arms, and looked down at Wayne from the height of the doorway. "Well, I know they can't stay here 'cause Ralph hates anything to do with God." Her arms were still folded. She moved away from the door and motioned us in. She was tall, with long dark hair, a matter-of-fact demeanor.

"Yeah," Wayne said. He spoke quietly. His arms were still and at his side, uncharacteristically. And then as the woman stood there in the hallway, he got down on one knee. "Anyway," he said, "I got all this responsibility."

"Just you?" the woman asked.

"Yeah." He was looking up, his hands outstretched now. She was looking down. Her arms were still folded.

"That's too much for one person." She pointed Wayne toward the living room.

"I know," he said, getting up.

I was trying to read Wayne's body language because I still didn't know what was going on.

"And did you talk to the council?"

"They'll give me anything I need but I gotta get some volunteers to help with some cooking."

She offered us seats on the living room couch. I sat down. Wayne stood. Traditional Northwest coast art decorated the walls: masks, prints, carvings. I noticed a videotape of a whale being butchered in Alaska that Ralph had apparently been watching for butchering practice. The woman sat down on the couch and marked the page in the book she was reading: *Your Erroneous Zones.* "Escape negative thinking and take control of your life," the cover said. She lit a cigarette and called Ralph at his desk in the prison in Clallam Bay, where he worked. He wasn't there. She left a message.

"Well, I'm sure he'll help you. I mean, I can't say, but he loves to cook and all," she said.

Wayne thanked her and walked back out in the rain.

When we got in the car, Wayne fell like a lump into his seat. "That was my ex-wife," he said.

64 / A Bullet

It was on a Friday night that the Shakers came.

Wayne greeted them alone. Donnie would have greeted them too but he was at the tavern in Clallam Bay, helping Arnie set up a karaoke machine, thought to be the first-ever karaoke machine on the west end of the Olympic Peninsula. I drove over and watched Donnie figure out the complicated wiring, and as soon as he did, Arnie broke into his karaoke rendition of "It's Now or Never," the Elvis Presley version. Arnie sang it in the same strong, deep voice that he uses when he is singing songs that have been passed down through generations of Makah. As I was walking out of the bar, a guy was stumbling over toward Donnie and Arnie and the karaoke machine, shouting at them: "Remember how you did it! Don't forget how you set it all up! You gotta *remember!*" I stood in the door looking back at this guy, convinced he was making some kind of important whale hunt allusion.

Later, I gave Wayne's mom a ride over to where the Shakers were staying. She wanted to meet them. She had been involved with the Shakers years before, and I was glad she was coming because Wayne didn't seem to know what they were about. She seemed to be going as a kind of self-appointed liaison between the Shakers and Wayne.

When we got to the house, the Shakers were just finishing the take-out orders of fish and chips that Wayne had bought for them at the Makah Maiden. Wayne looked as dressed up as I had ever seen him; he was wearing jeans, a white button-down shirt, and the jacket that had been given to him by Al Ingling, the veterinarian and ballistics expert—across the back, it said FIFTY-CALIBER SHOOTERS ASSOCIATION. He was with three Shakers, a man and two women, one of whom, Jean Smith, had had a vision of the whale hunt. Jean Smith was heavyset and she was blind. We all sat down in a circle around a little table. Jean Smith was at one end of the room and Wayne ended up at the other, directly across from her. The man set up a candle on the table. He set out a cross that was made of two-foot-long two-by-fours. He closed the curtain so that we couldn't see the little bit of sunlight left in the ocean view out the dark window. Jean Smith began talking.

She started by saying, "Well, I had a hard life, a really hard life, I'll tell you that."

She went on about her life, though not in a way that I could follow. But then Wayne's mom began talking. She welcomed the Shakers and she explained that she once was part of a Shaker church. "I know the Shake," she said. "I used to clean houses in town with the Shake. But the boys, they don't know the Shake. They don't understand. I just want you to know that."

Jean Smith nodded. Wayne sat perfectly still and said nothing.

Wayne's mom went on in what sounded to me at first like a kind of rambling speech but which I then took to be a kind of testimony. She told a story about seeing Satan in a man's hand, and she told a long story about a man making a trip without a car from Canada to Neah Bay, where he was not able to cross the road, where the devil stopped him, right there in the middle of the road. It was an amazing story. I could see it happening. Maybe it was because the room was extremely warm, but when she was done, my heart was pounding.

Wayne's mom finished by describing a time when she was in a boat that went over in the rough sea. She remembered that she was underwater and she didn't know where the surface of the ocean was: she was trapped and scared. She remembered a presence—something that allowed her to stay calm, to stay quiet, so that then she somehow heard the direction, she found the rope, she figured out the way to swim and made it to the top. She remembered having patience and clarity, and there, in the empty living room, she thanked God. "I hope the whaling crew will have it," she said. "I hope they will have clarity."

Jean Smith and the other Shakers nodded, mumbled affirmations, and soon the male Shaker was standing and repeating, "Mercy, mercy, mercy," and shaking a rack of bells and raising his arms and then saying over and over, "Mercy come down on Neah Bay."

The male Shaker was shaking and singing what sounded to me like a Native Americanized version of an old Latin mass. He was shaking around the room. In a minute, he was shaking over Wayne, who was sitting perfectly still. The man shook and shook over Wayne, ringing the bells, singing. The man shook until he seemed to be exhausted, until he wept.

Then the other woman stood up and began chanting and singing and shaking the bells, which were so loud by now that they pierced my ears. She shook the bells all around Wayne. She shook the bells within inches of his head. She touched him and pressed his arms as if she were trying to press something out of him, until she too cried and moaned and seemed exhausted and spent. All the while, Wayne stared straight ahead and sat perfectly still.

Now, Jean Smith got up very slowly from her chair. She made her way slowly across the room and did the same thing to Wayne. When she was done, she shook him so hard that I thought he might fall off the chair. Wayne's face stayed blank. He looked as if he were a kid who was being lectured.

At the end, after three long hours of chanting and of praying and of weeping, when the intensity of the Shakers was beginning to dissipate in the room, when there were only a few lingering sobs and sniffles and moans but the bells were still ringing in my ears, Jean Smith looked at Wayne and said that she had cleansed him of the hatred and evil that had been in him, she had guided him through this land of the dead, through a hall of ghosts.

"In a way, you've taken a bullet for your crew," she said. "All the hatred, all the bad things that have been said to you—I took them away." She added, "You've opened the door."

Again, Wayne sat perfectly motionless.

Just before midnight, the Shake was over. The next day Wayne would meet the Shakers again and introduce them to the crew and the Shakers would announce that in their vision the crew successfully hunts a whale and they would bless the canoe ("We didn't let the women bless the canoe," Wayne explained later). The crew was glad to hear this but when the Shakers blessed the canoe and then them, when they rang their bells and prayed and shook until they sobbed, the crew looked at Wayne as if to say, "What did you get us into?"[5]

On that first night of the Shakers' visit to Neah Bay, as soon as the Shake was done, Wayne sprang up from his chair. He acted like he'd just gotten his hair cut. "Okay then, we'll see you in the morning," he said to the Shakers, all business. "Pick you up for breakfast."

He gave his mother the keys to the van he had borrowed to get over to the Shake, and he shot out of the house. Outside, he called Ralph Butterfield on his cell phone just to make certain Ralph would cook the following evening. And then, under the clearing black sky, with stars flickering behind the thinning veil of clouds, he got out a cigarette.

[5] Melville once took his friends Nathaniel Hawthorne and Evert Duyckincks to see a Shaker service and both of them hated it. Duyckincks said the preacher resembled "an escaped maniac." Hawthorne was upset about the way the women looked at him and that men slept together. He called the Shakers "a filthy set." Melville had a great time.

Wayne looked drained, tired. "You know, my grandfather taught me to stay away from that God stuff," he said. "He taught me to worship my ancestors."

He lit his cigarette and shook out the match. "Boy," he said, "the things I do for this job."

65 / A Leak

Wayne was ready to hunt a whale, and so was the crew, who had, most recently, paddled out around Tatoosh Island on a rough ocean day of swells and crashing waves and had survived, to their surprise. The gray whale migration was at its peak, and the number of protestors present seemed to be at a low point: neither Sea Shepherd nor In the Path of Giants was there. Some people were questioning whether the television news trucks would return: the attention of the mass media was on Serbia, where the United States had just begun a bombing campaign. Wayne noted the headlines. "Maybe this will help us," he said.

Wayne had already gathered together all the gear—the guns, the harpoons, the lines, the floats. Dan Greene was back in town after having been off fishing for several days; his boat was ready to go again as the support boat. The tribe called in the whale biologist from the National Marine Fisheries Service who would monitor the hunt and the biologist came to Neah Bay and waited. It seemed like everything was falling into place, even from a ceremonial point of view. Because difficulties had arisen over the past fall about what songs would be sung upon the taking of the whale, Arnie was composing an all-new whaling song. He was writing the music; the museum was helping him with the words.

Wayne still couldn't get a whaling permit from Denise, however. She was doing her job as executive director of the hunt; she was executing the rules, but to Wayne's exasperation, she insisted that everyone on the crew pass the drug tests and the certification tests, and some of the crew members hadn't even taken the tests. She even wanted Arnie to take the drug test, which made Wayne laugh, given that Arnie was Mr. Health Food, Mr. Herbal Tea. Then, on top of fighting Denise, Wayne was beginning to argue with

Theron again. Theron could scare away a crew—he'd done so before. The longer they waited, the more crew unity was in jeopardy.

Days went by. More crew members took more drug tests, brought their levels down. One day, Wayne was messing around on the computer at the fisheries office—he was trying to figure out the internet—and he found a Web site reporting that the hunt was imminent, and he worried that the protestors would be back in force any day. "We can't take any chances," he said. The next day reporters were calling him from Seattle and a TV satellite truck arrived in town, the first since the spring. "We got a leak in this town," he said. He was at the whaling commission's office when the reporters started calling him, asking him if it was true, if he were indeed about to go for a whale. Wayne talked to Keith Johnson. "Put it to sleep if you can," Wayne said. Wayne left the fisheries office through the back door.

66 / Anchored

More and more I left the shanty and pitched a tent in the woods on the shore of Lake Ozette, and sometimes, while sitting down before my camp stove and searching the sky for stars and planets, or even while lying in my sleeping bag and listening to the wind, I attempted to take a sort of abstract view of the hunt, and consider how the great enterprise was being cobbled together, the sometimes seemingly half-baked ark with which the Makah believed their culture might be saved. In doing so, in coldly pondering the logistical requirements of the whale hunt, in mulling over the roles of the government monitors that were involved and the possible variations in the gray whale migrations, and in listening to all the protestors insist so adamantly the whalers-in-training couldn't catch a whale, I often wondered myself if they could do it, or if they would even try, even *without* protestors around. It seemed so difficult, so complicated, not to mention dangerous. Sometimes, I wondered if the Makah whale hunt might remain an oral tradition forever. But one day, I took a trip out to an island and watched Wayne tie up the boat we were in and, after that, I didn't have any doubts: I was suddenly and almost inexplicably convinced that they would hunt a whale.

It was a warm and sunny spring day, April Fools' Day,[5] and we were on a little excursion to Waadah Island. Wayne was going out at low tide to dig clams. He was digging clams for the clams but also to help out a graduate student in anthropology who had been studying subsistence food patterns in the village and needed some photographs of the kinds of shellfish found in the area. She and Wayne had recently become friendly.

Wayne took a shovel and an empty wall-compound bucket and we rode the harbor boat out to the island. The island itself is small and covered with hemlock and alder. There is a foghorn on its backside, where you can see the long rocky promontory that juts out into the strait, a little Giant's Causeway. Personally, I had always wanted to get over to Waadah Island because some of the old people in town had told me that there was one goat living there, left over from a little herd that the Coast Guard had once kept on the island. They'd said that on some days, at sunset you could see him standing on the little bluff at the southwest end of the island, looking out at the town. Conversely, some of the young people said that this was absolutely not true, that the goats had all been hunted.

When we got to the island, Wayne tied us up to a rusty old ladder off a weathered pier, and devised the complicated anchoring system that so impressed me and seemed simple to him, a no-brainer. Here are the specifics:

Wayne sent me and the graduate student up the ladder and onto the pier. The tide was going out, and if he left the boat simply tied to the ladder then it would be sitting on the rocks in an hour. With that in mind, he tied a line to the anchor and left the anchor positioned precariously on the edge of the boat, poised to fall in. He held the line that was tied to the anchor in his hand and then he climbed the ladder part of the way and shoved the boat out into the water. When I saw Wayne pitch the unanchored boat off into the water, I thought, Great! There goes our way back! As the boat headed slowly away from the island, he watched it, holding on to the smaller rope as if he were about to execute some sleight of hand. He waited, and as the boat passed slowly over the rocks that would soon be

---

[5] Melville often wondered if life in general weren't some kind of an April Fools' joke; he wrote his wife's cousin, Henry Savage, as follows: "It is—or seems to be—a wise sort of thing, to realize that all that happens to a man in this life is only by way of a joke." Indeed, he set his last published work of fiction, *The Confidence-Man,* on a Mississippi riverboat on April Fools' Day. In the book, Melville notes that "the acutest sage [is] often at his wits' end to understand living character."

exposed by the tide, he pulled the rope attached to the anchor. The anchor fell off the boat and splashed and sunk, the boat now anchored off the current shore but within range of what in a few hours would be the new shore. A stroke of pure practicality.

When Wayne got to the top of the rusty ladder on the pier, he looked back at the boat, which seemed to be floating away but was in fact not floating away at all. That was when I no longer had any doubts that there would be a whale hunt.

After anchoring, we took a leisurely walk around to the back of the island. On the trail, I spotted an empty cigarette pack, freshly discarded. I pointed to it, and Wayne said, "Artifacts." On the opposite side of the island, I looked out on the blue water in the strait, and watched the blueness transform into mad whiteness as the water burst up through the stairlike rock formation. When we walked back, we were close enough to the old pier to see a Coast Guard patrol checking our boat—it appeared as though the Coast Guard thought it might be adrift at sea until, after an intensive investigation of Wayne's anchoring system, they figured out that it was indeed anchored. As the tide went down, we dug for clams for a while; the clams spat at us in the late afternoon sun from their beds in the sand between the rocks, in little auditoriums where the rock-like goose and acorn barnacles were seated. We'd filled the bucket with littleneck clams and oysters and mussels and a few sea urchins. Wayne explained to the anthropologist that people in town would make chowder and fritters from the clams.

When we had as many clams and mussels as we could carry, we walked back to the boat and were surprised to see some of the crew in the canoe just off the pier. They had been out paddling when they spotted the harbor boat that Wayne had taken and decided to try and sneak the boat away, to trick Wayne. When Wayne saw what they were up to, he shouted down from the hill. "You're fired!" he said. They mentioned that they had just passed a gray whale on its way out of the bay.

The other thing that I saw that afternoon was the hoofprint of a goat. The print was fresh and I borrowed the anthropologist's camera and took a picture of it.

67 / Red-Faced

The presence of whales and the lack of large numbers of protestors pleased Wayne and the crew, and there was one last break before the hunt, a pause, in which Wayne was nearly able to relax. It was Easter week—Holy Thursday, to be precise—Wayne and Donnie and Arnie were visiting with a relative, a man named Martin, a social worker from the Seattle area, who was a member of the Blackfoot tribe. I nearly relaxed too. For a second, I almost felt like one of the guys.

Martin is about five foot eleven, and solidly built, with hair cropped short enough to reveal a scar on the side of his head. Arnie had described Martin to me previously as being a very spiritual man, and I could see right away why he would think that. Martin was soft-spoken and very calm and, as you talked to him, he listened intently. Martin's wife, who was Arnie's cousin, was there too, as was Martin's teenage daughter. Arnie's wife was back in the house watching TV. Arnie told me that Martin's other daughter is married to the actor and singer Litefoot, who played the Indian in the film version of *The Indian in the Cupboard.* We were all sitting on Arnie's back porch. Donnie was showing me how to shuck the clams that Arnie had bought from a guy who drove by with buckets full of clams in the back of his truck—he'd dug them up by the Coast Guard station. Arnie was playing music on the stereo in his pickup truck: A CD entitled *Greatest Songs,* by Redbone, a Native American recording artist. Arnie was getting the sweat lodge ready; big rocks were heating up in a fire. Donnie was trying to get me to drink a royal honey and ginseng energy supplement. He said it would give me a lot of energy. I said I didn't need any energy, but I finally just took it, to get him to leave me alone. Donnie took some strawberry-flavored ginseng. Wayne sat in a folding chair on the back porch and watched me and Donnie shuck the clams as he had a smoke. Everyone was very relaxed.

While I waited anxiously for the ginseng to take effect, Donnie showed me the part of the clam to eat raw, which I was also hesitant about but then also relented about. After a while enough clams had been shucked to make clam and octopus fritters—a relative had brought by an octopus earlier in the day. So while the fritters were being made, Wayne and Arnie got Arnie's sweat lodge going.

Wayne assured me that it was okay that we sweated together.

"This is not an official sweat for the hunt or anything," Wayne said.

In fact, Martin's daughter also sweated with us. Martin told her it was okay. In a kind of subtle unspoken way, Martin seemed to be in charge of this particular sweat. At first, I thought he was explaining particulars about the sweat to me, and then I wasn't so certain. Wayne and Arnie and Donnie were also paying close attention. We stripped down to shorts and T-shirts and Martin reiterated that it was a very casual sweat, nothing formal. "Normally we would bless the lodge before entering, and bless the rocks, but we're not going to do that today," he said. He told us to enter the lodge clockwise, and he said that if we were to leave the lodge, we would leave by walking out in a clockwise direction. We all went in and sat down in the dark. Donnie brought in the hot rocks. One hit the carpet. For a minute, the air smelled of burnt indoor-outdoor polyester fibers.

As the heat came up and the air cleared, Martin took water and tossed it carefully on the rocks in four directions—east, west, north, south. The steam thickened the hot air; it stung as I inhaled. He threw sweet grass and cedar on the rocks. He spoke of the significance of these things. Then he sang a song, a prayer. He instructed each person to say something, to give thanks, to pray. Outside, Redbone was still singing his greatest hits through Arnie's car stereo; he sang, "We Were All Wounded at Wounded Knee," to a rock beat. Inside, it was dark and quiet, confessional-like. Donnie prayed for the hunt, as did Arnie, and I prayed that I could maybe have some idea of what was going on. Martin thanked Arnie for the sweat lodge and he went on to wish the whalers luck. He said some other things, all of which resounded in the hot darkness, lingered like the smell of cedar. Wayne was quiet, his head was down; he was trying to breathe. Wayne said, "I'm just praying for the same thing that I keep praying for, which is that we have a hunt and we get a whale and everybody comes back safe. That's all I'm gonna say."

We all got out of the lodge and jumped into a giant plastic tank, the kind they use to hold iced fish at the fish docks; Arnie had filled it with water from his garden hose. We sweated three more times and sang some more as Martin coaxed us. He talked about how tribes all over the country had traditional sweat lodge ceremonies that were different from place to place but similar: it was a gentle nondenominational sermon that was delicately delivered. And then the ceremonial portion of the sweat was over and Martin said that we could leave at any time. He said, again, we should leave clockwise.

Arnie got out after a little while, walking out clockwise, and then Wayne walked out. Wayne walked out counterclockwise, but I don't think he knew what he was doing—he looked so preoccupied.

I stayed in the sweat lodge for a while. Donnie was relaxing in the hot air, talking quietly with Martin's daughter. But I was having some kind of trouble. My head was starting to spin. It felt as if it were trying to get out of my skull. Donnie noticed and asked me if I was okay.

It was at this point in the sweat lodge that I had a vision. I had a vision of me being carried out of the sweat lodge on a stretcher.

I got out and Donnie looked at my face and said it was red. We decided it was the energy supplement. Later on, when we went in and ate delicious clam and octopus fritters on white sandwich bread, Donnie kept looking at me and saying, "You should see your face. Your face is so red."

68 / Whales Are Everywhere

The whales? you may now be asking. What about the whales? After all this winter, after having disappeared last fall, where were the whales? To answer this and other questions, marine mammal biologists and scientists from all around the Northwest and Canada and Mexico gathered in Seattle for a conference on the gray whale.

At the conference, it was announced that the population of the gray whale was still increasing. The total number of gray whales was estimated to be 26,600, up from 23,100 observed over the winter of 1993, up from 22,200 observed over the winter of 1995, up from near extinction several decades earlier. The National Marine Mammal Laboratory also reported that, during the previous fall, during the time that the Makah whalers and the press and protestors were in Neah Bay waiting and watching for whales, the gray whales swam farther offshore and swam faster at night, for reasons that were not entirely clear. It was further determined at the conference that the whales had appeared off the Washington coast about a month later than they had during previous winters. "We saw them start to migrate in the first part of December and then didn't see them," a gray whale migration expert was reported to say. "What happened is that the animals seemed to make up for lost time, and there were groups farther offshore than usual."

A report was released a short while later saying that underwater noise was threatening the ability of whales (and other marine mammals) to find mates or food and to escape predators. The Natural Resources Defense Council said that supertankers and military sonar equipment made the gray whales migration like being "in the middle of an acoustics traffic jam."

Also a gray whale floated up dead on the beach near Port Ludlow, and residents of the town asked that it be disposed of. The options included towing it out to sea and sinking it or bringing it to the local dump.

Around the same time, another gray whale floated up dead in Puget Sound just north of Seattle in Kingston, and the man who came upon it claimed that he had had a spiritual experience with a whale in the same spot as a boy.

For a short while during the spring, it seemed as if gray whales were dying everywhere. Off the coast of Baja, fifty-six gray whales died mysteriously, and scientists weren't sure why. They wondered if it had to do with the salt mining plants. One theory speculated that the whales might have been killed by the phosphorescent dyes that drug smugglers used to mark the water off the coast for drug drops. As to why the gray whales were dying around Puget Sound, scientists speculated variously that there was not enough food for the gray whales; that water temperatures had affected their migration or their food supply along the migration route; that the Bering Sea, as a result of overfishing and changing food supplies, had offered less food for the whales over the past summer.

Meanwhile, the Coast Guard station at Neah Bay was reporting frequent gray whale sightings. "The whales are here," the Coast Guard commander announced to one newspaper. "They're everywhere."

69 / Alone

In the beginning of May, Wayne just barely survived a coup attempt during which factions of the whaling commission tried to get him off the hunt.

In a meeting of the whaling commission, on a spring evening just days before Wayne planned to practice whale hunting with all the participants—the crew, the support boats, the gunners, and the harpooners—a powerful faction of the commission tried to get Theron Parker promoted to captain. A commissioner argued that the captain should be in the canoe, as opposed to Wayne, who would merely be on a support boat. In a long speech, he argued such an arrangement was more traditional. People present at the meeting noted that in the past, this kind of situation would have made Wayne fly off the handle. But on this occasion Wayne stood silently, even though he was furious inside, seething, even—somehow, he managed to appear calm, to hold his tongue.[*]

And in the end, another commissioner stood up for Wayne, said that Wayne had been working on this whale hunt for too long, said that it was too late to change.

Later a commissioner said of Theron, "He doesn't realize that the crew wins, not just one person."

The same commissioner told me that he had been impressed with Wayne. This was not something I was used to hearing people in Neah Bay say.

"Wayne was way out there on Front Street, all alone," the commission member said. "But he did a very good job of controlling himself."

---

[*] As his career wound down, after *Pierre* and *The Confidence-Man,* Melville became a quieter kind of writer, concentrating on poems, many of them self-published. As a poet, Melville wrote a book-length poem entitled *Clarel: A Poem and Pilgrimage in the Holy Land* in 1876. It is a debate between faith and doubt, in which neither side really wins. Melville's poetry received mixed reviews, but the reviews didn't matter as much to him anymore because most of his poems were privately printed. His family wondered if he had gone slightly insane. ("Pray do not mention to *any one* that Herman has taken to writing poetry—you know how such things spread," Melville's wife, Lizzie, wrote to her mother.) He was working at the Customs House, on a pier in New York City. "The customhouse was notoriously corrupt, and he was subject to political pressures that occasionally threatened his position. It was a grim situation at best, and Melville himself left no comment on it," one biographer wrote. These years have been called Melville's Silent Period.

70 / Wayne Meets Theron

On Mother's Day, with the pressure building for Wayne to hunt, he found himself seated in a booth at the Makah Maiden with Arnie, having a cup of black coffee, staring idly out at a protest boat. He was fresh from an anger management class, and he announced that he ought to buy his mother a new reclining chair for the living room. "The one she has now is kind of beat up," he said. He was also thinking about Theron Parker; he was thinking that the hunt was going to fall apart. Wayne was thinking that he was going to have to fire Theron pretty soon, if Theron wouldn't listen to him in this the final stage, and firing Theron was not something he wanted to do.

Theron was in the next booth, which made Wayne antsy. At that moment, Wayne and Theron were a study in contrasts: Theron, in the corner of his booth, his arms spread out, his flannel shirt open, wearing a black bandanna around his head, leaning back and laughing loudly; Wayne, hunched over his coffee, his Raiders jacket zipped up as if he were outside and cold, his face tied up with nerves, with sleeplessness and cup after cup of coffee. Arnie was drinking herbal tea and extolling a cabbage celery drink he had recently sampled.

Suddenly, Wayne stood up. He came out of his booth and looked straight at Theron.

"Theron," Wayne said, "could I talk to you for a minute, in the other room? In private."

Theron turned his head slowly, in mock surprise. He looked at Wayne and smiled calmly. "Not right now, Wayne," he said. "It's not a good time." He returned to his conversation with his friends. He laughed at something someone said.

Wayne stood perfectly still, looking at Theron. Eventually, he turned around and sat down without a word.

Later, outside the restaurant, Wayne would comment on Theron in little bursts. "If I fire him, I'll have an enemy for life," Wayne would say. "But he's making me do it. . . . He's not a happy camper. . . . Before he came along, everybody was a happy camper. . . . He can't talk like that. It's bad for morale. . . ." But there in the restaurant, Wayne just sat back down and looked at Arnie, who was silently telling Wayne to let it go—not to fire off at Theron in a rage—and then Wayne looked away, out the window.

For a while, neither he nor Arnie said anything. Finally, Arnie said, "Ass."

Up to that time, I had never heard Arnie say a bad word about anyone.

71 / Stuck

It was the day before the hunt, although no one knew it at the time—not even the crew, not even Wayne, who was pacing on the docks at the marina, worrying, sorting everything out in his head one final time.

Wayne was in the new support boat, a smaller, yellow version of Dan Greene's fishing boat that was as fast as any Zodiac, and I was with him. Wayne was worried about the engine in the new support boat. The engine had been fine on an excursion the previous day, a trip (with me along) out into a foreboding day of wind and hail and dark-tempered ocean: swells lifted the boat up two stories, from which Wayne raced back down into the steel green-blue, only to be raised up again. But today the engine seemed reluctant from time to time. Wayne was taking the boat out in pursuit of Dan Greene and Arnie in Dan Greene's boat, the always reliable big red powerboat that was today on its way out to search for the numerous gray whales said to be migrating in the vicinity. The day was clear and beautiful, but for Wayne it was as if he were still in the middle of the previous day's storm: winds were howling all around him. He was feeling pressure: pressure from Theron, pressure from the whaling commission, pressure from the tribal council to finally catch a whale. Wayne had not eaten since the day before. This morning, he was up at four-thirty, sitting on the couch, sitting in his mom's kitchen, thinking and worrying.

The support boat's engine sputtered then stopped then started up as Wayne moved slowly out of the marina. Then the engine coughed again, and Wayne stood in his orange Mustang suit, shut down the engine, and used a life preserver to jam the battery in place. He fiddled with the electrical system, mumbling about the probability of sabotage. For a minute, the engine seemed to recover. He pulled out of the marina and protest boats swarmed him immediately—like birds fluttering over the exposed back of a whale. Ahead he saw Dan Greene and Arnie. They raced up to him and then shut down their engine, which had overheated. Now both boats were smack in the middle of a small constellation of whale watching boats, Zodiacs. As if on cue, Dan pulled out two fishing rods, handed one to Arnie, dropped his lure, waited for a rockfish to bite. Dan smiled his sarcastic smile, then shouted calmly over to Wayne and motioned toward the protestors, who were still circling and watching.

"Do we know where they go drinking?" he said. He flashed a grin.

"The Breakwater," Wayne shouted back.

"Why don't we go down to the Breakwater tonight?" Dan said. He smiled again.

"No," said Wayne, shaking his head. Wayne was taking Dan too seriously; Wayne didn't get that Dan was kidding. "We don't do that anymore," Wayne said. "We're not gonna do that."

Wayne waved to Dan and Arnie and headed out of the harbor.

He went past the protestors and into the strait, pressing the throttle forward as more protestors scrambled into their boats and followed him down the coast. It was a trip through blues and greens and water so calm and beautiful that it seemed meaningful to me: the protean canvas for a single story, an invisible epic.

When the protestors caught up to him, Wayne stopped the boat. He stood up, unzipped the front of his Mustang suit, and reached toward his shirt pocket to pull out his cigarettes. So tense were Makah-protestor relations that I was concerned the protestors might take Wayne's motion as a reach for a gun. When I told this to Wayne, he misconstrued me. "Come on, I wasn't that bad," he said.

Wayne cruised down the strait and passed Tatoosh Island: today the Gut was almost calm beneath the gaze of springtime tourists at the end of the Cape Flattery Trail. The tourists looked down on Wayne and waved—at another anonymous fisherman; the rough waters allowed him through. He passed the Fuca Pillar, where the stories tell of a boy who climbed too high and got stuck and never got down, whose cries can still be heard in the wind of the cape. In a few minutes, Wayne turned hard to port and was in Skagway, the little cove.

The water was blue and smooth—nearly tropical—and everything seemed right and ready, and then Wayne's engine died.

The boat drifted. The protestors swooped down on us and circled the boat as if it were carrion. Wayne leaned over the back to check the propeller. He leaned and leaned and leaned some more so that his feet were off the deck and his hands were underwater and suddenly his feet were in the air and all the protestors could see were the soles of his boots, announcing in unison their brand name, which was also the name of the great Northwest river, the Great River of the West: *Columbia!*

Upside down, Wayne worked in the water for a while—muttering, occassionally swearing—and finally got back into the boat and lit another cigarette. He was quiet as the water lapped patiently at the boat, as the waves rolled into the coast a few hundred yards away and the protestors watched.

72 / Wayne

Wayne, the whaler, his face like the bark of a tree weathered in the hard winter winds that blow off the cape, his eyes crackling with bloodshot lines like the lines of spring morning frost on the windshield of the whaling commission van that lay nearly dead in his driveway. His body was hunched over in sleepless exhaustion, with the edginess that comes from too much coffee and made him ready to act, to strike, like the wild or perhaps hatchery-bred steelhead that lay in the pools of the Waatch.

On the boat, Wayne held his arms open, his elbows on his knees, as if pleading for consolation, as if wondering if he would find some unseen backup here in this almost final moment of truth. He jerked his head back and forth—he watched the protestors, eyed the engine, scanned the water for any sign of a whale or of Dan Greene and Arnie—so that his head was like the wary head of a raven ready to pounce on dropped groceries in front of Washburn's Market or fly off in fright, depending on the circumstance.

And sitting there dead in the water, sitting there at the edge of the rocks that were his home but were at this moment so far away, waiting in the cove where his fishing fleet had for decades tied up in the case of a storm, he spoke aloud to no one in particular. He said a few words that might even have been a soliloquy if he were the type of person predisposed to deliver a soliloquy or a speech of any kind, which he was not. He asked a question: "What else can go wrong?"

He drifted. He drifted some more. He finished his cigarette and went back to work on the engine until, finally, it was running. He turned the boat around. He cruised in slowly, the protestors following, the protestors attached to him now like barnacles to a whale.

He spoke again after another long measure of silence. "It's almost too much," he said, as his boat was entering the marina, as the protest boats were finally peeling away. "It's almost too much for one person," he said.

Silence again, followed by a sputtering resolution.

"I'm not gonna quit," he said. "They want me to quit. I'm not gonna."

73 / The Peak

The next morning, I drove up into the hills. I drove to Waatch Peak, a lookout. I drove my car slowly up the winding logging roads so that I wouldn't get a flat tire. I drove through a marsh, past little creeks, through recently logged areas and areas that hadn't been logged for a while or maybe never. Then, when I got to the clearing at the top, I took a camp chair out of the trunk of my car, grabbed my binoculars, and sometimes even sat on the roof of my car. Up there, on the peak, I felt like a character from a romantic German novel, hoping I might be enlightened, hoping to feel it all, to take notes and compare.[♭]

[♭] In his 1929 essay on Herman Melville, Lewis Mumford wrote two things that I am compelled to mention here in this final moment before the Makah hunt, in the time when the story of the Makah hunt was becoming past tense. The first is this long comparison of *Moby-Dick* to a symphony, which, for me, nicely encapsulates the tremendous emotional rise I was getting out of Melville's all-encompassing epic in these spring days: "*Moby-Dick* is a symphony; every resource of language and thought, fantasy description, philosophy, natural history, drama, broken rhythms, blank verse, imagery, symbol, is utilized to sustain and expand the great theme. . . . [N]ot a stroke is introduced that does not have meaning for the myth as a whole . . . Melville's instrumentation is unsurpassed in the writing of the last century: one must go to Beethoven or a Wagner for an exhibition of similar powers: one will not find it among works of literature." The other thing that Mumford said that I found interesting is this: "Melville sets out to teach us nothing: but at every step we follow eagerly and find ourselves making notes, instituting comparisons, seeing the world in fresh perspective." I knew this to be true. I had been taking notes on *Moby-Dick* for months and, though I already knew how the book ended, having read commentaries and biographies, having swum in as much *Moby-Dick*–related material as I could, short of seeing the movie, I'd saved the last chapters to read at the time when the Makah caught the whale (if they did), for the moment that I am now about to describe. And, as I sat up on the peak, I had the book in the car, so that I was thinking not only

The Olympic Mountains were behind me, still covered with a record snowpack on account of all the winter's rain. I could see off toward Vancouver Island, its clear-cuts still white. I could see the steepness of the peaks—the Waatch, the Sooes, the Makah—descend down in patches of second-growth green to the cream-colored lip of the beaches, to the points of sculpture-like rocks that marked the end of one crescent-shaped bay and the beginning of another. From the peak, I could see the Sooes River as it made one last blackened green turn before it spilled out into the Pacific and became ocean. From the peak, I could see the fishing boats and the protest boats. I could see the reporters from newspapers and TV. I could see the news helicopter as it came buzzing all of a sudden over the hill behind me, as it came shooting out of the populated region of America to the east (it scared the hell out of me). I could see the gut-red insides of the black whaling canoe. I could see the ocean. I could see the spouts of whales.

Here I sat, like the sailor up on the masthead, like a lame duck conductor looking over a uncontrollable symphony orchestra that consisted of a carved cedar canoe, a harpoon, a gun, Zodiacs, a black converted Coast Guard cutter blaring killer whale sounds, TV cameras being splashed with seawater, dozens of notepads, and Wayne Johnson—a symphony of discordant notes. Here I sat, sometimes calling up Wayne's mom on my cell phone to see if any whale hunt news had come on the television—she was watching the Seattle Sonics in the NBA playoffs and trying not to worry about her son, about "the boys."

Here I sat and saw the story that millions of other Americans in the Great Pacific Northwest watched live on TV in the comfort of their own homes. Here, overlooking the land of the People of the Cape, with the waters of their history being churned in my pretty good sight by the boats of protestors and the boats of media representatives and, of course, their own boats, I watched the story which would be told so many different ways by all the different people who would be involved or who would observe or would be touched in one way or another: Makah, Nuuchah-nulth, Native Americans, animal rights activists, conservationists, racist jerks, or white guys who were born far away, in New York City, such as myself. And from where I stood, the story went like this:

---

about the obvious crash of whale hunt events unfolding in the view beneath me but also about Melville and his book and his life and what the world might have meant to him, to the genius who was so private, so inward. I couldn't help but compare whale hunts. In fact, as impossible as it might seem, I sometimes felt as if I was seeing the art of *Moby-Dick* in life.

74 / A Hunt—Day One

And so the hunt began, even though it wasn't supposed to have begun, even though the crew had just been getting together to practice, to get out on the water with all of the equipment—the Makah whalers' first whale hunt in a generation was just supposed to be a dry run.

It was a warm, blue-water day; the sky was like a long, full chord that was in the perfectly tuned key of spring. The crew paddled the *Humming-bird* off the fir-trimmed beaches, past Shi-Shi, down past Ozette. They were just off Wedding Rock, where there are ancient petroglyphs of hunted whales, where there is archaeological evidence of centuries of whale hunting, where Wayne had lost his *Today* show cap. The idea was to merely practice approaching whales, to see what it was like to come up on them. Numerous whales were in the area for such an endeavor—gray whales, feeding, straining the mud for edible life on the Pacific's floor.

Protestors were there too. The Zodiac and speedboats of the Sea Defense Alliance were in vicious pursuit of the first-time whalers, and they seemed to sense the inevitability of the Makah hunt. They seemed furious in the tantalizing vicinity of their avowed enemy, like a sheepdog that senses a wolf descending on its herd. When the crew approached the gray whales, the protestors in turn approached the crew. The water exploded in a frenzy of modern whale hunt activity: paddlers paddled, the protestors' engine props foamed the water, the weight and bulk of the gray whale's fluke swirled the sun-sparkled ocean as the whale rose for air and then descended in its noble ambivalence. In the frenzy, as the protestors spun around the canoe and the support boat, the protestors threw things at the *Hummingbird*. They fired fire extinguishers, launched angry, shouted-out threats.

The crew needed help. In the back of the canoe, Andy put up the flags that Wayne had scrounged up for just such an occasion—the flags that said to the world (or at least to the U.S. Coast Guard) that the Makah Nation was in the midst of a traditional ceremonial whale hunt, an act of what the tribal attorneys had termed cultural subsistence. Via cell phone, the crew immediately had a permit. The Coast Guard was now obliged to protect them. The whale hunt had officially begun.

Arnie Hunter—the quiet whale commissioner, the supporter of

Wayne, the Queequeg-like prince—was on Dan Greene's support boat.[5] There was Donnie Swan, steadfast, able, still good-natured in the face of the protestors' squall, still calm, ready, like Stubb, with additional harpoons.[55] There was Keith Johnson, who would be on the island of Grenada in a few days for the annual meeting of the International Whaling Commission, where he would watch as Al Ingling presented a paper on the Makah's humane-kill strategy: Keith Johnson, whom I could never really figure out, to whom I could draw no comparisons.

Wayne was in town when the hunt accidentally began, back on the dock in Neah Bay when the whalers finally took off—a little like the way Starbuck was left on deck of the *Pequod* when the crew went off to hunt the whale, or so it seemed to me.[555] Wayne was taking care of last-minute details while the crew went out for practice. He'd only just secured Theron's cooperation—Denise and some of the commissioners had talked to Theron the day before. When Wayne heard on the radio that the hunt had begun, he cursed, and then ran down to the docks as fast as he could

---

[5] A comparison: If *Moby-Dick* were a buddy movie then Ishmael and Queequeg would be the buddies. Ishmael would be the fast-talking short guy and Queequeg, the strong, secretly funny silent type. It's a share-and-share-alike relationship; they sleep in the same bed. But Queequeg helps out Ishmael even more than he (though probably not Melville) knows, and that's the kind of relationship I think Wayne and Arnie had during the whale hunt; I thought Wayne maybe looked to Arnie for support sometimes.

[55] In *Moby-Dick*, the second mate is called Stubb, and although he is only fictional, he nevertheless reminded me, at this point, in a very tangible way of Donnie, if that seems possible. Ishmael, the narrator, describes Stubb thusly: "A happy-go-lucky; neither craven nor valiant; taking perils as they came with an indifferent air; and while engaged in the most imminent crisis of the chase, toiling away, calm and collected as a journeyman joiner engaged for the year. Good-humored, easy, and careless, he presided over the whale-boat as if the mostly deadly encounter were but a dinner, and his crew all invited guests."

[555] In *Moby-Dick*, Starbuck is the first mate, the crew member who seems to stand in Ahab's monomaniacal way, who is forced, by virtue of his position as first mate, to attempt to manage Ahab's anger. In the third and final day of the fictional whale hunt that is described in *Moby-Dick*, Starbuck pleads with Ahab to cease his pursuit of the white sperm whale. "'Oh! Ahab,' cried Starbuck, 'not too late is it, even now, the third day, to desist. See! Moby-Dick seeks thee not; it is thou, thou, that madly seekest him!'" By this point in my reading of *Moby-Dick*, and by this point in my observance of the Makah whale hunt, I was beginning to think of Starbuck when I thought of Wayne, and vice versa. "Looking in his eyes," Melville writes, "you seem to see there the yet lingering images of those thousand-fold perils he had calmly confronted through life." I also thought of Wayne when I read these lines: "'I will have no man in my boat,' said Starbuck, 'who is not afraid of the whale.' By this he seemed to mean, not only that the most reliable and useful courage was that which arises from the fair estimation of the encountered peril, but that an utterly fearless man is a far more dangerous comrade than a coward. . . . For, thought Starbuck, I am here in this critical ocean to kill whales for my living, and not to be killed for them by theirs." Wayne seemed especially Starbuckian in real-time comparison to Theron.

get there; he jumped into the little yellow support boat and raced out to the scene of the hunt.

There was method in the over-sea madness. Arnie and Dan shouted encouragement from the support boat, signaled to the canoe when they saw a whale rise to the surface to breathe. In the canoe, Darrell Markishtum, sitting on the wooden slats that made do for seats in the wide curve of painted-red cedar, was paddling with vigor when a whale was in sight, with less vigor when a whale had disappeared. Andy Noel held his paddle—the canoe's man-held keel—hard on the right, hard on the left, depending on the whale. And in the bird-beak–like extension of wood that is the bow of the *Hummingbird,* as the big canoe cut through the water like a knife, sat Theron Parker, who had come around and finally decided once and for all to deal with Wayne, at least for the time being.

Theron paddled with the paddle that he had power-sawed from lumber and then carved and painted. He sat alongside a harpoon that was a thick dowel attached to a machine-shop-made tip that the tribe-appointed veterinarian had prescribed. The crew was short one man—it was only supposed to be a practice hunt, after all—but Theron seemed to be making up for it. He dug at the water with his trademark ferocity, paddling so hard that the *Hummingbird* made a wake, which, viewed from above, was a billowy and bottomless triangle that spread out across the bay, which was zipped through by the protest boats.

The *Hummingbird* was, of course, not an actual traditional whaling canoe. The traditional whaling canoe that was being carved in the longhouse across from the museum still wasn't finished. But now in Neah Bay, on the first day of the whale hunt, the *Hummingbird* was the de facto traditional whaling canoe. It was going to do. Indeed, it might have been mistaken for just another traditional canoe of the Northwest coast's people on a noncontroversial trip to another village, to a paddling event, only now there was a big silver boat circling it and harassing it, only now there were news helicopters flying overhead and a National Marine Fisheries Service biologist watching to see if the Makah hunted the whale in the manner that the IWC and NMFS and the tribe had agreed they would.

And incredibly, after all the posturing, all the guarantees and promises, the scores of press conferences, after they had offered money to the towns-people of Neah Bay regarding information leading to word of the execution of the hunt, Sea Shepherd, the leader of the protest, was not around. Captain Paul Watson, on board the *Sirenian,* set sail in the Strait of Juan de

Fuca for Neah Bay as soon as he got word. Also incredibly, the In the Path of Giants team was not there either. Steph Dutton and Heidi Tiura and their boat, *Sea Dog*, were in Monterey, California, where they had begun to work with a whale watching company that ran cruises out of the bay. Of course, when they heard the news—the Internet and television networks all over reported that the whale hunt had begun—the In the Path of Giants team was on its Web page supporting the protests, pleading for people to send money to the protestors who were still in Neah Bay. On the first day of the hunt, all defense of the whale was left to the Sea Defense Alliance (Sedna), the sentries who had patrolled Neah Bay over the spring. It was as if Ahab had left the ship to the crew and gone belowdecks to read and write letters, to take a nap at a really pivotal moment. It was implausible, impossible-seeming, even though it was, in fact, happening. At least that's how I saw it.

For their part, the whales were in the water, maybe cognizant of what was going on above them, maybe not—it depended on whom you talked to, what you had read, and also what you believed. The whales surfaced, blew watery air from their mucous-filled blowholes, inhaled, dived to the floor of the ocean, and strained the muck for food.

Very soon, the first modern traditional whale hunt began to resemble a whitewater dance in an amphitheater of sea cliffs. Each time a whale surfaced, the Makah canoe paddled toward it. The protest boats countered by circling the Makah, by racing toward the gray whale itself, to scare it away. Sometimes this seemed to work, though then other whales would surface. Whales were still everywhere off the coast of Cape Flattery: the great buffalo herd of a migration was in full swing on the Baja-to-Alaska underwater coastal highway. The cape was in the midst of the giant-marine-mammal rush hour.

It was up close that the event was most dramatic, in the shouts and taunts, especially as sung on the protest boats, on which people palpably dreaded the death of a cetacean, feared for the life of the whales. The men and women protesting the hunt—and their number was growing by the hour—sprayed fire extinguishers at the tribal members, at one point firing off flare guns. They shouted comments regarding the Makah men's sexual prowess—anything to intimidate the crew, who were, for the most part, in their twenties and not accustomed to whale hunts, much less being taunted and threatened by anti–whale hunt activists while in a canoe and hunting whales.

In the writhing, cold water a few feet above the careening silvery gray shadows, a protestor shouted toward the crew: "Go home!"

Donnie shouted back: "We *are* home!"

Arnie was on the support boat with more harpoons and floats and the whaling rifle, the large elephant gun. Arnie watched one of the protestors racing by the edge of Dan Greene's boat. The protestors shouted menacingly: "We've got a gun!"

Arnie smiled and shouted back: "We've got a bigger one!"

At one point, the Makah reported to the Coast Guard that they had been threatened with guns, that they were being harassed. The Coast Guard, the blue-capped men in their orange flotation suits, boarded the main Sedna vessel, the *Bulletproof.* They found no guns.

The action continued. There were more threats, more whale sightings, more paddling, until finally, to the absolute horror of the activists, to the simultaneous amazement of the paddlers, Theron Parker rose in the bow of the canoe with the harpoon. A gray whale was before him. It was in range of his steel-tipped wooden dowel. The knuckled-back whale swelled out of the water and then began to roll down toward the blueness, at which point Theron brought back his arm and launched the harpoon. The steel shaft dived into the water. The whale rolled. The harpoon missed.

Soon, TV helicopters and seaplanes arrived and the modern yet ancient ceremonial whale hunt was being covered live on TV in Seattle. Soon, the Makah headed north to the center of their legally mandated hunting zone, to where the Coast Guard felt they could better protect the little group that was, in the eyes of the U.S. government, exercising the rights of their treaty. Soon, Wayne was on the scene. He had more crew members with him, more bodies for the canoe, reinforcements. Soon, Theron stood again and missed again. Soon, two members of Sedna had been taken out of their Zodiac and brought to shore, where they were detained by law enforcement officials. Later, they posted bail in Port Angeles, and the judge told them not to travel west of the Elwah River, a now-dammed but once great salmon run that flows out of the Olympic Mountains and into the strait whose very waters were perhaps washing past whales, past protestors, past the Makah canoe.

Finally, in the still-sunny afternoon, the hunt was over for the day. In the warm spring evening, with the red sunset behind the peaks on Cape Flattery, Neah Bay's population was expanding again. It was fishing season and sport fishermen were coming into town to troll for the salmon, both wild and hatchery, to fish for halibut where once only the Makah fished. But the hotel rooms were all booked too: reporters came back, in cars and planes and satellite trucks. Neah Bay was again motel-room-booked, restaurant-stuffed, in total first-time whale hunt mode. On a noneconomic note, on a note that did not come under the heading of logistics or court-order-related details, there were eight eagles circling over the west end of town, soaring, in full view.

Critiques rolled in with the tide. In the Path of Giants posted a headline on its Web site: MAKAH TRIED & LEARNED IT ISN'T AS EASY AS THEY THOUGHT.

One of the reporters who stood on the edge of Neah Bay with a bright white light in her face looked into the eye of the camera and seemed energized with the whaling and the protesting and the return of general commotion to the sleepy village. "For the first time in seven decades," she said, "the Makah made an attempt at harpooning a gray whale but missed."

The reporter interviewed Keith Johnson. He looked at her and at the camera. He was elated but serious. "We didn't strike the whale," he said. "It was over the top of the tail. He rolled just about that time. But we're learning."

The crew paddled to Shi-Shi beach, where they made camp for the night, and lost one person—one guy just couldn't stick around. The support crew rode the boats around the cape and landed back in town. Wayne walked in off the docks. A reporter offered Wayne a microphone.

"There were quite a few whales out there," he said. He seemed tired, but also calm, washed through with exhilaration. "We got up on 'em a few times and, well, when the time's right, we'll get one," he said.

Wayne spoke with the crew and talked to council members and whaling commission members. He talked to Arnie and Donnie. He got home late, and when he did, the phone was ringing. It was Ralph Marschalleck, the director of the German film crew. Ralph wanted to know if the hunt could wait. The film crew would be arriving from Germany very soon.

75 / A Hunt—Day Two

The next day dawned clear, and the crew went out again, but the sky quickly clouded over, turned a woolen gray. The sea went dark off the cliffs. The ocean billowed like a sheet in the wind with nine-foot swells, which were still manageable for the canoe, and then with three-foot-tall wind waves, which were not. The National Weather Service issued a small-craft advisory. The crew had difficulty maneuvering in the wind, as opposed to the whales, which were spouting and diving again out in the waters off Cape Flattery, possibly the same whales as the day before, possibly different ones—no one seemed to know. The protestors, on the other hand, were back and more prepared. The *Sirenian* had returned and Captain Paul Watson stood on the bow and sent off Zodiacs and played killer whale sounds. Again, the boats of the Sea Defense Alliance swirled around the canoe's crew. Again, the Coast Guard watched the protestors, prepared to move in. As it happened, the protestors had an ally onstage that day. A new group of players descended on the windswept whale hunting scene: a pod of orcas, which were also, like the Makah, hunting gray whales.

From the vantage point of the peaks, the sandstone sea stacks seemed half-mooned around the arrangement of boats. Far offshore, at the back of the Pacific Coast stage, a break in the thick sweater of clouds allowed crepuscular sunshine to rain on the very edge of the horizon; the heavenly light backlit the commotion of the outboards, the paddles, the tin drone of angry loudspeakers. Overhead, the news helicopters hovered like albatross, waiting for a death, an end. People in the little houses and trailers around Neah Bay were following the action, as were TV viewers all over the Northwest. I stood on the peak and watched the maneuverings and felt faded into the background. I called Wayne's mom, and I could hear her TV on in the background. "I hope they're okay," she said.

At the end of the day, one protestor was telling reporters that the crew was desperate, that they were going after any whale they could find and not the mandated migrating adult gray whales, not the whale without a calf that the tribe had agreed it would attempt to hunt. But the crew didn't seem as desperate as it did inexperienced. Desperation was more obvious in the aspect of the protestors, who were tearing about in their ships, burning fuel that some of them could barely afford, furrowing

through the sea, on behalf of the whales, on behalf of their sentient cocrea-
tures. The Coast Guard videotaped the anti–whale hunters, watched from
the edge like interested gulls.

Wayne called off the hunt early on the second day, so that the crew did-
n't even count it as a hunt but as a practice abandoned. Dan Greene's boat
towed the canoe to Makah Bay and then the canoe paddled the rest of the
way to shore, while the protestors backed off. The *Hummingbird* cut
through the waves as they crashed into Sooes Beach. The crew paddled
into the wide mouth of the Sooes River, which greeted them as a brackish
and serpentine refuge. The river turned the canoe inland and then south,
and then the crew paddled past Gary Ray's farm, beneath the bridge on
the road down the beach. They rolled the canoe up the bank of the river
and put it on the military surplus trailer and drove into town along the
muddy road, in a ragtag caravan, horns honking, flannel-shirtd arms waving, shouts of tired cheers. Downtown, they went into Andy Noel's house
and got warm, dried out.

Wayne came in at the dock. He was upset about the protestors, about
the taunts, the threats, the near misses that came as the defenders of the
whales spun by the canoe and the support boats. In a way, he couldn't
understand their anger. Wayne was shaking his head as he lit up a smoke.
"Somebody out there's gonna get killed," he said.

Donnie stood next to him. "Yeah," Donnie said.

A reporter was nodding. "That would really put this thing over the
edge," the reporter said excitedly.

Wayne looked curiously into the reporter's eyes.

"Yeah," Wayne said.

On the third day and for a few days following that, the crew rested;
they waited for Wayne to call for another hunt.

In the interim, picketers stood at the reservation property line: CANOE OF
FOOLS, a placard read. SOON THE OCEAN WILL BE A BLOODBATH, said
another. The restaurant was filled with headlines that were pored over with
coffee and toast: THEY'LL DO IT—NO PROBLEM, one said. Another
announced, GOAL OF THE MAKAH HUNT: SPIRITUAL REVIVAL. Once again, all
the issues were recapped in newspaper stories, and by the news anchors who
were speaking overhead on the TV. Once again, the letters to the editor
began pouring in. There were a few new wrinkles in the story of the
Makah whale hunt, one or two new angles, such as the fact that gray whales

246 / Robert Sullivan

had been washing up dead along the coast and in Puget Sound all winter, for reasons that were not yet clear, if they ever would be. Addressing that particular matter, a wire service report added this note: "Some scientists wonder if grays may be recovering a little too fast for their own good. There is a finite number of amphipods in the Bering Sea, and some experts speculate that gray whales may be approaching their carrying capacity—literally overgrazing their Bering Sea pasture." The press waited and watched for the canoe and wondered nervously if they were going to be stuck again in Neah Bay for another long time.

Canoes from tribes around the Olympic Peninsula began arriving in Neah Bay to show their support. By the weekend there were canoes from the Quileute tribe, from the Puyallup, the Tulalip, and the Hoh nations—canoes from the Canoe People, canoes driven in on trailers towed by trucks and cars. The other tribes took a risk in supporting the Makah. The Puyallup high school was evacuated after a bomb threat was called in, for instance, the caller citing the Puyallup's support of the Makah. But the other tribes came on behalf of their own treaty rights too. It was like an old fish-in.

On the day that the first canoe arrived in support of the Makah—the canoe from the Puyallup Nation—John McCarty was in Clallam Bay to greet the visiting paddlers as they made their way on the stretch of final winding road down to the reservation. When I saw John, I wondered what was going on; I wondered for a minute if he was holding an anti-Wayne press conference. He wasn't. He was just standing there alongside his wife, Ginger, both of them smiling, even beaming, as if they had had no problem with the hunt or their fellow tribe members at any point, as if everything were right in the world.

"We got help," he said.

In between hunts, I stopped in on Wayne, who was at home early in the morning, sitting at the kitchen table, in jeans and a T-shirt, making calls. His nephew was there, an eight-year-old boy who was so excited about the hunt, about his father, who, as one of the crew, was on TV, about the fact that his cousins and uncles were out hunting a whale. The little boy asked Wayne if he could hunt a whale too, if he could be out on the boat someday. "Can I, Uncle?" he said.

Wayne looked at the boy exhaustedly. Wayne's mom called the boy over.

"Maybe someday," Wayne said.

The German film crew had been calling again and asking Wayne to wait, to hold the hunt off—telling him that they were on their way and that he should remember the documentary. Wayne sipped coffee from a coffee cup decorated with various cetaceans that made me think of whale murals, that made me think of whales, that made me think of Wayne.

Wayne.

Wayne got dressed. He shaved. He went into town. He went to the Makah Maiden. He went into the back room. He sat down with George Bowechop, who all along had been helping maneuver the crew through the bureaucratic details. Wayne said, "We got some official whale commission business to do." Wayne sat before George as George looked over Wayne's papers, over all the lists and to-do lists he'd been carrying around for months, over all the stipulations, spiritual and nonspiritual, imposed by the whaling commission. George, officially examining the work of the whaling captain, nodded solemnly. Wayne—upright in his chair, at attention, sitting quietly and joke-free, as if the Shakers were still blessing him, still hovering over him with bells and sweaty prayers—looked as if he was being inspected.

Wayne was somber, humbled, nodding, with a winter of preparations behind him, with the worries of the hunt on his shoulders, with a cup of black coffee. He was the man people said he shouldn't be and couldn't be. Wayne was the man in charge.

More days passed, some of them beautiful, flat-oceaned sea days that went by without whale hunts, that seemed like such perfect days for whale hunting to those not actually involved in the whale hunt that the press and the protestors began to wonder if the crew had given up again, if the hunt would once again be called off. Also a few key people were out of town: Keith Johnson, the president of the whaling commission, was now in the Caribbean, on the island of Grenada, traveling with the American delegation to the IWC, and preparing to see Al Ingling, the veterinarian/ballistics expert, give his testimony on the theoretical execution of a humane kill, a testimony in which Al would compare using the whale gun with breaking the neck of a chicken. Denise Dailey was there too.

But the hunt hadn't been called off. Wayne was just pausing, on behalf of the visitors who had come with their canoes; he was making sure that they all had places to stay and food. It was the only way, he said. He also wanted the crew to rest. In the meantime, the canoes of the Canoe Nations all paddled together in Neah Bay, while the protestors taunted them, while the Coast Guard watched more and more anxiously.

The sky was giddy with blue. In the hills just off the beach, the mud-slides were dry and nearly red in the warming spring sun. Tiny waves lapped gently on the beach before the Makah senior center. Children ran in packs along the shore and shouted and waved. A friendly cameraman from Seattle gave four little girls a microphone and they pretended to be reporting live from the Olympic Peninsula: they knew the ritual instinctively.

The protestors waited too. They waited in their boats at the entrance to Neah Bay, they took their positions just off the breakwater. Occasionally, the *Sirenian* came into the Makah harbor and addressed the town through its loudspeakers, which blared: *"Don't murder whales!"*

The press busied themselves with whale hunt–related stories. Television stations interviewed Helma, Arnie Hunter's mother, on how to go about cooking a whale. (She told them that she planned to smoke some of it in Arnie's backyard.)

At a press conference, on a warm spring day, reporters asked Ben Johnson questions that—at this point—seemed to reveal the reporters' own innermost whale hunt coverage desires:

"Any pressure to get out there and hunt?" one asked.

"Not at all, not at all," Ben Johnson said. "We live here," he went on, his hands in his pockets, shrugging his shoulders, "and we're going to do it when it's all perfectly set."

One of the TV crews asked if they could get a spot on the Makah support boat, with Donnie and Wayne: they wanted to get better video footage of the hunt.

"I don't think so," Ben Johnson said.

The TV crews griped about all the access that the German film crew always got. "What if we had German accents?" a cameraman asked.

As for the Germans themselves, they still weren't around, though they were due in soon. One night Ralph called and said to Wayne, "Hello. This is Ralph. Do you remember me?"

As the days passed, I was staying in my tent out behind the Cape Motel, in view of the shanty, which some fishermen were occupying. I was happy for the nice days, but the rainy days were okay too: the spring rain seemed to wash a brighter green into the place. As it rained, I sat in my tent in the afternoons and in the evenings reading and thinking about whales and the Makah and the trip that the whales had just taken from Baja to Neah Bay on their way to Alaska and I finished *Moby-Dick*.[5] The sky poured and sometimes hailed, all of which I enjoyed now, so that I fell asleep and slept completely soundly, as if I had been drugged, as if I had become one with the Olympian rain, like moss. Mostly, I wondered if Wayne could take much more waiting, if the stress would get to him. Even in these final days, I was running into people who would volunteer that Wayne couldn't do it, that he would crack under the pressure, that, in the end, he would screw it up.

I saw Wayne again on Friday night. He had called for another hunt the next morning. Wayne's own car was still broken down, but late on Friday afternoon, he convinced the anthropology graduate student to drive him out in her car to see the crew—Wayne and the anthropology student had been spending more and more time together. Wayne was worried that the crew would be hungry; he wanted them to have food, to have energy for paddling—even if *he* wasn't eating. He got groceries and brought them down to the paddlers, who were camped on the beach with the canoe. When the crew saw him, they told him that they were fine, that they had already eaten. They pointed to the carcass of a deer.

Early the next morning, on a rainy Saturday, the whale hunt was once again officially on—the second big hunt day. The canoe was out in the water along with the official support boat, which carried Wayne and Don-

5 It was when the Makah whale hunt was finally happening, after I had spent a long time flipping through *Moby-Dick* and through the rest of Melville's works and biographies and other Melville-related literature, that I happened to talk to a Massachusetts-born literary scholar. He said to me what I had been unable to say to myself all along: that, in a way, the Makah whale hunt was the opposite of *Moby-Dick*. *Moby-Dick* is a book that builds to a symphonic climax of symbols after a long accumulation of steadily juiced-up details. The Makah had their symbols—the whale hunt and the whale—and they worked toward their earthly goal, the death of a whale, and an accompanying acceptance of death. At the time of the hunt, when I was relishing the final chapters of *Moby-Dick*, and realizing that it would soon end, I read Ahab uttering these words to the earlier-mentioned Starbuck and saw them as the theme of this, my subtext: "Ye two are the opposite poles of one thing; Starbuck is Stubb reversed, and Stubb is Starbuck; and ye two are all mankind. . . ." Given the cultural and personal significance of the hunt to the Makah, and given the tremendous moral and creative energy that, if you ask me, fairly jump off the pages of *Moby-Dick*, I subsequently found them to be semi-sacramental representations of each other—i.e., two sides of the same coin—and after the hunt was finally over, when I sat down to write, I attempted to construct this account accordingly.

nie as well as a mysterious shooter, the Makah tribal member who would fire the rifle at the whale in an attempt to perform the humane kill. The shooter was not featured in the press reports; he wanted to be incognito, even to his neighbors in Neah Bay. The shooter was picked up at the edge of the docks and dropped off before the support boat anchored, so that he wouldn't have to talk to the press or to anyone else. He arose from the dark when the time was right, from out of nowhere, Fedallah-like.

Some of the television stations cut back and forth between the basketball playoffs and the whale hunt, which was being covered live again. Usually, the canoe was in one television frame and the whale was in another: man and nature kept separate by virtue of a nonpanoramic camera. But from time to time, when the canoe neared a whale, the images merged. And the overlay of these two images was a palpable shock: the synthesis of a year of previously recorded footage of the Makah hunt and previously recorded footage of the gray whale.

The crew paddled for ten and a half hours. At one point, Theron Parker stood up again and launched his harpoon, and it looked as if it struck the gray whale and subsequently was shaken from the whale's great tail but the crew decided instead that the tail of the whale had slapped it away. Afterward, Donnie tasted the tip of the harpoon and said that he was certain it hadn't gone into the whale.

Wayne rotated paddlers, but the crew grew weary, their arms tired from hours of paddling, feeling like heavy clay. Their timing was off, but they felt they were getting better. They paddled after whale after whale, followed as the huge mammals strained the bottom of the coast, rose, blew out air, breathed, submerged, all relatively effortless. At one point, the crew asked Wayne to bring out Eric Johnson, the captain from the previous fall, their friend. Eric had not taken the requisite whale hunting qualification exams. But Wayne consented—he did it for the crew—and a boat brought Eric out on the water. Eric's Achilles tendon was still in a cast, but by dusk, when there was no whale, when the misty rain had soaked the paddlers and their windbreakers and sweatshirts, when they were too tired to whale hunt anymore, the cast was gone anyway: it had dissolved.

The protestors kept fighting, vigilant in their attempts to thwart the hunt—a concerned and caring Ahab-ian pack of whale rights activists, all madly intent on one thing. But they were losing boats. The Coast Guard sought to maintain the court-appointed exclusion zone around the whale hunting canoe (a distance of five hundred yards); each time the protestors broke into the exclusion zone, the Coast Guard impounded their craft. Four boats were impounded by the Coast Guard that day. At one point, Sedna's boat, the *Bulletproof,* a large silver powerboat, appeared to skim over the back of a gray whale. At this, the Coast Guard moved in immediately and went back to the Coast Guard base to examine their videotape, to see if a gray whale had been unlawfully harassed. After all, the hunt was taking place in a national marine sanctuary and, even during a whale hunt, the Coast Guard had to be certain that the non–whale hunters did not harass the whales.

Notably, the *Sirenian* had not been seized. Captain Paul Watson, the strategist, almost the only activist left with a boat, stayed out of the way of the canoe. He continued to blare killer whale sounds from loudspeakers. He videotaped the crew, the support boat, watched for the gun. At one point, the canoe paddled hard toward the *Sirenian,* and the big black boat went quickly in reverse; seemed to back away.

On TV, Watson was interviewed via cell phone by a TV reporter. He was asked if he would continue to harass the whales, if he knew it was illegal.

"You know," Captain Watson said, "I don't know what kind of a crazy farm I've just run into here but these guys want to blow a whale apart with a fifty-caliber machine gun and everybody's concerned that we might get too close to a whale. The fact is that they want to kill this intelligent, beautiful animal, blow it apart with an antitank gun, and everybody's focusing on, 'Oh, Sea Shepherd might be too close to a whale.' I think it's *ludicrous.*"

The newscaster at a desk in Seattle offered color commentary on the whale hunt, on the paddlers who were paddling through the lunch hour without a break, without food. "Susannah," he said to the newscaster who sat beside him, "this is very tiring for these guys."

Cut to a weatherman, who smiles and motions to the weather map: "The weather in Neah Bay ought to be favorable for the Makah whale hunt."

Cut to another newscaster, who says, "We're actually going to take a short break right now, but we'll be back with the Makahs."

Cut to the basketball coverage, previously scheduled.

Around this time, Wayne, on Dan Greene's boat, out in the rain in the ocean, heard his cell phone ring, answered it at no charge to himself (when he chose his cell phone payment package, Wayne bought the cheaper cell phone coverage plan that makes it necessary for the caller to pay for the cell phone call). Ben Johnson, the duly elected leader of the Makah Nation, told Wayne that, as captain of the whaling crew, he ought to order the whaling gun to be fired from the boat: the crew could harpoon the whale after it was already dead. Wayne, in the rain, with his free hand gesturing as the helicopter hovered over him, said he couldn't do that right now, in this particular instance. The crew had worked too hard, he explained. They wanted to harpoon the whale, like the old whalers, as they had practiced. Wayne, who had carried the gun in the newspaper pictures, who six months before had wanted to use the gun and forget the harpoon—Wayne said no to the gun.

The crew paddled on until dusk, trying to harpoon a whale, until Wayne called the hunt off one more time.

The sun set slowly that night, and a long black cloud—an island-shaped phantasm, a shadow peninsula with black mountains and dark hills—floated out along the strait to shut out the bright red sky. Beneath it all, the crew got together and prayed, stood on sacred tribal land and passed around an old harpoon. An elder gave them a song that had come to him in a dream, in which he had foreseen the whale giving itself up to the young men without a struggle. The protestors headed down the strait for dinner and rest. Sea Shepherd cruised down the strait to refresh its arsenal of boats. One of the Tulalip tribal members staying in Neah Bay had a dream that featured a great celebration.

76 / A Hunt—Day Three

On Monday, at just after 5 A.M., the crew met at the Makah Maiden for breakfast. They called for their checks, but Joddie, the woman who ran the restaurant, told them not to bother; it was on her. She said, "Go out and catch a whale." Within an hour, the canoe was paddling out into the ocean from off the coast. The crew paddled so quickly, in fact, that they almost beat the support boat to the scene; Wayne, Donnie, Dan Greene, Eric Johnson, and the shooter were just arriving when the canoe began hunting whales off Cape Alava. The sky was cloudy and drizzling but the sea was calm. A breeze blew out of the Olympic Mountains and down off the Makah peaks and held the sea down like a hand.

There were no protestors anywhere to be seen. The *Sirenian* was not there. Captain Watson had sailed east, down the strait to the San Juan Islands, to replenish the protestor fleet, which had been almost completely commandeered by the Coast Guard. At that very moment, as it happened, the *Sirenian* was on its way back to Cape Flattery. For a long time after the whale hunt, the members of the whaling crew and many other people in Neah Bay believed that the protestors had overslept because they had been out drinking late the night before. That wasn't the case—the protestors had been out late a few nights before. Nevertheless, that was how the story would be remembered in Neah Bay. Also remembered was that the Makah were out on the water all alone.

Or at least they were relatively alone. Employees of the National Marine Fisheries Service were on the water at the scene; their small aluminum craft was manned with biologists ready to observe, to see if the Makah would hunt the whale humanely. And the media representatives were there too— a boat filled with television crews made it out to Cape Alava to film the hunt. But the other press boat, the one that had been hired to take news-paper reporters and newspaper photographers to the scene of the hunt, had broken down just as it pulled out of Neah Bay. It was stranded. After months and months of moment-by-moment coverage, these reporters were not able to view the hunt at all, not even on TV, where, thanks to the helicopters, the coverage was once again live.

The canoe and its harpooner, the powerboat and its rifle shooter, the sec-ond harpooner and the somewhat confident but increasingly concerned whaling crew captain were all appearing on the morning TV shows. At the bottom of the television screen, hardly intruding on the modern version of a mythic event, the time and the temperature were displayed for the sake of the suburban commuter who was about to get into his or her car, who was a five and a half hour drive from Neah Bay.

This morning, with the whaling canoe moving closer and closer to one whale, with the specter of this whale moving closer and closer to the sur-face, to the waters parallel to the ceremonially carved canoe, with the whale hunt about to become an actuality, a done deed, the morning tele-vision host announced the following to the commuter at home, as if he were calling a prizefight or watching the police chase a runaway car: "Time clearly is running out for this whale."

The whale for which time was running out was a gray whale, one that had presumably spent the winter in a lagoon off the Baja Peninsula, perhaps in Guerrero Negro, which is a nice place—I can attest to that. Viewed on TV, viewed from the top of the peaks, even viewed from a boat in the water, the whale was theoretically on its way north to the Bering Sea. It swam, submerged, surfaced, blew a plume of briny mist.

And now, on TV and in real life, in windbreakers and sweatshirts, in wet suits and baseball caps, the crew of the *Hummingbird* spotted one gray whale amid an estimated twenty-six thousand. The crew of young men, who had been chosen by their families and questioned and had sometimes failed and other times passed the tests they took to qualify as whale hunters, who had practiced paddling together and fought with one another and wondered if they were worthy of their great ancestral whale hunting heritage and even if their fellow crew members were worthy and had from time to time wondered who was talking to the protestors or to the press—this crew paddled toward this gray whale, targeted it for the hunt.

The support boat fell back—Dan Greene slowed his boat down. Donnie, Eric Johnson, and the shooter watched, readied the harpoons, the gun, the final details. Wayne—the appointed conscience of the event—barked out orders that weren't so much orders as concerns, harried reminders. He was a kind of transformed being.

Wayne could see, as could anyone in range of a TV set in the Great Pacific Northwest, that the whale was ahead of the canoe but the canoe was gaining. The crew paddled fast and hard, sore still, but experienced after two full days of on-the-job whale hunt practice, skilled even. They paddled in strong-shouldered unison, except for Theron Parker, who was almost half a stroke ahead of the rest, who paddled faster and harder, who seemed possessed. The crew was paddling a stroke a second—they seemed to be shouting, even if they weren't: *stroke ... stroke ... stroke ...* —and by the count of seven they had crossed the path of the whale. Viewed from above, the whale made the thirty-five-foot-long canoe look small, its fluke outstretching the canoe, its dozens-of-tons bulk making the majestic, carved-out coastal cedar tree seem fragile.

Stroke ... stroke ... stroke ... and by the count of ten, Theron pulled his paddle out of the water. Quickly but carefully, still looking ahead at the water, watching for the gray, barnacle-covered hump, Theron placed the paddle down in the bottom of the cedar canoe. Then he picked up the harpoon—grabbed it by the specially designed neoprene handles, glanced toward the line behind him, the floats. Theron stood in the canoe and waited. At his back, the paddlers continued to paddle in practiced unison, their windbreakers fluttering in the wind, their clothes sopped with splattered seawater. Andy used his paddle to steer, and in a quick spare second, pulled his cap down tight, the one that said NATIVE.

On the support boat, Wayne sat hunched, concentrated, face tightened, head ringing, looking like an expectant father after months of labor—the Starbuckian Wayne.

The whale floated with a celestial ambivalence, with a nonmaniacal glissando that made the cold, gray water appear warm, inviting, almost Baja-like. The whale was so large as to once again seem as if it were a feature of the coast, a small moving portion of Cape Flattery. The whale turned slightly, back toward the ocean-cutting canoe, and then, after its last undisturbed blow of water, as it reached the surface, as it white-watered the ocean for a brief second, the gray whale touched its sky.

A collision of events was about to occur, a coincidence of phenomena: underwater instinctual mammalian migration and a man-based need to define itself—the latter, in this instance, against the ocean-backdropped hum of modern existence. And yet, although the Makah were being watched by the television-viewing public (either now or later on the evening news, the local *and* the national version), although a photograph of the event would appear on the front page of newspapers ranging from the *Peninsula Daily News* to the *Seattle Post-Intelligencer* to *The New York Times*, there were no whale hunt protestors to be seen. The Makah whale hunters were still out on the water with only their canoe and a whale.

Theron took his footing, the gray whale before him, just below the surface. The whale was still turning, its barnacles now touching the surface of the Pacific, rippling the sea with white streaks of resistance. Andy steered the *Hummingbird* straight, held his paddle tight to the side of the canoe. The crew kept paddling. Theron leaned back. And then he launched the harpoon. The harpoon landed in the whale.

So short was the path from canoe to whale that the shaft of the harpoon was still in Theron's reach. He grabbed it. He gripped it. He pushed the harpoon into the whale, put his weight into the harpoon, attempted to plant it deeply. And then quickly, he sat down. He sat down and he braced himself hard. He held on to the side of the canoe as the harpoon began to submerge. He leaned back, suddenly humbled, because the whale that had just been struck was now directly beneath the bow of the canoe.

The gray whale rolled to its right; it nearly rolled completely over. This move by the whale, this visually elegant gesture, would later be interpreted differently by the different groups of people involved in or observing the hunt (just as every other aspect of the hunt would be, not to mention the hunt itself). The whalers and many other people in Neah Bay took it as a sign that the whale had already given up, that it was surrendering itself to the crew, and that the whale somehow considered the crew worthy. To some of the people against the hunt it was an indication that the whale didn't know yet what had just happened. It was an indication that the whale was freaking out.

Either way, the roll of the whale caused the harpoon shaft to rise from the water yet again.

Theron reacted quickly, leaning over to yank the shaft out as it seemed to stand up before him. The tip of the harpoon remained embedded in the whale, the line to the harpoon point held fast. In that instant, Theron hurriedly tossed out the rest of the line in the cedar boat, for fear the whale would wrench it from the canoe. The paddlers continued to paddle. Theron threw out the large, beachball-sized rubber float, a float that in the old days would have been made of inflated sealskins, probably mostly because in the old days the whale hunters couldn't get ahold of beachball-sized rubber floats. At that, the crew began to paddle backward. Just off the bow of the canoe, the whale's tail slapped the surface—a tremendous slap of the tremendous fluke—causing a crash and a wave. And then the whale disappeared.

It was at this precise moment that the weather began to turn. It was as if on cue, as if it were happening in a novel, as if life were attempting to match art—not that life and art didn't already seem to be doing a pretty good job mimicking each other here out on the ocean with a whale pulling a hand-carved canoe. Two minutes later, the sea went from calm to rough. Several more seconds passed until the line that ran from the canoe to the whale down to the Pacific Ocean went taut. A white wake broke before the canoe's bow as it suddenly lurched forward. Theron pulled hard on the line to keep it in the front of the boat. He held it with all his strength—because the canoe was being towed by the harpooned whale.

Now the support crew moved in. Dan Greene steered the boat toward the whale as it sped off, dragging the canoe. Behind Dan, Wayne shouted to Donnie, telling him to get a second harpoon, to be ready to throw. Wayne watched as the shooter raised his rifle. The shooter took patient aim, trailing the underwater shadow that was the harpooned whale—

when all of a sudden the press boat moved in, crossing his line of fire: TV cameramen from Seattle were in his sights. The shooter stopped abruptly, broke off his aim. He waved his arms toward the press boat; he tried to wave them away. The rest of the crew on the support boat; he shouted frantically at the press boat. In that time, the whale submerged again, wallowing in the dark underwater shadows, moving away—its death prolonged.

The whale continued to pull the canoe. Dan Greene looked ahead of his boat and watched the line on the canoe as it was being dragged. He positioned the chase boat alongside the gray whale as it dived shorter dives and took shorter breaths.

Wayne watched, shouting and waving his arms. He stood silent from time to time and from a distance appeared as if he could be in prayer, as if he were treading water in the idea that someone might get killed, that the risks were still great even without the taunting and the threats of the protestors.

The shooter took aim again, the drone of the boat engine and the ocean and the wind enveloping him. Eric Johnson, who was assisting the shooter, stood and waved off the press boat. Then he quickly kneeled down and plugged his ears. The elephant gun went off once, and then again. The bullet proceeded smoothly through the water in a thin, straight streak of pure white, an air-filled line. The line went just over the submerged head of the whale. It missed. The whale still pulled the canoe.

Wayne turned to Donnie, who was ready as always, still Stubb-like. Wayne told Donnie to harpoon the whale a second time. Donnie had his harpoon ready. He waited, aimed. Wayne watched, standing in his Raiders jacket, holding on to the side of Dan's boat. Donnie sighted the whale, stepped to the side of the boat, leaned back, and launched a second harpoon. He threw it as if he'd always thrown harpoons, as if he knew exactly what he was doing—as if he were a whale hunter of old. And he hit his target dead on. The harpoon sank into the hard-boiled-egg-like flesh of the whale. And with Donnie's thrust, the whale's tail slapped the water once again, only this time with a more daunting force. Donnie braced himself. The great creature seemed to shudder. For a long time afterward, Donnie would remember that moment, and he would remember that the whale seemed to understand the threat, to feel the pain.

At this point there was a momentary panic on the support boat because they couldn't find any more bullets. Wayne raced frantically up and down the deck looking for bullets until the shooter realized that the gun was still loaded. Then the shooter fired again. Another bullet left the gun, another underwater streak of white, this one hitting the whale's brain. The report of the rifle rattled through the wind and off the gray cliffs of the coast, off the sea stacks and the fir-tree-covered islands. And as if by a dark magic, the water turned suddenly red. The whale writhed, its body contorting on the surface, the harpoons jutting and then disappearing and then jutting from the water again like a marker. The whale was dying, its strength fading. In a few seconds the whale was dead.

On the water, when they saw what the support crew had done, the crew prayed. They rested their paddles on their knees. Theron stood at the bow of the canoe, the rising winds and waves now tossing the boat about. Theron looked down on the other men in the canoe and he led them in prayer.

It was just as the whale was killed that Sea Shepherd's *Sirenian* arrived at the scene of the kill, charging furiously through the rising wind waves, leaving a raging white wake. The *Sirenian* came to a full stop near the Makah canoe. The *Sirenian* blared its horns, the black boat bobbing in the water, crying with loudspeakers, mourning the whale, and for its own sake. The Coast Guard watched as the protestors seethed.

In Seattle, one of the news stations cut away, deeming the death of the whale too violent for broadcast.

From the support boat, Wayne watched the crew pray and then he noticed that while the crew had prayed the whale had all a sudden sunk. This was a shock to Wayne. He hadn't planned on the whale sinking so quickly; he had thought it would float for a little while. But it had sunk without commotion, without drama. This began to make sense to Wayne when the whale hunt was over; in the old days, he and Donnie later reasoned, not being killed outright with a gun, a not-quite-dead whale probably floated longer and was less difficult to tow. And now as he sat there looking out on the place where the whale had disappeared into the deep water, Wayne saw that the water was becoming even rougher.

When the whale was killed, the breakfast crowd at the Makah Maiden cheered. People all over town knew almost immediately. Across from the street from the restaurant, working on the construction crew building the new post office, Micah McCarty, kneeling in the mud, heard the cheers and the car horn honks. He smiled; he kept working; he had a job. Reporters and cameramen shot past him in trucks and cars and all through town like a school of fish, asking anyone they could find the same question over and over: "How do you feel?" At the restaurant, a television producer announced to no one and everyone at the same ecstatic time: "New York is going *crazy* for this!" Helicopters came in from the ocean, from over the scene of the hunt, and dropped off videotapes of the whale hunt. News crews raced their satellite trucks down to Sooes Beach and parked where they thought the whale would be brought in, still not understanding that very little if anything about this whale hunt conformed to expectations. Soon townspeople drove down to the beach too. The paddlers from the other tribes drove down with the trailers carrying their canoes. It was an impromptu vigil on an improbable cold and stormy day. People sat out on the sand in beach chairs, wrapped in blankets and cheap plastic ponchos, holding umbrellas that kept turning inside out due to the wind.

I walked down to the beach and stood in the rain, watching the gray ocean's stormy churn. I wondered if the crew would ever make it in and I ran into Harriette Cheeka, the poet, with her mother; Harriette was carrying a tape player, playing a tape recording of old family songs through a bullhorn. She said to a little girl, "You're going to see a whale today."

The rainy wind bent back the scruffy pines and raked the gray sand. People stood around for hours in the rain, until the wind and then the hail finally got to be too much and everyone went to their cars. The Makah police chief was watching the scene at the beach. (He had offered his resignation after Sea Shepherd had publicized the felony that he had been charged with while police chief of an Indian nation in Nevada, but, until his replacement was hired, he was still in charge.) He chewed on his cigar from beside his Jeep. He was getting reports on his radio that the crew was having trouble, but he kept a calm face.

On the beach and back in town where the dogs ran through the streets as they did every day, where the fishing boats went in and out of the marina as if nothing had happened, almost everyone was oblivious to the fact that the whale was not yet secured. The whale and the canoe and the crew were drifting south in the stormy water, down the coast, away from the ancient whale hunting grounds, away from Cape Flattery and Neah Bay; they were drifting past Cape Alava to an area where the Coast Guard might not be able to protect them anymore. And they were worried about losing the whale.

On the water the crew finished praying, and then they held their paddles in the air and cheered; they began paddling euphorically through the stiff wind waves toward the support boat. There was no more cheering on the support boat. Donnie and Wayne were talking hurriedly. Donnie was pulling off his sweatshirt, getting down to his dry suit, getting ready to dive in and attach a line to the whale, which was now dangling by a harpoon line, just above the ocean floor.

According to the original plan, Donnie was going to use his diving equipment to do this. But when Donnie picked up his tanks on the deck next to Wayne and turned the valve to check the air, the tanks made a distress call: *pshhhhhhh!* There was a problem with his register. Donnie told Wayne that he would dive without his tanks—he would hold his breath. But Wayne was concerned that Donnie might get tangled in the line. Wayne was worried about something going wrong. He would not allow Donnie to dive without the tanks.

"No," Wayne said. "We're not gonna get somebody killed."

Their eyes fastened. Donnie reminded Wayne that they could lose the whale.

Wayne was adamant. With semi-mythic strength, Wayne resisted the temptation: he thought he would rather lose the whale. "We're not gonna risk it," he said.

After that, they had to come up with a new plan.

While Wayne and Donnie were thinking, the crew paddled the canoe alongside Dan Greene's boat, a happy gam. The men on the support boat helped the crew out of the canoe and on board the boat. The whalers shook hands and hugged; Dan Greene held his boat steady. Theron hugged Andy. Andy walked over to Wayne, who was sitting down on the boat, holding his head in his hands, trying to come up with a way to get the whale secured. When Andy walked over to hug him, Wayne didn't notice at first. Andy shouted: *"Wayne!"* Wayne stood up and smiled. They embraced. Then Wayne stopped smiling and looked down at the water again. The wind was howling now. The rain was coming down in cold, hard sheets.

A half hour passed, and the whale was still sinking. A harpoon line broke. Other crew members volunteered to dive in and attempt to tie up the whale, but Wayne would not hear of it. They radioed for help, for new air tanks, and in a few minutes a boat was on its way out of the marina, on its way out of Neah Bay, around the cape and down the coast. In the meantime, the crew decided to pull the whale up by hand. From the edge of the support boat, a dozen men pulled and heaved on the one line that was still attached to the whale.

More time passed. The replacement diving tanks had not yet arrived. The boat was drifting. There were reports among the protestors that the Makah had lost the whale, that the whale had completely sunk and the hunt had been a complete disaster, which was still Wayne's great fear. In the rain and wind, as the sea tossed their boat up and down, the Makah first pulled and then strained to raise the whale from the water. On the count of three, they managed a crowded heave, a strain through a tangle of arms on a three-ton mass of flesh. The dead whale rose a few feet. The men rested. They pulled some more, rested again. Still more time expired, and then the whale rose higher in the water. In fact, the whale rose on its own accord—quietly, with no theatrical vortex, no cosmic display. The gases in the decomposing, medium-sized Leviathan—churning and reacting and oxygenating—gave the whale a buoyancy in death, brought it to the surface, up toward the rainy gray light.

The whale—its sleek, geologic silhouette giving way to a gray flatulence in postmortem—was now within a dozen feet of the surface. Finally, with Wayne's consent, Donnie put on his mask and dived into the ocean. He slapped and kicked at the water and dragged the rope around the whale's tail, and in doing so, hugged it. On the boat, gazing into the reflectionless water, Wayne seemed to be holding his breath in unison with Donnie. Finally, Donnie attached a line and then lifted himself back into the boat, pulling off his mask and smiling his wry smile. When Donnie came back aboard, Wayne was, for the first time in weeks, calmed down, almost relaxed. He was thinking that the whale hunt was about to be over.

By now, Arnie Hunter was on the scene to assist and a big boat from the Makah fishing fleet, the *Heidi*, had arrived. The line to the whale was attached to *Heidi*'s hydraulic winch. Before the line was attached, the fisherman, Sonny Peterson, asked Wayne and Donnie how Donnie had attached the rope. Wayne told him that they had attached the line with one-quarter-inch stainless steel snaps, which are frequently used on gill nets. Peterson looked at Wayne and shook his head and said that one-quarter-inch stainless steel snaps would never hold.

Wayne started to worry again. Donnie put his diving mask back on and went into the water once more. He tied on a new line, attached it with a bowline knot. He dived down and reappeared; he bobbed in the choppy water surrounding the whale. And as soon as Donnie was back on deck, the snaps on the first line broke. On the *Heidi*, the whaling crew started home. They waved and cheered—to one another and to the cameras following them on the water and in the air. Wayne waved to the press boat. He gave the thumbs-up. He almost looked relieved. The whale was dragged in behind them, the glorious bloated trophy rolling in an inglorious plume of white water. The trip around the cape and through the stormy ocean took six hours.

The rain let up some late in the afternoon, just before the whale was brought to the village, to the beach in front of the senior center. As soon as the news crews got the tip, their trucks left Sooes Beach and parked downtown again. At the entrance to the harbor, the dead whale was unfastened from the fishing boat and tied up to the canoe, so that the canoe could pull the whale to the shore. The *Hummingbird* paddled in the midst of a small fleet of Northwest canoes from the Hoh, from the Puyallup, and from the Quileute. The Coast Guard ships were behind the canoes, and behind the Coast Guard ships were the protestors. News helicopters swarmed in the sky. The only people missing were the German film crew, who were apparently still traveling.

Theron was shirtless in the front of the canoe. He raised his paddle in the air to acknowledge the cheers as they rose up from the crowd assembled on the beach. The whale was landed in the low tide; its body rose up and down with the bay's little waves, as if it were still breathing, as if the tide were a respirator. Theron climbed up on the whale, slipped off, climbed up it again, and stood triumphantly. Andy did the same. Then Darrell climbed onto the whale and then the others. A helicopter hovered over the whale and the whalers, a photographer dangling from its open door. Out in the harbor, the *Sirenian* blared its horn angrily (enraged now that the whalers had stood on top of the whale). The crowd—what seemed like the entire village—cheered and applauded. People were wearing cedar headbands and baseball caps, wearing button blankets and those cheap plastic raincoats that are milky clear plastic. They were carrying drums and singing songs, the words rising out over the carcass into the woolen clouds and the rainy afternoon light.

The tribe held a small ceremony to mark the event. A stretch of the beach was roped off with yellow police tape. The reporters were asked to stand back from the ceremony, off to the side or up on the hill, which is where the people in town who had mixed feelings about the hunt or were against it completely were also standing. Ben Johnson used a small megaphone to speak to the crowd. "The Makah made history today," he said.

Then George Bowechop was asked to speak. He walked slowly, from the front porch of his house, made his way across the road, across the wet sand and down the beach to where the whale lay, where the small waves lapped against its fluke. On his front porch, George's daughter-in-law, Janine, the director of the Makah Museum, filmed the event with a video camera. She panned across the bay, filming all the canoes and the crowd and the whale hunters, and she thought for a moment that she was filming the past.

Wayne and Donnie and the rest of the support crew came ashore down at the marina, instead of at the beach. Smiling, they walked along the shore to the beach, past the reporters, who congratulated them, past the bait shop, past the soda machine, past the boat launch and the little wooden pier, where the crew had taken their swimming tests.

Donnie hugged his daughter, who smiled at him and touched his face as he kissed her. Donnie hugged his mom, who had given him a whale rattle the night before: she was beaming. Arnie was wearing a cone-shaped cedar hat, and walking around and smiling and telling reporters the same thing over and over in his quiet and matter-of-fact bear-like way: "It was like we came full circle." He also said, "I'm a true believer in the strength of prayer."

Wayne was flitting in and out of the crowd. He looked as if he wasn't certain of what he should do but knew he should be doing something.

All eyes and TV cameras were on Theron now. As the drums beat, Theron stood on the whale and held his hand in the air. He sprinkled eagle feathers on the whale, according to tradition. He strode up the beach with an emphatic majesty, still bare-chested in the cold rain. Carrying a whale rattle and wearing a blanket on his bare back, he went to a parked car to acknowledge his elder, to be respectful. And after he did, he turned to speak to reporters for the first time. Rather than growling, as he had always done before, rather than getting upset at the microphones and telling the reporters exactly where they could go, rather than being a jerk, he was solemn.

"We prepared for about a year," he said. "We prayed to our creator."

At this point, they began to cut up the whale.

I could see the whale from afar. It was a magnet of black, a hillock of flesh that beckoned in a dark way: the waning symbol. When the yellow tape came down, I walked down to the beach. I peeked in through raincoats and sweaters and windbreakers and fleece outerwear and saw the shiny gray skin, the barnacles, a hugeness that later the protestors would say was not that huge but that looked huge to me. I looked around at the hills and the bay and the strait and the furry clouds and the rain: the view seemed to emanate from the wet blackness of the whale, to expand out from it and the small crowd of commotion. Every detail became more detailed, became charged in an electrical way, as in a great vibrant mural.

I walked around the crowd that surrounded the whale, so that finally I was standing near the eye of the whale, watching the photographers and the TV cameramen take pictures of the eye, the sad-looking eye, the closed-down portal of consciousness. I talked to the biologists who inspected the gray whale and determined it to have been a three-year-old female that was nonlactating and that had died quickly when the bullet went through its brain—they pulled the harpoon out and showed the bent stainless steel shaft. They showed me the whale lice, *Cyamus scammoni*, the silver-dollar-sized creature named for the sort-of-great gray whale hunter, Charles Scammon, and placed one in my hand, where it grabbed at me and pinched me, which let me know that it was real.

I watched tribal members photograph the whale. I watched them photograph themselves with the whale. I watched the television cameras film the tribal members photographing themselves in front of the whale. I watched the children—running around and laughing and chattering—eat the whale's white blubber, which was rubbery and creamy-looking at the same time and was sliced in freezer-door–shaped slabs: the blubber tasted of brine and was chewed and chewed by everyone around and then spit out, impossible to digest. I watched the men who were carving the whale: Andy and Darrell, Ralph Butterfield, and a whaler from Alaska, a friend of the Makah. The Alaskan whaler was leading the carving of the gray whale; he was showing the newly-returned-to-whaling tribe exactly how to go about it. Bright, bloody hunks of red meat were cut carefully off the clean white bones of the whale's chest cavity, and the meat was stacked on blue plastic tarps, several supermarket freezers' worth. Crew members and tribal members took it away. The whale slowly diminished in size, in the manner of a Thanksgiving turkey.

I looked for Wayne, and I finally found him wandering around the carcass, which seemed beside the point for him. I realized he was still on the job. He smiled and shook hands but as the people greeting him passed, his face flashed back to a serious, almost morose concentration. He was watching to make certain the event continued to proceed smoothly, to see that the crew members received whale meat, that the whale meat was stored away for the potlach that would come in a few days. He roamed along the edges of the event, asking the crew members questions. Once in a while he laughed.

Wayne went home and took a shower and stopped in at the community center, where there was a dinner. I stopped by. I saw Donnie there, arms folded, standing by the door, and I saw Arnie. I asked them how they thought Wayne was holding up. Arnie said that Wayne was probably exhausted. "He's not used to that kind of responsibility," Arnie said.

A little while later, Wayne suddenly found himself at the front of the community hall. Someone asked him to say a few words. He started to say something, but then he got nervous. Someone shouted for him to speak up, but he couldn't. It was too much for Wayne. The whaling captain seemed to be trembling. He walked off.

Back out at the beach, in the dark, the carving of the whale continued. It seemed as if it would never be completely butchered—the detail that would not go away, death lingering. Late into the evening, the crew kept carving, and the government biologists kept taking samples. At around eleven o'clock, as his mother dragged him away, a little kid cried, "I want to *stay*!" At midnight, the tide was coming in and an attempt was made to pull the whale carcass farther up the beach with one of Wayne's giant military surplus trucks, but even in its partially eaten-away form, the whale would barely budge. Klieg lights illuminated the carcass, giving the beach the look of a crime scene.

By one o'clock, there was still some meat on the bones of the whale, and the Alaskan whale carver who had been leading the carving was getting at the intestines. He was trying to convince the Makah to save the intestines, but none of the Makah seemed interested. A few people showed up with some dinner on paper plates for the men still working on the whale— salmon and potatoes. Andy was there, working hard alongside the Alaskan whaler, but they needed more help. It was raining again. The Alaskan shouted out to the small crowd that stood in the cold dark: *"Are there any Makah?"* No one responded. One of the reporters decided to help the whalers and so waded into the bloody midnight water and assisted in the unraveling of the whale's guts.

77 / After a Whale Is Dead

VLADIMIR: (Pause) We have kept our appointment and that's an end to that. We are not saints, but we have kept our appointment. How many people can boast as much?
ESTRAGON: Billions.

— *Waiting for Godot* by Samuel Beckett

The morning after the whale hunt had finally succeeded, the dead whale was still there, only it didn't look much like a whale anymore. It looked dead. Dogs sniffed at the whale's remains as it sat beneath a blue tarp on the beach, rocks weighing down the tarp, the sky white with low rainless clouds. A tribal police officer guarded the carcass.

I spent the night in the shanty and woke up early. I drove over to see Wayne, who was just waking up on his mother's living room couch. He looked exhausted, having been up for so many days in a row. He got up and poured a cup of coffee. He sat down at the kitchen table and listened to his mom, who was sitting in her chair in front of the TV and thinking of going downtown and finding a television reporter who was commenting on a few of the negative remarks aired by the protestors (she didn't).

"You pulled it off," I said to Wayne. He was rubbing the sleep from his eyes. "Now you can run for tribal council," I kidded him.

His mother smiled. "That'd be good," she offered. "Then we could fight openly," she said.

A TV crew knocked on the door but Wayne told them he'd give a press conference later. Then he took a shower and got dressed and drank a cup of coffee from his whale-art–covered mug and went downtown.

"Come on," he said, opening the door. "Let's go see who hates me."

At the restaurant, the hunt was being replayed on all the network news shows, and the canoe and the crew and the whale were on the front page of *The New York Times*. The Seattle papers were filled with stories about the hunt, with headlines ranging from TRADITION RENEWED (the *Seattle Post-Intelligencer*) to TRADITION VS. A FULL-BLOWN PR PROBLEM (*The Seattle Times*). Some of the reporters expressed amazement: for example, one of the TV reporters from Seattle spoke over a shot of the whale being harpooned and said: "It was like something out of a Makah legend." But mainly, the tribe was criticized. The protestors had held a vigil in Seattle. *The Seattle Times* reported receiving four hundred calls and E-mails regarding the hunt and said that comments were running 10–1 against the hunt. There were letters to the editors about the hunt having been barbaric; about the whale's innocence; about the Makah having taken advantage of the whale's trust. Captain Paul Watson, firm in his belief that the Makah hunt was illegal, proclaimed the United States a pirate whaling nation: "Today, with speedboats, military weaponry, and the draconian assistance of the U.S. government in stifling all dissent, American whalers managed to blast a whale out of existence in American waters on the pretext of cultural privilege." On their Web page, In the Path of Giants was seething: in a banner headline of anger, Steph and Heidi wrote: DAMN THE MAKAH FOREVER.

For the follow-up coverage on the day after the whale was killed, reporters were milling around the carcass, wondering about a press conference. They were talking to the high school shop teacher, who had an idea to assemble the bones of the whale back at the school. Donnie was there with his daughter; he was smiling, chatting at ease. And Micah was there. Micah seemed okay about not having been on the crew. When the reporter asked him how he felt, Micah, the eloquent one, said, "There really are no words to describe it."

Next to Micah, a little boy sitting on his father's shoulders pointed to the whale and said, "What's that?"

"That's a whale," his father replied. "That's for our Indian tradition. That's for our rights."

"Oh," the little boy said.

Later, at the press conference, Wayne seemed as if he was anxious to talk about getting another whale hunt going as soon as possible. But Ben Johnson played down Wayne's enthusiasm and the timing of the next hunt. Instead, Ben talked about the death threats that were coming into the tribal voice mail system. He also said that Keith Johnson and Al Ingling and the rest of the tribal delegation to the IWC meeting in Grenada had been explaining how a humane kill might proceed when news came through that the crew had gotten a whale. Most of all, Ben Johnson commented on plans for the upcoming potlach. Indians from all over the Northwest, from Vancouver Island and British Columbia, from around the West would come to Neah Bay to celebrate, to eat the whale. It would be the ritualized public end of the whale hunt.

Days passed. For his part, Wayne, as captain of the whaling crew, decided to compose a short speech for the potlach. The night before the celebration, he paced in his house, stayed up late working on his speech, which was not so much a speech as a simple list of people he wanted to thank, including the crew, Donnie, Arnie, the whaling commission, a whale biologist with the National Marine Fisheries Service, and a few others, including his ancestors, his grandfather, and the whale. He read it over and over. He vowed to read it carefully, not to be nervous, to stay calm.

The next day, on the first Saturday after the whale hunt, the potlach began. There was a parade through downtown Neah Bay. The paddlers led the parade, pulled along in their canoe by a car. Theron sat in the front, continuing to bask in his glory. At the potlach in the gymnasium, there were dances and speeches and gifts for everyone, as in the days of the great chiefs: toys for the children, pots and pans, appliances, blankets and dishtowels. It was a huge gathering; the floor of the high school auditorium was filled with folding tables and folding chairs for the nation and its guests. Plates of blubber and whale meat were passed out, along with salmon, potatoes, and Jell-O. Later, the floor was cleared and people filled the bleachers and listened to more speeches and watched the dancing. Ben Johnson said, "The Makah have a living treaty. We're whaling again." Al Ziontz, the tribe's retired Seattle attorney, said that when he began working with the Makah there had very few actual fishing rights, even though fishing rights had been delineated in their treaty; now, it was noted, the government was enforcing the tribe's right to whale. Even John McCarty gave a speech on the greatness of the Makah. Theron walked through the room like a reigning monarch. He spoke with a Masai lion hunter, with a chief from Fiji, both of whom had heard about the whale hunt and were in the Seattle area and decided to drop in and celebrate and eat whale.

During the festivities, Wayne kept his speech in his pocket. He sat alongside Arnie at a table in the front of the room. He was ready to stand up before the crowd. He felt pretty good. He had joked with a reporter that he had brought the guest of honor to the potlach, the whale. He went outside the hall to have a cigarette a couple of times. But when it came time for him to get up, he didn't. He and Arnie never got the chance. They were passed over. The people in charge of the festivities never got around to letting Wayne speak. This made Wayne so angry. This made Wayne very angry, in fact, that he left his table and walked disgustedly over to his house. He sat there on the couch all night. He didn't want to talk to anybody.

I was one of the last people to eat the whale. When I sat down at the potlach, Donnie immediately came over to my table and handed me a plate of whale meat. I looked down at the plate. I looked over at the undercover protestors, the ones who had infiltrated the event. (They were the non-Indian-looking people standing along the back of the gymnasium wall and scanning the room with scowls on their faces and not eating the whale.) Then I tasted the whale.

Donnie watched me, which made me feel a little bit honored and a little bit nervous at the same time. "Good, huh?" he said. I nodded. I chewed. I chewed some more. The whale was a little tough. It tasted sort of like beef, or maybe venison or elk, neither of them meats with which I am terribly familiar, I suppose it tasted like whale. I can think of no better place in this story than here to describe the particular taste sensations I experienced in minute detail, except that I can't. The eating of the whale was a kind of a hyperconscious experience. It was the most overexamined meal I ever had. I continued to chew. I swallowed and speared another piece with my fork and chewed some more and looked around for the salt and pepper but didn't see any and then smiled at Donnie and at the people across the table, and so forth, and the entire time, all I could hear was a voice in my brain that was shouting, *You're eating a whale!* The next morning, I packed up my tent and decided to splurge on a big celebratory breakfast at the restaurant, after which I drove home and wondered if I should have eaten the whale. I don't know whether it was the sausage I had at breakfast that morning or the whale I had for dinner the night before, but on my way home my stomach got very upset.

Prior to my drive home, just after I ate the whale at the potlach and before I went to my tent, I walked over to Wayne's house. I'd heard that he was very upset. A couple of people had seen him walk out of the gym. Now the whole town was in the auditorium and he was at home. When I got there his boots were outside the door and the only light I could see was the light of the TV, which cast a quivering blue. I stood there on the dirt road wondering if Wayne was okay with the whale hunt being over but I couldn't bring myself to knock on his door.

I walked back to the potlach. On the way to the gym, I recognized Ralph Marschalleck, the German documentary director, who was walking around in the darkness. I introduced myself. He remembered me. "We missed the hunt," he said.

I said that I was sorry.

He said that he and his film crew had been one day too late. He repeated himself: "We missed the hunt."

I found out later that Ralph was upset with Wayne. Ralph had wanted Wayne to wait for his film crew to arrive from Germany before hunting the whale.

On the drive home, I picked up a man who was walking alongside the road, who had just plucked some salmon berries from a bush and was dusting them off. He got into the car and told me that he was on his way back to British Columbia, and that there wasn't enough room for him in his relatives' car and he had volunteered to hitchhike. He said that he had grown up in a Nuuchahnulth village on the coast of British Columbia. He talked a lot, and in so doing he told me about his town on the coast of British Columbia and about his language being taken from him and about how he had recently stopped drinking and about how the whale hunt had made him feel renewed, so alive. I dropped him off in Forks, and drove alone back across the Olympic Peninsula. I drove down the coast, alongside the glacier-covered mountains, through the thick, green, springtime forests, and when I got home I passed days of thoughtfulness in which I couldn't get Neah Bay out of my mind. I wanted to think that the drama was done, that there was an ending, the way there was an ending in *Moby-Dick*. I tried again and again to imagine it had all ended in some way, and in so doing I spent a lot of time wondering about Wayne.

When I drove back up to Cape Flattery the next week, it was low tide, the lowest tide of the year, and the sun was bright and stark, like an X ray—Neah Bay felt completely exposed. I stood on the bluff overlooking Sooes Beach. There were no news vehicles or protest vessels. School children were playing in the sand: it was the annual end-of-the-year family-and-student picnic. The sky was perfectly blue, the salty air perfumed with the rich scent of tiny Nootka roses that bloomed in the roadside brambles, that were tickled by the cool wind off the sea. I got back in my car and drove along the dry road and walked down to the water to see the ocean floor uncovered, to stare at the starfish, the mussels, the barnacles, clinging tight.

Late in the afternoon, I went over to Wayne's house. I knocked on the door; he was sitting on the couch and putting his boots on. We caught up a little.

He said that since the hunt he had gone over to Victoria for a day of vacation but that he'd not been able to relax because when he tried to go into restaurants with the anthropologist, he had been kicked out: people recognized him from TV as the captain of the whaling crew. He said that he had seen his son in Seattle, and had had a good talk with him. He said he hoped his son would stay out of trouble. We talked a little about Donnie, who had already gotten a job at the tribal fisheries department, doing stream surveys. And then Wayne played me a videotape of the whale hunt that one of the TV reporters had sent him. He put it in the TV set and he did the commentary; he was intent, leaning into the screen. "See that. That's when the press boat got in the way. We could have shot the whale right there," he said. He shook his head. "Oh, well," he said, "it all worked out."

We watched the tape some more—the canoe paddling ferociously, Theron launching the harpoon, the great effort to secure the carcass—and Wayne continued to commentate. "There's Donnie," he said. "Donnie and Arnie—they were probably the two most important people on the crew. Most important to me, anyway. I couldn't have done it without them."

As Wayne spoke, I realized that he was watching the tape even more intently than I had first noticed, and I realized that there was a sadness in his voice. When the tape ended and he turned toward me to head for the door, I saw that his eyes had welled with tears. My heart sank; I asked him if he was okay. "I don't know what's going on," he said. He was quiet. He rubbed his eyes. "Those anger management courses are working a little too well," he said. Wayne put on his boots.

He'd gotten his car fixed, so we drove over to the tribal center to pick up the whaling crew jackets that had just come in. Wayne worried that they were too big, that they might not fit the crew members. We drove over to Arnie's house, and Wayne gave Arnie a jacket out of the box.

"Try it on," Wayne said.

Arnie tried it on. "How's it look?" Arnie said.

His wife looked up from the TV. "Good," she said.

"Is it too big?" Arnie asked.

"You'll have room to grow," Wayne said.

We sat around after that and talked about the complications that had begun to arise in the aftermath of the hunt. The German film crew was so upset with Wayne that they wrote a letter to the tribe claiming that the tribe had reneged on its deal to allow them to document the hunt. Wayne was in trouble for having allowed Eric Johnson on the support boat when he hadn't been certified. There was talk of giving Wayne a few dozen hours of community service as punishment for his procedural improprieties.

Wayne was hoping to go whale hunting again that fall, a hunt with his family. There were other families organizing for a hunt: Theron was trying to arrange one and John McCarty was too. On that afternoon, Wayne was not interested in helping the other families out. Hearing him talk, I wondered if maybe Wayne was still trying to figure out what the whale hunt had meant to him personally; I wondered if he was perhaps trying to figure out what he'd ended up with in the end, aside from a dead whale, that is. Of course, I couldn't say what he was thinking. I didn't really know.

We left Arnie's and went outside. Wayne was having a smoke, and I looked up at the sky and mentioned that Neah Bay seemed so beautiful that day, so lovely under the ceiling of summertime blue, and I asked him how it looked to him. He practically snapped at me.

"I just want to get the hell out of this town," he said.

I stood there like a jerk. Wayne finally broke the silence. "No, it's really beautiful," he said. "This really *is* the only place for me." *

---

* Just as Melville suggested that art seemed to imitate life in some respects, I found it difficult to distinguish between Ishmael and Melville from time to time, especially now when I happened to be thinking of both of them in relation to, among other people, Wayne. Something that Ishmael says in *Moby-Dick* at this time struck me with regards to my relationship as a reporter to Wayne: "Disect him how I may, then, I go but skin deep; I know him not, and never will." If you could ever know anything about Melville, who seems a difficult character for a biographer to pin down, you could perhaps know that he himself felt unknown in a way. Melville's professional career as a writer was just about over after *Moby-Dick* and *Pierre*, and he was completely out of the novel-writing business after *The Confidence-Man* but he kept writing. He privately predicted great things for his work. After he retired from the Customs House, he roamed the used-book stores in downtown New York and stayed at home writing poetry and working on his one final work-in-progress, *Billy Budd*, which his wife packed away at his death. Some biographies seem to paint him happier when he died than he was during the time of his commercial failures. "All his life he had pondered the mystery of death, and at times he was dangerously obsessed with the idea of suicide," writes Laurie Robertson-Lorant, in *Melville*. After he gave up the publishing business, he thrived. Melville seems to have been drinking less, and his relationship with his wife appears to have been on the mend (there was talk of divorce at one point and an undying rumor that he once pushed her down the stairs). In his desk when he died there was a clipping that said: "Hold fast to the dreams of youth." And in his last days he underlined a line by Balzac that said: "Your destiny is a secret between you and God." When he did die, after two years of bad health, the author of *Moby-Dick*, the masterpiece, was barely remembered even by the famous moniker, which he loathed: The Man Who Lived Among the Cannibals. He slipped away almost imperceptibly. His obituary in *The New York Times* referred to him as Henry Melville. He was called Hiram in another. Several writers considered writing biographies about him but didn't.

*   *   *

Over the summer and into the fall, I stayed in touch with Wayne, while visiting Neah Bay and points around the peninsula. When I finally began typing up my account of what I had seen at the Makah whale hunt, I realized that people were stepping forth all around with *their* accounts. There was a television documentary being made in Seattle, and I saw a long posthunt report that a Canadian TV station did. I kept running into other reporters who said they were thinking of writing a book about it all, and one reporter made a point of telling me that she had decided against doing so because it was the Makah's whale hunt and therefore no one but a Makah could effectively say what had happened. At one point, Wayne told me that he was thinking of writing a book about the hunt too. He wanted to tell people his version of events, but then eventually he decided against it. The German film team, meanwhile, had figured out a way to finish their film. It seemed as if everyone who had survived the ordeal had a story to tell.

I kept checking in with Wayne. For a while, he seemed to be doing okay. He was still seeing the anthropologist, and he had run into a few bouts of work. For instance, he and Donnie both fished the river for salmon in the fall. Wayne caught a couple of good nets full, while Donnie easily filled the entire back of his pickup truck. They sold the fish for twenty-five cents a pound.

At the end of the summer, people in Neah Bay began to plan for the next whale hunt. At first, Wayne still didn't want to help anyone who wasn't part of his own family; he had lingering resentments. But then Wayne mentioned to me that he had had a change of heart, that he would not stand in the way of other families as they set out to whale. He said he would even lend Theron a hand. "It's good for the tribe," Wayne said. At the end of the summer, Wayne and Arnie went to Seattle for the weekend. Wayne was still having some trouble getting served in restaurants but they had no problem getting into the Native American salmon festival. There were a lot of tribes there. During the event, a man from a tribe in western Washington approached Wayne and asked him if he was the captain of the whaling crew. Wayne hesitated at first, eyeing the man cautiously. The man extended his open hand. "I just wanted to shake your hand," he said. That afternoon, Wayne stood and drummed and sang songs with Arnie and his family. It was the first time he'd ever done so. I asked Arnie about Wayne. Arnie said, "He's starting to realize who he is."

Whenever I fooled myself into thinking that Wayne had settled into a steady post–whale hunt existence, Wayne surprised me. A couple of times over the winter, Wayne called me up and left a message that I should call him back as soon as I could; he sounded completely down and out and even said as much. I called his house immediately but his mom said she hadn't seen him and she even said that she was worried about him. I'd heard he was worried about his son. I knew that he was going through a rough period with his girlfriend. Also, he wanted to get a trailer of his own but the bank wouldn't give him a loan. In fact, he seemed to be realizing that all that work and all that concentration he'd put into the whale hunt didn't pay off immediately, if at all; that the whale hunt was not an end in itself; that as significant as it was culturally and politically and even spiritually it was still only a whale hunt; that it was over.

I couldn't get in touch with him and I was worried. Finally, one day I got him on the phone. "There's a rumor that I went off the wagon and I was spotted in a cocktail lounge in town," he said to me. "There's been people saying that, but they got no proof."

I was having problems figuring it all out myself. I was nearly overwhelmed. I was thinking about Wayne and the whale hunt and all the time I'd spent in Neah Bay and elsewhere pondering traditions and protests and whales, and, I was asking over and over, *Where does it end?* I felt as if I were sinking into a vortex from which I might not pull out. And so in the middle of a grim winter, in the longest, darkest days of December, I decided to visit Neah Bay one last time.

I dropped in on everyone I'd met before the hunt had begun. I saw George Bowechop. He was helping to draw up a statement in response to the governor of Washington, who had reportedly told Sea Shepherd the following: "I have always been against the hunt." George took phone calls and scribbled copious notes on a long yellow legal pad. He told me that he was satisfied that the whale hunt was a significant moment in the legal history of the Makah Treaty, a kind of successor to the fish-ins of the fifties and sixties. He said that young people would be able to look back and see what it meant to be a Makah not just in the museum but in the newspapers and in the courts.

I saw Gary Ray. He was trying for the third time to be elected to the tribal council ("Third time lucky," he said), using the same poster he had the last time he ran with the same Theodore Roosevelt quote as his campaign slogan: "The work we do for ourselves follows us to the grave. The work we do for others lives on forever." I remembered him saying before the hunt began that a lot of the young men were on a teeter-totter that could go up or down depending on how the whale hunt proceeded; I asked him which way he thought the teeter-totter was headed. "Up," he said. "Definitely."

Arnie was at his VFW trailer. He said he was closer to getting his VFW post a lifetime charter, and he took me into a back room to show me some cranberry leaves that he was drying out. "It makes great tea," he said.

The word around the reservation was that the Germans were due in any day to show their film of the hunt. They had resolved their differences with the tribe and bought some film footage of the hunt from one of the people who had videotaped it. There were plans to show the German film on a big screen in the school gym. Some of the reviews of the film were already in. People were saying it focused on Micah McCarty, John McCarty's son, and although that upset some people, it made me want to see it more. Micah struck me as a pretty cool guy, with or without the hunt. I thought I could understand why the Germans liked him.

I had a Pepsi with Donnie at the Makah Maiden. His girlfriend was expecting a baby and he said he was excited about that, though he was not going to get married yet. "I'm too young. I'm twenty-three. I've got a lot more to experience," he said.

Donnie told me that Theron had asked him to be on the crew that he was putting together for the next whale hunt, which seemed imminent. Donnie had declined. He didn't like the way Theron was running his crew, and he had his doubts about Theron's abilities as captain—specifically, doubts as to whether Theron should have harpooned the gray whale so close to the canoe, just as it was turning beneath the canoe. "When I harpooned it, it really snapped its tail. It was huge," Donnie said. He was shaking his head. "Somebody could get killed out there."

And besides, Donnie said, Theron couldn't hunt until they came up with a new plan for storing the whale meat. The fish-storage freezer that had been used to store the whale meat after the last hunt was currently filled with government-surplus butter and cheese. It had been moved there a few weeks before, when the government-surplus butter and cheese storage building was condemned. In addition there was a problem with the new whaling canoe. It had cracked shortly after it had first gone into the water and it would take a while to repair.

I asked Donnie if he had had trouble getting served in restaurants the way Wayne had. "No," he said. He grinned. "But people know who I am and all."

Money was a problem for Donnie, as it was for all the crew members. He had been working at fisheries lately, and on that day he had been diving at the bottom of Lake Ozette, his face freezing in the winter lake water, checking on the habitat of the endangered sockeye salmon. But this job was up at Christmas, in just a few days, at which point he would be unemployed. He was thinking of moving to Port Angeles temporarily and getting work there. A big construction project was due to start up—the decommission of the Elwah River Dam, an old dam that blocked the Elwah as it ran out of the Olympics. Before the dams, the Elwah salmon run was mythic—hundred-pound salmon were commonplace—and there was hope that when the dam came down the salmon might be revived, like an old tradition. Donnie had the idea that if he worked in Port Angeles he could still be on the reservation on weekends.

"The thing is," he said, "it's tough having no money all the time."

Then I went to see Wayne. When I'd called the night before to make certain Wayne was at his mom's house, she answered the phone. "Oh, things are finally starting to calm down around here after the hunt," she said. She told me that people in the neighboring towns were starting to look her in the eye—though she did have a problem with her chiropractor, a man off the reservation who wouldn't see her after he found out that her son had hunted the whale. "I just don't understand all the anger," she told me.

When I saw Wayne, I asked him how it was going and he said that it had been difficult for him right after the hunt but that he was feeling better now. He had completed his anger management classes and after a few more parole hearings, the assault charges would be erased from his record: on paper, it would be as if he had never hit the guy he'd hit; it would be as if it never happened. "I've been sober all this time," he said.

I noticed a computer on Wayne's desk. It turned out that Wayne had learned how to use E-mail and he was staying in touch with other whalers and keeping an eye on the protestors. He was checking up on Sea Shepherd's conservation campaigns. He could see that In the Path of Giants was still running California whale watching trips. He said he thought that Sedna had disbanded. "It was hard on us, but it was harder on all of them; we were already here," he said. He was working for the whaling commission on a part-time basis, getting some whaling equipment together, running errands down to Fort Lewis for surplus goods. Denise had been relieved of her whaling commission duties and was back working as a biologist in fisheries. "I'd try to get Denise's job if only I had more education," Wayne said.

Working for the commission wasn't enough money to live on so he was getting ready to put an application in to work on the Elwah River Dam, the same job that Donnie was applying for.

When Wayne told me this, I went off soliloquizing about how important it would be to be working on the restoration of the great Olympic Peninsula river, and I got all emotional about Wayne being involved in the return of the salmon run, until Wayne brought me back down to earth.

"Yeah," he said, "and it pays good too."

He said that if he did get to work on the dam, he could maybe drive a truck, because he was qualified for that. He would have to live in Port Angeles. He added that he might miss the next hunt if he got the job but that if he could make some money he might be able to come back and whale hunt again.

We made plans to meet for breakfast the next morning. I left and went for dinner at the Makah Maiden and walked around for a while. The moon came out briefly over Neah Bay. It was full and bright and it danced behind the clouds over the bay. The papers were saying that the moon was the closest to earth it had been in years. This assertion made me really look at the moon, at the light it cast on the bay, on the peaks, on the trash-lined street, on the little homes. This assertion made me examine the moon and wonder if it was somehow more significant, and I began to think it was.

I went to sleep in the shanty, and when I woke up in the morning it was still dark and a storm had come up. At the beach, the sea was a riot of white foam, the waves smashing to the shore; the clouds churned endlessly, like dark smoke from a faraway fire. I was enjoying walking in the rain, when I saw Wayne and Arnie sitting at a table in the restaurant, having coffee and tea, respectively. I stopped and watched them for a second, as they talked and laughed: Arnie smiled, Wayne threw back his chin. They laughed in a rectangle of light that lit up the dark storm morning that was captioned by the restaurant's neon sign: OPEN.

When I went in, Arnie was his old confident self and Wayne was upbeat, as if overnight he had come up with some new makeshift plan, a new scheme to go on. After breakfast, as I was about to leave, Wayne stood outside in the rain and smiled a big smile. He shook my hand firmly. The wind was howling and the rain was soaking his sweatshirt.

I wished him luck however it all worked out, and he shook his head. "You know," he said, "I'm just now coming back to life."[♭]

[♭] In Britain, where *Moby-Dick* was first published, the first editions had no ending. The publisher had cut the last chapter in the version of the book that Melville intended to be published. Ishmael, the narrator of the book, survives the wreck of the whaling ship. He alone survives, and in the one-page coda-like finale, the book is revealed to be his recounting of the tale, the single version of the whale hunt story, which is, as I've been trying to say, the opposite position that I, as one of many Makah whale hunt chroniclers, find myself in. In Britain, readers couldn't possibly see what Melville was going for—or at least they couldn't see how he tied it all up, how it all ended—granted, of course, some stories don't have endings. In Britain, there would be—and was—the obvious complaint, which went like this: well, if everyone died then who is this Ishmael character and how did he get a chance to write down this incredibly long and detailed and Shakespeare-influenced tragedy? The British reader also couldn't see that the way in which Ishmael survives is to embrace death—literally, by holding on tight to an airtight wooden coffin that, in a very funny scene, is made into a life buoy. (Queequeg looks like he's going to die for a long and humorously melodramatic moment and then doesn't, so the ship's carpenter, the representation of Martha Stewart–like practicality on board the *Pequod*, converts the no-longer-necessary coffin into a life buoy, so as not to waste wood.) Ishmael embraces death and then is reborn, bobbing up through the cedar-chip-filled vortex into which went Ahab and the version of Starbuck that was too weak to hold back Ahab's anger. Ishmael, on the other hand, is carried up in a "cunning spring"—which is something that I have to say I really hoped Wayne might find. If the Makah whale hunt was arguably the opposite of *Moby-Dick*, the one where the natives are in control, as opposed to the evangelical white guys, then it seemed as if *everyone* ought to be able to survive, to rise on their own cunning spring. Not reading of Ishmael's survival would be like pulling the metaphysical rug out from underneath the reader, an experience I could relate to as an observer of the unending Makah whale hunt. I can only imagine that Melville, for his part, when he heard that the British publisher had left the ending off, must have gone through a lot. Then again, that's a little like the way I experienced the ending of *Moby-Dick*. After I had finished reading it, someone told me that I had read the wrong edition; that there were better editions available—more complete, edited to better express the author's supposed true intent; that the version of *Moby-Dick* that person had read was better. This made me laugh for a long time, until I really felt for a moment that you could call me crazy.

NOTES

I referred to numerous books and articles written about the Makah and Cape Flattery. Some of the most helpful were *The Indians of Cape Flattery* by James G. Swan; *The Makah Indians: A Study of An Indian Tribe in Modern American Society,* by Elizabeth Colson; Ruth Kirk's *Tradition & Change on the Northwest Coast*; and *This Is My Song: The Role of Song as Symbol in Makah Life,* a study of Makah songs and rituals written by Linda Jean Goodman. Ivan Doig's book on James Swan, *Winter Brothers: A Season at the Edge of America,* is a beautiful description of the modern Northwest and of the Northwest that James Swan encountered in the late 1800s as a white settler who never quite settled in with whites: (I listened to the unabridged audiotape version as I drove to Neah Bay in the winter and once got a speeding ticket, I was so engrossed.) I read numerous newspaper stories by Lucile McDonald, who first transcribed the Swan diaries. Her book *Swan Among the Indians: Life of James G. Swan, 1818–1900* begins with the following entry in Swan's diary: "'I knew the Makahs well enough to believe myself safe. I had been careful never to lie to them, even in a joke, and I carried no weapon when I went among the Indians. I have always found that a civil tongue is the best weapon I can use. The promiscuous wearing of firearms among the Indians during peace is more likely to provoke hostility than anything I know. It certainly does not inspire them with confidence.'"

Information about the dig at Ozette came from various sources, especially contemporaneous newspaper reports of the time written by Hill Williams, then the science editor of *The Seattle Times*. Also helpful were reports in the *Port Angeles Evening News* and *The Port Angeles Daily News*; an article entitled "Olympic's Pompeii," by Earl Clark, published in *National Parks,* June 1981; and the books and articles of Ruth Kirk, especially *Hunters of the Whale.* Information about the ancient whaling practices of the Makah came from Swan, from reports in the bulletins of the Bureau of American Ethnology (specifically in bulletin 124, published in 1938 and written by Frances Densmore); and from *The Whaling Equipment of the Makah Indians* by T. T. Waterman which was published by the University of Washington in 1920. A paper entitled "A Reassessment of Westcoast (Nootka) Whaling" written by Christopher B. Wooley, was given to me by whaling commission members. Also helpful was an article in the *Pacific Northwest Quarterly*, vol. 33, 1942, entitled "Reminiscences of a Whaler's Wife."

I learned about the revival of canoe carving and canoe culture in general by reading, David Neel's book *The Great Canoes: Reviving a Northwest Coast Tradition*, which includes an essay by Tom Heidlebaugh, entitled, "The Canoe Way of Knowledge." I also read about the canoe trip in the *The Forks Forum*, the Forks, Washington newspaper, and I watched a video, *Paddle to Seattle*, which was produced by the Quileute tribe. For information on the use of cedar in general on the Northwest coast, I read *Cedar : Tree of Life to the Northwest Coast Indians* by Hillary Stewart.

For information on the potlach, I referred to Ruth Kirk's *Tradition & Change* and to *Peoples of the Coast* by George Woodcock and *An Iron Hand Upon the People: The Law Against the Potlach on the Northwest Coast*, by Douglas Cole and Ira Chaikin. A book in which I read about traditional carvers carving nontraditional goods in a traditional fashion is called *Shapes of Their Thoughts: Reflections of Culture Contact in Northwest Coast Indian Art* by Victoria Wyatt. For explanations of Northwest coast art in general I turned to the extensive writings of Bill Holm.

In all of the chapters that involved any aspect of whales—everything from whaling to whale art to the history of antiwhaling movements—I referred over and over to *Men and Whales* by Richard Ellis, which, like my edition of *Moby-Dick*, I carried with me at all times during my stay on the Olympic Peninsula. Ellis is encyclopedic on every conceivable aspect of whales and whaling, Melvillian in the scope of his detail. Additional information on Captain Paul Watson came from *Sea Shepherd: My Fight for Whales and Seals* by Paul Watson as told to Warren Rogers. Some whale facts came from the book *Whales of the World* by Phil Clapham and from *Guardians of the Whales: The Quest to Study Whales in the Wild* by Bruce Obee and Graeme Ellis. Much of the information on gray whales came from *Gray Whales: Wandering Giants* by Robert H. Busch, and *Gray Whales* written by David George Gordon and Alan Baldridge. I found the story of the discovery of the first humpback whale sounds in the book *Tales of Whales* by Tim Dietz. The musicality of whale sounds is discussed at length in *Among Whales* by Roger Payne. The *Paddler* article referred to is entitled "Paddling in the Path of Giants," written by Paul McHugh, and it appeared in the August 1998 issue.

Information about slavery in the Pacific Northwest came from the book *Indian Slavery in the Pacific Northwest* by Robert H. Ruby.

I read stories about Kwatee in, among other places, *Indian Legends of the Pacific Northwest* by Ella Elizabeth Clark. I also listened to an LP recorded by Helen Peterson, a Makah, in 1976, that is entitled *Song and Stories from Neah Bay*.

The gray whale biologist who gave me the name of the whale-watching firm in Guerrero Negro was Bruce R. Mate, a gray whale expert at Oregon State University. The gray whale biologist who gave me Bruce Mate's name—and supplied me with valuable insight on the habits of gray whales in the environs of Cape Flattery—was Patrick Gearin. While in Mexico, I consulted the Lonely Planet guidebook and *The Forgotten Peninsula: A Naturalist in Baja, California*, by Joseph Wood Krutch. Information about Charles Scammon came in large part from *Scammon: Beyond the Lagoon: A Biography of Charles Melville Scammon* by Lyndall Baker Landauer and from Scammon's own works, including *The Marine Mammals of the North-western Coast of North America, Described and Illustrated: Together with an Account of the American Whale Fishery*, which was first published in 1874.

The entry on Karl May was drawn mostly from a bibliographical essay written by Karl W. Doerry and included in the *Dictionary of Literary Biography*, vol. 29, which is entitled *Nineteenth Century German Writers, 1841–1900*. The quote from Albert Einstein came from a blurb on the back of my copy of *Winnetou*; other blurbs are by Hermann Hesse ("May is the most brilliant representative of a truly original type of fiction—i.e., fiction as wish-fulfillment. . . .") and Albert Schweitzer ("What I liked most in May's writings was the courageous stand for peace and mutual understanding which inspires nearly all his books . . ."). I also read a book called *Spaghetti Westerns: Cowboys and Europeans from Karl May to Sergio Leone* by Christopher Frayling in which it is mentioned that, after he lost the Russian Front during World War II, Hitler instructed his general staff to read the Winnetou novels again. The address of the Web site for the Karl May Museum is www.karl-may-museum.de/indexe.html. At the

Karl May on-line trading post, you can buy things such as Karl May CDs and a walnut armchair just like the one May sat in when he pretended he was Old Shatterhand. As you browse, the Web site plays a tune, "Yankee Doodle Dandy."

In the chapter dealing with Indian fishing rights, I referred to *Ecocide of Native America: Environmental Destruction of Indian Lands and Peoples* as well as an article entitled "In Usual and Accustomed Places: Contemporary American Indian Fishing Rights Struggles" that I found in an essay collection entitled *The State of Native America: Genocide, Colonization and Resistance.*

For information regarding Olympic flora and fauna and the geology of the area, I mainly consulted Dan Mathews' *Cascade-Olympic Natural History: A Trailside Reference.* Additionally, I carried the *National Audubon Society's Field Guide to the Pacific Northwest and Olympic National Park* by Tim McNulty.

In writing about the day-to-day news events leading up to and including the modern-day whale hunt, I drew from all the published reports from the newspapers that offered extensive daily coverage of the Makah whalers—a list that includes *The Seattle Times, The Peninsula Daily News,* and the *Seattle Post-Intelligencer.* I also read Associated Press reports and watched videotapes of the reports on the Seattle television stations. (For this, I am especially indebted to Laura Moix.) For the final whale hunt scenes I referred repeatedly to the KIRO-TV video coverage of the hunt.

With regard to the Melville-related footnotes,[b] my reading on Melville was haphazard, to say the least. Mostly, I read the Melville books that the Multnomah County Library happened to have on its shelves. Those included *Melville* by Edwin Haviland Miller; *Herman Melville's Moby-Dick,* a col-

---

[b] The mark used to denote footnotes in this book was chosen with an eye to the following passage from Chapter 55 of *Moby-Dick*, "Of the Monstrous Pictures of Whales": "As for the bookbinder's whale winding like a vine-stalk round the stock of a descending anchor—as stamped and gilded on the backs and title-pages of many books both old and new—that is a very picturesque but purely fabulous creature, imitated, I take it, from the like figures on antique vases. Though universally denominated a dolphin, I nevertheless call this book-binder's fish an attempt at a whale; because it was so intended when the device was first introduced. It was introduced by an old Italian publisher somewhere about the 15th century, during the Revival of Learning; and in those days, and even down to a comparatively late period, dolphins were popularly supposed to be a species of the Leviathan." The old Italian publisher that Melville is referring to here is Aldus Manutius, who first used the dolphin and the anchor as the trademark of the Aldine Press in Venice in 1502. The trademark was intended to symbolize speed and firmness, and was only later referred to by printers as a colophon, a Greek word that means "finishing touch."

lection of essays edited by Harold Bloom and included in the Modern Critical Interpretation series; *The Long Encounter: Self and Experience in the Writings of Herman Melville* by Merlin Bowen; *Melville's Reviewers* by Hugh Hetherington; *The Example of Melville* by Werner Berthoff; and, *Melville and the Comic Spirit* by Edward H. Rosenberry, in which I learned that a year before Melville's death, an article in *Harper's* referred to him as a noted "minor humorist." (The *Harper's* article was entitled "American Literary Comedians.") The Melville book that I treasured and consulted most continually was *Melville: A Biography* by Laurie Robertson-Lorant.

ACKNOWLEDGMENTS

Gillian Blake, Giulia Melucci, Rachel Sussman, and Nan Graham at Scribner; Zoë Pagnamenta, Julie Bush, Zelimir Galjanic, Sarah Manguso, and Andrew Wylie at The Wylie Agency; Anna Wintour at *Vogue*; Alex Heard, Catherine Bouton, Gerald Marzorati, and Adam Moss of *The New York Times*; Gully Wells, Ted Moncreiff, and Eric Crites at *Condé Nast Traveler*; the Makah Cultural and Research Center; Makah Tribal Fisheries; The Lost Resort; The Cape Motel; The Makah Maiden; the public libraries of Port Angeles, and Clallam Bay and Multnomah counties; The Arbor School of Arts and Sciences; Sunflower School; James Leinfelder; Peter Quinn; Manny Howard; Larry and Sarah Rossin; Bonnie Loetscher; Tracy Chambless; Jennifer Sepez; Brian and Ted Gamble; Jerry Cronin; Richard Pliskin; Sarah Morgan and Mark Oldani; Deborah Mandelsberg and Jeff Cole; Patty Torcia; Marsha Weber; Joan Shipley; Greg Radich; Satoru Igarashi, Dana Dodd; Margaret Lamason; Pat and Mary Hoglund; Robin Olesen and Peter Wegner; Todd Waterbury; Laura Moix; Patrick Conley; John "Jack" Conley; S. McPherson; Mia and David Diehl; Matthew "Matt" Sharpe; Elizabeth Sullivan and Helene Bourget; Jill Desimini and Dan Bauer; Linda and Donald Desimini; Robert E. and Mary Elizabeth Sullivan; Samuel Emmet and Louise Grace.

I wish to thank Sadie Johnson, Arnie Hunter, and Donnie Swan for all their time, and I am indebted to all the residents of Neah Bay and to all the members of the Makah Nation who were kind enough to talk to me and show me around, most especially Wayne Johnson.

A Whale Hunt

1. Robert Sullivan begins *A Whale Hunt* with a series of primary documents—newspaper columns, letters to the editor, tribal songs, etc.—detailing the story's central conflict. Why do you think Sullivan chose to open the book this way? Do you think the chosen excerpts are biased toward one side or the other? If so, do you think this influence was intended?

2. Why do you think Sullivan refers to *Moby-Dick* and the life of Herman Melville throughout the book in footnotes? How does the shape of *A Whale Hunt* compare with the shape of *Moby-Dick*? Lewis Mumford is quoted as saying about *Moby-Dick*: "Melville sets out to teach us nothing." Is this true of Sullivan?

3. Neah Bay's unique history is evident, yet there are signs that it could be any remote town in modern-day America. There are moments in the book when the town's old and new cultures are shown coexisting, as when a crew member passes "in an old sedan out of which music was blaring." How did these contrasts affect the book's tone? What was your strongest impression of Neah Bay's culture?

4. What has made the whale such a strong symbol of the animal rights movement? How would the story have been different if it revolved around the hunting of another animal? Would it have been as emotionally compelling?

5. To what degree do you feel compassion toward certain animals? Are your feelings dependent on the kind of intelligence exhibited by the animal or the animal's ability to feel pain? How strong are your animal-rights convictions? Were they altered at all by reading this book? Why or why not?

6. How does Sullivan use humor to navigate the issues raised by the hunt? And how does humor matter to the people involved in the hunt?

7. Paul Watson called the Coast Guard's focus on protestors' activities during the whale hunt "ludicrous." Do you agree? Throughout the story, did you feel the protestors were treated fairly? Should they have been given more or less leniency for their actions?

8. At one point, Wayne Johnson says: "This thing has become so much more than we ever imagined. Now, it's like we have to do it . . . with all the media and all the people watching us, we have to do it." What effect did the media and the protestors have on the hunt? Would the Makah effort have stalled without its fight against this organized resistance? Do you think most traditions are made stronger or weaker by outside resistance?

9. Recall the intimidating strength of Theron Parker, the reluctant leadership of Wayne Johnson, the steadfast opposition of Paul Watson. Which person's emotional reactions most closely mirrored your own? Who would you like to have learned more about?

10. Were there times in the book when it seemed the hunt would never be completed? When did it seem least likely to occur? Did the events leading up to the hunt strongly foreshadow its success or failure? How?

11. Early in the book, and again toward its close, the tribe's members talk of the hunt's spiritual meaning. Some crew members downplay the spiritual aspects of the hunt, while others pray and take part in other ceremonial rituals once the hunt is finished. Does spiritual intent affect your judgment of the tradition and, if so, how? Are there traditions in your life that are only understandable within their spiritual context? If so, what are they?

12. Sullivan writes: "In the end, it seemed ridiculous to try to experience a whaler's religious experience; it seemed absurd to attempt to simulate someone else's spiritual tradition." Do you agree?

13. Sullivan refers to the tribe's expedition as a "modern yet ancient ceremonial whale hunt". In what ways is it modern? In what ways ancient? As we judge traditions across cultural boundaries, what role should history play? To what degree do you partake in traditions because of their historic importance?

14. How does America's historic treatment of Native Americans affect your feelings about the tribe's desires? How does Sullivan handle this component of the story?

15. Discuss the aftermath of the whale hunt and how you think it will affect the future. Are the Makah likely to continue their tradition? Will protest die down or increase? What do you think will happen to the people featured in the book?

Browse our complete list of guides and download them for free at
www.simonsays.com.

Printed in the United States
By Bookmasters